Film Clowns of the Depression

Film Clowns of the Depression

Twelve Defining Comic Performances

WES D. GEHRING
Foreword by Ray E. Boomhower

McFarland & Company, Inc., Publishers
Jefferson, North Carolina, and London

ALSO BY WES D. GEHRING
AND FROM MCFARLAND

*Joe E. Brown: Film Comedian
and Baseball Buffoon* (2006)

*Mr. Deeds Goes to Yankee Stadium: Baseball
Films in the Capra Tradition* (2004)

Frontispiece
The laid-back director Leo McCarey (left) with
Harpo Marx on the set of *Duck Soup* (1933).

(All photographs are from the author's collection)

LIBRARY OF CONGRESS CATALOGUING-IN-PUBLICATION DATA

Gehring, Wes D.
Film clowns of the depression : twelve defining
comic performances / Wes D. Gehring ; foreword by Ray E. Boomhower.
p.   cm.
Filmography: p.
Includes bibliographical references and index.

ISBN-13: 978-0-7864-2892-2
(softcover : 50# alkaline paper) ∞

1. Comedy films—United States—History and criticism.   I. Title.
PN1995.9.C55G424   791.43'617—dc22   2007000555

British Library cataloguing data are available

©2007 Wes D. Gehring. All rights reserved

*No part of this book may be reproduced or transmitted in any form
or by any means, electronic or mechanical, including photocopying
or recording, or by any information storage and retrieval system,
without permission in writing from the publisher.*

On the cover: The catalyst for Groucho's political paranoia in
Duck Soup (1933) is gifted straight man Louis Calhern (right),
with Chico (left) and Harpo Marx

Manufactured in the United States of America

*McFarland & Company, Inc., Publishers
Box 611, Jefferson, North Carolina 28640*

To Sarah and Emily,
and my Depression era parents,
from whom...

Contents

Foreword by Ray E. Boomhower	1
Preface	3
Introduction	7
1. Charlie Chaplin's *City Lights* (1931)	11
2. Eddie Cantor's *The Kid from Spain* (1932)	27
3. Mae West's *She Done Him Wrong* (1933)	38
4. The Marx Brothers' *Duck Soup* (1933)	51
5. Laurel and Hardy's *Sons of the Desert* (1933)	67
6. Will Rogers' *Judge Priest* (1934)	80
7. W.C. Fields' *It's a Gift* (1934)	96
8. Joe E. Brown's *Alibi Ike* (1935)	110
9. The Marx Brothers' *A Night at the Opera* (1935)	126
10. Charlie Chaplin's *Modern Times* (1936)	140
11. Laurel and Hardy's *Way Out West* (1937)	152
12. Bob Hope's *The Cat and the Canary* (1939)	164
Epilogue	176
Filmography	181
Chapter Notes	183
Bibliography	195
Index	205

Foreword

By Ray E. Boomhower

Located approximately five miles from the Golden Dome at the University of Notre Dame, Mishawaka, Indiana, offered to those who grew up there during the 1960s and 1970s few, if any, advantages over life in larger communities. Small corner grocery stores and bakeries offered convenient last-minute shopping opportunities for harried housewives, and the city's park system flourished with regular summer programs for bored youth and free lighted tennis courts for sports enthusiasts.

At that time small-town Indiana was not too far removed from the days of the Great Depression, offering limited entertainment options for young people. Fortunately, for a film buff like me, Mishawaka did have at least two movie theaters within easy walking distance of my home on West Battell Street. I can still remember enduring the hot, muggy trek on summer days to the nearby River Park Theater to enjoy a special "kiddie matinee" featuring a large tub of popcorn, an ice-cold soft drink, and an afternoon of cartoons and features in air-conditioned comfort. The films offered, usually along the lines of Godzilla battling some space monster or Roy Rogers rescuing Dale Evans from bad men in black hats, did little to stretch our young minds.

As I grew older, the city began to change as local businessmen turned to the past to entice customers. The old Kamm's Brewery along the Saint Joseph River became a series of shops and restaurants dubbed the 100 Center. Included in the new businesses was a movie theater that, in addition to regular Hollywood fare, sometimes featured classic films from the past. Intrigued by the promise of seeing a movie in black-and-white, I took a chance and sat through a 1932 Paramount Pictures release called *If I Had a Million*. The film examined what happens when a dying tycoon played by Richard Bennett, disgusted with his relatives' lust for his fortune, gives his money away to eight people picked at random from the city directory.

Those who receive the largesse from the eccentric millionaire include a cynical prostitute, a henpecked husband, a prisoner on Death Row, and a lowly office clerk. My favorite segment, however, involved two former vaudevillians, played expertly by W. C. Fields and Alison Skipworth, battling a series of careless drivers, termed "road hogs" by Fields. The duo's antics had me convulsed with laughter and I realized for the first time how important movies such as this one must have been for an American public dealing with the grim economic realities of the Great Depression. I also vowed to take advantage of any showing by the 100 Center theater of films from the 1930s.

My days as a teenage devotee of movies from the Great Depression came sharply into focus when I read Wes D. Gehring's latest book covering twelve pivotal films from that classic age of screen comedy. I was delighted to discover the inclusion of my favorite movie from that, or any, time, the Marx Brothers' *Duck Soup* (1933). At a later age, I appreciated the film's skewering of government ineptitude and preening patriotism (the endless playing of the Freedonia national anthem), but when I first saw it I enjoyed it for what it was—a comedic masterpiece. After all, even Groucho Marx, when asked about the movie's political significance, reportedly said, "What significance? We were just four Jews trying to get a laugh."

As well as reminding me of favorites from the past such as *Duck Soup* and Charlie Chaplin's *Modern Times* (1936), Gehring's book has rekindled my desire to search my local video store and library for such films as Mae West's *She Done Him Wrong* (1933), Joe E. Brown's *Alibi Ike* (1935), and Bob Hope's *The Cat and the Canary* (1939). These Hollywood clowns of the Depression era offered comfort and support during trying days, something that is needed even in the best of times. These clowns showed a resilient spirit not only on screen, but in their real lives as well. Each of them offers an instructive lesson for those who have fallen and hope to rise again.

Ray E. Boomhower is managing editor of the Indiana Historical Society's popular history magazine Traces of Indiana and Midwestern History. *He is the author of several biographies on notable Hoosiers, including Gus Grissom, Lew Wallace, and Ernie Pyle.*

Preface

> With entertaining insight, author Peter Novick has said writing history is like trying "to nail jelly to a wall."[1]

As in life, chronicling comedy history is about making choices. My family has always been fascinated by funny films. Screen comedians were central to my upbringing. But while laughter ruled, there was minimal analysis. Consequently, most of my adult life has been spent exploring a youth filtered through films. Almost all of my two dozen books are about screen comedians and various movie comedy genres. And while I enjoy the inspired Novick history-writing analogy about trying "to nail jelly to a wall," the twelve focus film selections for this text all have strong comedy credentials. After a lifetime of study, these were not difficult decisions. Granted, three of my selections feature personality comedians sadly neglected today: *The Kid from Spain* (1932, Eddie Cantor), *Judge Priest* (1934, Will Rogers), and *Alibi Ike* (1935, Joe E. Brown). But they were comedy legends at the time, and their laughter legacy, as showcased in these movies, merits rediscovery by today's connoisseurs of comedy. Of course, even this book's more familiar figures, such as Charlie Chaplin and the Marx Brothers, are often simply relegated to being recognizable pop culture icons — whose work is also neglected. This book attempts to address this problem.

Along related lines, I am reminded of *New Yorker* writer Peter Schjeldahl's observation, "A thing is mysterious if you don't know what or how to feel about it, and wish you did. Mystery is a lack not of information but of meaning."[2] History attempts to provide both information and meaning, by way of perspective. And that is the goal of this text, too. However, whether these movies are "new" to readers, or are familiar friends, this text is ultimately a celebration of the screen clowns that continue to gift us with laughter.

The 1930s are routinely considered sound film's greatest comedy era. Though this "golden age" encompassed various comedy genres, clown comedy is the most basic type. With that in mind, this work examines twelve pivotal pictures from the Depression decade: *City Lights* (1931, Charlie Chaplin), *The Kid from Spain* (1932, Eddie Cantor), *She Done Him Wrong* (1933, Mae West), *Duck Soup* (1933, Marx Brothers), *Sons of the Desert* (1933, Laurel and Hardy), *Judge Priest* (1934, Will Rogers), *It's a Gift* (1934, W.

C. Fields), *Alibi Ike* (1935, Joe E. Brown), *A Night at the Opera* (1935, Marx Brothers), *Modern Times* (1936, Charlie Chaplin), *Way Out West* (1937, Laurel and Hardy), and *The Cat and the Canary* (1939, Bob Hope).

Growing up as part of the first television generation, I was lucky enough to see all of these pictures, and many more, via early broadcasts on the small screen. Ironically, Hollywood of the 1950s, which was then at war with television, initially felt it was punishing television by not allowing post–1948 films to be shown. Instead, television networks created programming which would now rival some of the classic movie stations on today's cable. My youthful viewing was further complemented by ongoing movie comedy tutorials from my parents — children of the Depression and avid film fans. This inspired foundation was invaluable during my graduate school path to a doctorate in film comedy studies.

While some of the comedians in this text, such as Chaplin and the Marx Brothers, have generated a great deal of analysis, funnymen like Joe E. Brown and Eddie Cantor are all but forgotten. Even knowledge of the great Will Rogers often is limited to the serious student of American humor. Having written extensively on film comedians and comedy genres, I am well aware of gaps in the literature. This text attempts to address these shortcomings, as well as compare these clowns to comedy contemporaries treated more kindly by history. Plus, this study takes the unique slant of focusing on pivotal screen clowns of a given decade ... by way of select films. Most other movie comedy books attempt either a total history or a select period which showcases a mix of various comedy genres. In contrast, I have filtered a memorable decade through twelve memorable movies — all connected by being the same comedy genre type: clown. I am confident that this will make all the difference.

Several major libraries on both coasts were instrumental in my research. As with all my books, whether biographies, or criticism texts, my first stop is the Performing Arts Library of the New York Public Library at Lincoln Center. Its vast period clippings files of film artists and individual movies are critical to any serious cinema study. (During the 1930s the most detailed and insightful American film criticism was provided by a host of New York–based newspapers.) Complementing the Lincoln Center is the New York Public Library's main branch at Fifth Avenue and 42nd Street — particularly the microfilm "tombs" (dead newspaper) department. Leads from Lincoln Center often can be further fleshed out at the "tombs."

On the West Coast the Academy of Motion Picture Arts and Sciences' Margaret Herrick Library in Beverly Hills is also a necessary stop, especially for clippings files. (These holdings often underline the importance of the New York newspapers — all of which are well represented.) Another important West Coast stop is the Cinema and Television Library of the University of Southern California, which houses the private papers of numerous entertainers.

A number of friends were central to the writing of this book. Film historian Conrad Lane was sometimes a sounding board for the manuscript. Historian and editor Ray E. Boomhower wrote the book's foreword. Joe and Maria Pacino provided research assistance and a place to crash when I was in the Los Angeles area. My department chair at Ball State, Nancy Carlson, was supportive and helped facilitate university financial help. Janet Warrner supplied valuable editorial advice, while Jean Thurman was responsible for computer preparation of the manuscript.

For me, as for most writers, the craft ultimately comes down to the love and support of family. Their "safety net" makes all things seem possible. My rooting section includes my parents, my sister Sue, and my daughters Sarah and Emily, who also doubled as research assistants. Thank you one and all.

Wes D. Gehring
Spring 2007

Introduction

> In order to laugh at something, it is necessary (1) to know *what* you are laughing at, (2) to know *why* you are laughing, (3) to ask some people why *they* think you are laughing, (4) to jot down a few notes, (5) to laugh. Even then, the thing may not be cleared up for days.
> — Robert Benchley in 1938[1]

While gifted humorist Robert Benchley (1889–1945) has some affectionate fun in his charmingly vague case against interpretation, the passage of time weighs in strongly on giving his comedy colleagues from the 1930s a closer look. This book examines the decade's most basic type of comedy — the clown, or personality comedian — as genre. With its concentration on the Depression era, the study bases its analysis on twelve important pictures. Each of the dozen merits an individual chapter, in which the movie is both closely critiqued, and considered a mini-microcosm of the comic world of its main funny person or persons. The twelve films are: *City Lights* (1931, Charlie Chaplin), *The Kid from Spain* (1932, Eddie Cantor), *She Done Him Wrong* (1933, Mae West), *Duck Soup* (1933, Marx Brothers), *Sons of the Desert* (1933, Laurel and Hardy), *Judge Priest* (1934, Will Rogers), *It's a Gift* (1934, W. C. Fields), *Alibi Ike* (1935, Joe E. Brown), *A Night at the Opera* (1935, Marx Brothers), *Modern Times* (1936, Charlie Chaplin), *Way Out West* (1937, Laurel and Hardy), and *The Cat and the Canary* (1939, Bob Hope).

While these are signature clown comedies of the 1930s, they continue to resonate with audiences years removed from the Depression. Along these lines, my favorite film, regardless of the era, is *Duck Soup*. As a child of the 1960s, I was fascinated by this Marxist masterpiece. And this movie was largely the catalyst for my becoming a film comedy historian. Similar testimonials can be made for each of the movies in this text. To illustrate, award-winning actor John Lithgow was moved to be an actor by the automatic feeding device in *Modern Times*, where poor Charlie is a comic guinea pig for a culinary torture device. Lithgow remembered this golden moment from childhood as the time "when I almost died laughing...."[2]

The personality comedian components constitute the main thrust of the individual chapters, but this is not to suggest that all clown films exist independent of other comedy genres. Indeed, there are few pure examples of any phenomenon. Personality

Leo McCarey and Mae West on the set of *Belle of the Nineties* (1934), which McCarey also directed.

comedians often have an affinity for the thematic comedy genres. Such ties are actually born out of the clown personae themselves. For example, the comic absurdity of the Marxes sometimes lends itself to dark comedy, seen in the war-related scenes of *Duck Soup*. The folksy, crackerbarrel axioms of Will Rogers celebrate populism, especially in *Judge Priest*. Bob Hope's flip-flops between comic antihero and egotistical wise guy are nicely attuned to spoofing, such as the horror film reaffirmation parody found in *The Cat and the Canary*. Reaffirmation is an edgier, more subtle approach to parody, and Mae West also explores this genre, as it relates to melodrama, in *She Done Him Wrong*. Finally, Laurel and Hardy embrace the more traditional broad-based type of parody in *Way Out West*, which comically derails the Western.

While this text concentrates on the comedy stars of these pivotal pictures, "success," as the old axiom goes, "often has many parents." Thus, in three cases a now celebrated director undoubtedly helped elevate a vehicle to memorable movie status. Leo McCarey directed both *The Kid from Spain* and *Duck Soup*. When one considers that McCarey also teamed and molded Laurel and Hardy in the late 1920s, with *Sons of the Desert* closely following a McCarey scenario (though he was not directly tied to the picture), one feels as if he should receive special billing with the comedians.[3] After all, McCarey is the only director to ever put a personal stamp on a Marx Brothers movie, while still making it easily their best picture. *Duck Soup* is also arguably the most acclaimed of the films examined herein; the American Film Institute called it one of the five funniest movies ever made—sharing company with *Some Like It Hot* (1959), *Tootsie* (1982), *Dr. Strangelove, Or: How I Learned to Stop Worrying and Love the Bomb* (1964), and *Annie Hall* (1977).

Joining McCarey in the unique director status for this text is John Ford, who megaphoned the Will Rogers picture *Judge Priest*. Ford is a pivotal populist auteur, who raised the artistic crackerbarrel level of *Priest*, as well as his two other collaborations with Rogers—*Dr. Bull* (1933) and *Steamboat Round the Bend* (1935). Just as the Marx Brothers and Eddie Cantor were best showcased by McCarey, Rogers' time capsule pictures are the trio he did with Ford. However, while this collaboration also seemed to impact Ford's later populist outings, particularly his Westerns, neither the Marxes, nor Cantor, had a discernible impact on McCarey.[4]

In studying the twelve focus films, the best of the personality comedian crop for the 1930s, a significant companion picture or two by the same comic or team often come under special scrutiny, too. One such example has already been hinted at in the previous paragraph, the Will Rogers–John Ford film trilogy. A better analysis of the central *Judge Priest* is achieved by an awareness of the two other collaborations. Along similar lines, a critique of Joe E. Brown's inspired *Alibi Ike* is enriched by comparisons with his two other excellent diamond comedies—*Fireman, Save My Child* (1932) and *Elmer the Great* (1933). Conversely, the comic range of an artist can also be gauged by the diversity of parts over a small window of time. For instance, the chapter on W.C. Fields' greatest film, his antihero classic *It's a Gift*, also examines the comedian's best huckster (his other persona) picture, *The Old-Fashioned Way* (1934), which opened the same year.

Surprisingly, or maybe not so surprisingly, given comedy's tendency to be escapist, of this text's twelve pivotal pictures, only Chaplin's *Modern Times* deals directly with the Depression and related themes, such as unemployment and street violence between the police and leftwing workers. One could also argue that there is a metaphorical Depression connection in Chaplin's *City Lights*, especially the class consciousness implied by the millionaire (Harry Myers), who, when sober, never recognizes the comedian's Tramp. But this is not to imply the other focus films are without realistic flourishes. Mae West's *She Done Him Wrong* is highlighted by her signature sexuality (what West comically called the "linen battlefield"[5]), not to mention veiled references to prostitution. Laurel and Hardy's *Sons of the Desert* and W. C. Fields' *It's a Gift* explore the world of henpecked husbands with such attention to detail that the pictures are both funny and unexpectedly poignant.

Still, all things considered, there is an often otherworldly nature to these movies. Three of the films are set in earlier time periods — *Judge Priest* and *She Done Him Wrong* return to the 1890s, while Laurel and Hardy are *Way Out West* — shortly after the Civil War. Both McCarey movies, *The Kid from Spain* and *Duck Soup*, take place in zany foreign lands, with Cantor in a mythical Mexico only Hollywood could produce, while the Marxes are citizens of Freedonia — yet another of the film capital's entertainingly fictitious European settings for comedy. Throw in the baseball escapism of Joe E. Brown's *Alibi Ike* and the haunted house backdrop for Bob Hope's *The Cat and the Canary*, and one would be hard-pressed to date most of these movies to a Depression-related timeline. Even Chaplin's more "1930s conscious" films often segue to sketch material reminiscent of earlier Tramp movies — which are much less time-specific in their origins. In fact, this was an occasional period criticism of *Modern Times*— not delivering on its topical promise.

Yet, one should hasten to add that the greatest gift one receives from personality comedy — the ritualistic capacity which repeatedly brings one back to the comedians' works — has a special relevance to the Depression. Cinema clown comedy of any age is about *resilience*, both physical and spiritual — that is, funny characters comfort us in our short lives with their comeback comedy. They are like the mythical bird, the phoenix, which burned on a funeral pyre and rose from the ashes to live through another cycle. This can embrace the cinematic slapstick of a comedy character flattened one moment, only to be totally revived in the next frame. Or, this analogy can be applied to tragic tendencies in the real life of the comedian, such as the comic genius of W. C. Fields ... tempered by his alcoholism and a torturous real-life estranged marriage — both of which fuel *It's a Gift*. He fashions laughter from personal pain — resilience indeed. As comedy historian Neil Schmitz observed,

Humor ... [is] the hardest piece of work given to man ... [in order to] beguile himself, make the wrong right, convert pain into pleasure, [and] forgive error. To this extent, periodically, we are all humorists. We take the kick and love the brick [of slapstick revenge].[6]

To draw humorous life lessons from pain can be both endearing and enduring, as this text's dozen movies demonstrate. And even though most of the comedy classics examined herein are not self-consciously Depression pictures, all of them embrace a comic resiliency which had probably never been more needed than in the Depression. But whether one is chronicling the malaise which accompanies either an economic depression or the more general psychological variety — a dose of comic resilience is always a *timely* antidote. Fittingly, these twelve films have been treating various forms of depression since the 1930s. What's more, for many of us they represent the background music of our lives.

CHAPTER 1

Charlie Chaplin's *City Lights* (1931)

> Why did I continue to make non-dialogue films? The silent picture ... is a universal means of expression. Talking pictures necessarily have a limited field.
>
> — Charlie Chaplin in 1931[1]

While this chapter on Chaplin's *City Lights* opens the text for strictly chronological reasons, being the first film released of the twelve movies showcased herein, it is fitting to begin with for another reason, too. Chaplin (1889–1977) is quite simply the greatest comedy auteur in the history of cinema. His ability to write, direct, perform, produce, and compose the music for one groundbreaking picture after another is unprecedented. But with all of Chaplin's classics, *City Lights* has consistently garnered some of his highest critical praise. For example, acclaimed film historian Arthur Knight would write upon the 1972 re-release of the movie, "At this late date, it seems as pointless to re-review *City Lights* as it is to essay a critique of Michelangelo's works in the Sistine Chapel."[2] Moreover, the seminal early film critic James Agee accorded the picture a unique honor in his groundbreaking essay, "Comedy's Greatest Era" (1949). Agee's description of the poignant conclusion, where the once-blind flower girl finally sees Chaplin's romantically frustrated Tramp and finds him wanting, also has a poetry of its own:

> [Chaplin's Charlie] recognizes himself, for the first time, through the terrible changes [disappointment] in her face. The camera just exchanges a few close-ups of the emotions which shift and intensify in each face. It is enough to shrivel the heart to see, and it is the greatest piece of acting and the highest moment in movies.[3]

This is no random bit of exaggerated praise. Through the years, scholar after scholar has seconded Agee's "greatest scene ever" verdict on *City Lights*' finale. For instance, film historian and sometimes director Peter Bogdanovich would observe in 2000, Agee's "'the highest moment in movies' [statement] ... certainly remains a valid judgment."[4] Given these kudos, it should come as no surprise that "for many it [*City Lights*] is the summit of Chaplin's art."[5]

Before further examining the inspired comedy of *City Lights*, one has to note the outright bravery of the production. The movie opened well over three years after the part-talkie *The Jazz Singer* (1927) established that sound films were the wave of the future. Why did Chaplin continue the silent tradition when the rest of the movie industry was jumping to sound? First, it allowed cinema's premier clown to maintain the universality of his Tramp character. Chaplin's little Charlie "spoke" a language understood around the world — pantomime. Anything else, such as adopting English dialogue, would have undercut the everyman nature of his character severely. Chaplin's writing and interviews from this period would also apply that same universality to all of silent cinema, celebrating the specialized art form it represented.[6] Chaplin screen contemporary Mary Pickford articulated this sentiment in the most provocatively succinct manner when she stated, "It would have been more logical if silent pictures had grown out of the talkies instead of the other way around."[7]

Second, an international character also could be equated with an international box office. Being confined to one language would limit Chaplin's large market abroad. Good business for others dictated a transition to sound, while just the opposite was true for Chaplin, though he did add a synchronized score and sound effects to *City Lights*. When the picture opened to rave reviews, period commentators were quick to endorse Chaplin's decision to remain with the universality of silence. Famed movie columnist Louella O. Parsons wrote on the eve of the comedian leaving for *City Lights*' London premiere, "He is now the sole actor who can show his picture in its original form in Europe."[8]

Like Soviet filmmaker and theorist Sergei Eisenstein, Chaplin believed that sound could be used as an additional tool in what would still be essentially silent cinema. The comedian was appalled that early sound films so surrendered themselves to this new development, especially when the sound quality was often very primitive. Chaplin even satirized this technical limitation at the opening of *City Lights*, where two pompous public speakers "broadcast" distorted sounds instead of words. And on the eve of *City Lights*' release, Chaplin revealed that he had gained creative strength through being "submerged by correspondence from every portion of the world lauding him for his stand against talking pictures."[9]

A third reason to continue the silent tradition, suggested by his oldest son, Charles Chaplin, Jr., was purely to save the Tramp figure, which had become his father's alter ego. Because if Charlie's universality was not to be compromised with a voice, the character itself would need to be retired. But with sensitive insight, the comedian's son wrote, "[K]nowing my father, ... he simply could not make the move that might destroy the Little Tramp. *City Lights* was my father's signed reprieve."[10]

A fourth and final factor in Chaplin staying silent might simply have been tied to what was then becoming the comedian's production tradition — the lengthy gestation period for his films. When shooting on the 1931 *City Lights* began in late 1928, Chaplin had already been working on the story for nearly a year! Though the autumn 1927 release of *The Jazz Singer* signaled the birth of the sound era, many initially felt that both silent and sound pictures would co-exist. Moreover, even with the first full-length, all-talking film, *The Lights of New York*, opening in July of 1928, only 1300 American movie theaters (of 20,500) had sound installations by the end of that year.[11] Many period pictures were released in both sound and silent versions, given that the majority of theaters were not yet wired for the "talkies." And while the general public was fascinated by sound (fueled, in part, by the huge new popularity of that 1920s phenomenon — radio), cinema critics and connoisseurs were quick to mourn the artistic loss of silent film's often subtle expressive imagery in the rush to record talking heads. Indeed, as late as 1939, pioneering movie historian Lewis Jacobs would write in his watershed study, *The Rise of the American Film*:

> [With] the incorporation of spoken dialogue as a permanent element of motion pictures ... [the] technique lost its sophistication overnight and became primitive once more; every phase of the movie medium reverted to its rudiments. The interest in artistic film expression ... was stifled in the chaos that the advent of sound produced.[12]

Thus, among the intelligentsia, Chaplin's defense of the pantomime art of silent cinema was much embraced upon the eve of the sound revolution. It also helps explain why, among the new kings of saturation sound comedy (the Marx Brothers), the darling of the critics was *silent* Harpo. Still, as Chaplin's *City Lights* shooting schedule stretched from late 1928 until late 1930 (an amazingly long production), with a January 1931 premiere, the American film industry had now completely converted to sound.

Besides Chaplin's brave bucking of the transition in American cinema, he had even seen his major silent comedy rivals (Buster Keaton and Harold Lloyd) convert to sound. Though we now date the beginning of this duo's decline from their first starring sound pictures, *Welcome Danger* (1929, Lloyd) and *Free and Easy* (1930, Keaton), both movies were box office smashes, with audiences curious to hear how their formerly silent stars sounded. If these developments did not give Chaplin pause during his lengthy *City Lights* shooting schedule, Lloyd's technological about-face on *Welcome Danger* probably gave the creator of the Tramp some sleepless nights. That is, Lloyd initially shot *Danger* as a silent movie. But after an early preview, Lloyd decided to largely re-shoot the entire picture as a talkie! *Danger* went on to become Lloyd's top-grossing movie. (Harry Langdon, often considered the other silent comedy pantheon member, with Chaplin, Keaton, and Lloyd, self-destructed his career by poor artistic choices *before* the coming of sound became an issue.)

Of course, the slow, creatively drawn-out process that doubled as the Chaplin style was not the only thing that extended the production schedule of *City Lights*. The Tramp's world in this picture fluctuates between interactions with two contrasting characters — a blind flower girl (Virginia Cherrill) and a forgetful millionaire (Harry Myers). But for director Chaplin, the not always benevolent dictator of the set, his actors sometimes created production exasperations. Henry Clive, who was originally cast as Charlie's millionaire friend, stalled on doing a comic drowning scene until the water in Chaplin's pretend river (the studio pool) was warmed. The comedian turned several shades of red and promptly fired Clive. Through the years, reports have varied on just how much film footage of Clive had already been shot. But to start over with any new major character (as was the case with Myers) would have been time-consuming. This was especially true for a director like Chaplin, who went to great lengths acclimating his performers to their characters. In fact, the comedian would act out each part for every scene in minute detail, even involving minor players. Child actor and later film director

Robert Parrish, who played the small part of a peashooting newsboy in *City Lights*, would entertainingly describe Chaplin's "acting-all-parts" directing style:

> As [Chaplin as the Tramp] passed in front of our corner, [fellow newsboy] Austin Jewell and I raised our peashooters. Chaplin said, "No, wait!" and promptly stopped being the Tramp and the blind girl and became two newsboys blowing peashooters. He would blow a pea and then run over and pretend to be hit by it, then back to blow another pea. He became a kind of dervish ... seeing and cane-twirling as the Tramp, not seeing and grateful as the blind girl, peashooting as the newsboys ... [F]inally he had it all worked out and reluctantly gave us back our parts. I felt that he would much rather have played them all himself.[13]

Chaplin's working relationship with Cherrill, who played the blind girl, was more complicated. Having trouble casting the part, the comedian was struck by Cherrill's appearance at a prizefight—a popular Hollywood sports outing in the years before major league baseball came to the West Coast. She reminded him of blonde beauty Edna Purviance, Chaplin's long-time leading lady and lover early in his film career. A screen test was arranged, and besides being photogenic, Chaplin would later write, "she had the faculty of looking blind. I instructed her to look at me, and she could do it."[14] Along related lines, the 1931 director of the National Society for the Prevention of Blindness would write Chaplin in praise of Cherrill's "strikingly realistic and most touching" performance: "You have rendered a double service by giving us in one stroke a great artistic production and a true picture of loneliness and helplessness which is the fate of the blind."[15]

Cherrill was quickly signed for the part, despite her lack of acting background. While that would give most directors pause, Chaplin saw it as an advantage, enabling him to completely make over the novice performer. Purviance had been an amateur, too. (This *Pygmalion–My Fair Lady* controlling approach by Chaplin might also explain why his leading ladies, with the exception of Paulette Goddard, seldom went on to successful solo careers.) Moreover, Cherrill's lack of silent film technique was merely part of a larger challenge Chaplin faced on *City Lights*. As he wrote in his autobiography, "Since the advent of talkies, which had now been established for three years, the actors had almost forgotten how to pantomime. All their timing had gone into talk and not action."[16] Consequently, Chaplin would not be reinventing a metaphorical "pantomime 101" just for Cherrill.

Of much greater concern for Chaplin, however, were the nocturnal habits of his new leading lady. In real life Cherrill was a twenty-year-old, recently divorced free spirit who was originally in Hollywood visiting society friends on an extended holiday. But when her appearance frequently showed signs of the previous night's partying (hardly the desired look for the stereotypical virginal maiden of a Chaplin film), the comedian seriously considered replacing her. The prime candidate was Georgia Hale, his heroine from *The Gold Rush* (1925, *City Lights*' only rival as the greatest of Chaplin's pictures).

Hale was still intimately involved with the filmmaker, and a surviving *City Lights* screen test of the actress suggests she could have handled the part of the blind girl. Indeed, Chaplin told Hale she had the part and added, "This is what I've been trying to get for weeks."[17] Though Hale was placed under contract, the comedian's publicist,

1. Charlie Chaplin's *City Lights* (1931)

Charlie Chaplin as the Tramp, with the blind flower girl (Virginia Cherrill), in *City Lights*.

Carlyle Robinson, eventually convinced him Hale was not suited for the part. Still, Chaplin continued to second-guess his selection of Cherrill. The comedian next tested a teenaged blonde beauty named Violet Krauth, who would later find minor fame as the actress Marian Marsh. Once more, Chaplin found the screen test favorable. But Robinson again helped derail this substitution (with the support of another Chaplin assistant, Alfred Reeves). Ultimately, Cherrill was retained as the blind girl, after Chaplin gave her a stern pep talk behind closed doors. (Maybe the comedian's insecurity about Cherrill came from the fact that *City Lights* was that rare Chaplin production in which he was *not* romantically involved with his leading lady. Obviously, an intimate relationship can represent a control factor all its own.)

So where does one begin to critique *City Lights*—that is, if one is willing to further explore the artistry of a cinematic equivalency to "Michelangelo's works in the Sistine Chapel"? (To defend the critical revisiting of great art, one has only to remember that watershed works often reinvent themselves with the passage of time. Moreover, through the re-examination of established truths, revisionist insights often surface.) My choice for a *City Lights* starting point would be its conclusion. There are three pivotal reasons for this decision. First, if the movie's close is the greatest moment in the history of cinema, why would one think of looking elsewhere for an opening? Second, this ending represents the first time in Chaplin's creative career that he had worked out the conclusion *before* beginning the production. Now, while this flies in the face of most creative writing texts, where one's *finis* is to be strongly in place before creatively working to that end, most silent comedians simply improvised their stories. Film historian Gerald Mast has poetically likened Chaplin's improvisational storytelling as so many "beads on a string." And in point of fact, personality comedy (silent or sound) is more character-driven. It is seldom about the story. One goes to see a favorite clown do his or her specific comedy shtick; story is simply backburner fare. Along related lines, Mark Twain skewers critics who look for story structure in humor by opening *Huckleberry Finn* with the comic warning, in part—"persons attempting to find a plot in it will be shot."[18]

Possibly because of Chaplin's *City Lights* epiphany, with regard to the conclusion, this is the comedian's most structured story. Acclaimed drama critic and author Walter Kerr goes so far as to suggest, "*City Lights* may also be read as a structural exercise, with great satisfaction. It is the most ingeniously formed, immaculatory interlocked of Chaplin's experiments in combining comedy with pathos."[19] This Kerr statement also segues to the third reason for beginning with the conclusion of *City Lights*—pathos has never been more effectively showcased, whether one is discussing Chaplin, or the merry milieu of any other comedian. No one better defines the magic mix of comedy and pathos than Chaplin. His unique handle on this marriage of funny and sad has made him the idol of both film fans and other comedians, such as Jerry Lewis—"If you're going to aim for the stars, why not pick the best [Chaplin]? And the one thing that Charlie had—in spades—was something I'd barely tapped into [early in my career]: pathos."[20] Lewis is such a student of Chaplin's artistry along these lines that this Charlie disciple also articulates one of the better takes on comedy and pathos:

> Great comedy ... always goes hand in hand with great sadness. This is the grand Circle of Life, the mixture of laughter and tears. You can be funny without tap-

ping into strong emotion, but the humor is more superficial. Funny without pathos is a pie in the face. And a pie in the face is funny, but I wanted more.[21]

What makes the *City Lights* conclusion the definitive example of pathos and comedy? Well, Chaplin had been working toward this sort of tour de force ending for years. A special comedy component of the Chaplin milieu had always been as a caretaker for vulnerable young heroines, who often later broke his heart. One could start with his *The Tramp* (1915), which the comedian's landmark early biographer, Theodore Huff, has called "the first Chaplin classic."[22] His Tramp rescues a farmer's daughter (lovely young Edna Purviance) from robbers but sustains a minor leg wound in the process. As Purviance nurses Charlie, he is the happiest of potential lovers. But when her sweetheart returns, the Tramp sees the writing on the wall and stoically saunters down life's highway, propelled by what poet Carl Sandburg winningly described as those "east-and-west feet."[23] This would be Chaplin's first use of pathos, a phenomenon he later described as follows: "I dislike tragedy. Life is sad enough. I only use pathos as a means of effecting beauty, for so much of the tragic is in all beauty."[24]

Another pioneering example of Chaplin pathos involving a heartbreaking heroine, *The Bank* (1915) finds his office janitor falling for yet another unattainable leading lady (a typist played by Purviance). This time his hope for romance is fueled by a dream in which he thwarts a bank robbery and rescues her. But as he kisses Purviance the illusion dissolves into merely a smooch of his mop! Chaplin author Isabel Quigly wrote, "*The Tramp* had shown the pathetic, the lyrical and the rapturously joyful Charlie; *The Bank* showed Charlie the tragedian."[25] Of course, not all Chaplin pictures go this poignant pathos route. In fact, the catalyst for my own book on the king of comedy and pathos was that Chaplin was just as likely to be capable and get the girl, such as in *The Gold Rush* and *Modern Times* (1936).[26] But there is no denying that the preferred comfort zone for critics involved Chaplin and pathos. And the common denominator for these films invariably had him losing the heroine.

Ironically, Chaplin's leading lady from *City Lights* is not lost to an Arrow Shirt type hero, *à la* the young man of *The Tramp* or the equally dashing aerial artist of *The Circus* (1928). The Charlie of *City Lights* is competing with his own creation: The blind girl thinks her benefactor is a handsome young millionaire. The Tramp allows this innocent misperception to stand. Indeed, Chaplin tweaks his perennial outsider into the most unselfish of saviors. Falling in love with a beautiful blind girl, Charlie moves the proverbial heaven and earth to acquire the necessary cash for a sight-producing operation. While his assorted odd jobs (from street sweeper to boxer) do not pan out, his sometimes friendship with the forgetful millionaire (who only remembers the Tramp when he has been drinking) proves more profitable. But there is an unfortunate catch. Shortly after receiving the money, an unrelated robbery attempt at the millionaire's mansion makes it appear that Charlie is a thief. Though Chaplin's underdog initially escapes and gets the operation funds to Cherrill's character, he ultimately is caught and does jail time.

Now flash forward to sometime in the future. The Tramp is just out of prison, and he has not looked so bedraggled since his Mack Sennett beginnings (1914). The blind girl is not at her normal flower-selling location. But one knows she is on his mind, because of the attention Charlie gives a discarded flower in the street. Put upon by the aforementioned pea-shooting newsboys, the Tramp accidentally finds himself near Cherrill's new florist shop. The comic altercation between Charlie and the newsboys amuses the now obviously sighted flower girl, who views the Tramp through the plate glass window of her shop. Still clutching the flower, often symbolic of the fragility of life and love in the Chaplin world, Charlie suddenly sees Cherrill and is frozen in place. He is overjoyed that she can see, yet overwhelmed about what this means for them. Unfortunately, while Charlie sees yet another idealized heroine on a nineteenth century romanticized pedestal, Cherrill and her assistant see only a laughable hobo apparently smitten by her beauty. They even kid about a "conquest." Worse yet, Cherrill expresses her pity by offering the Tramp a coin and a fresh flower. Embarrassed, Charlie shakes off his shock and starts to move away. But Cherrill comes into the street and manages to stop the Tramp, placing a coin and a flower in his hand. This is a brilliant stroke by Chaplin, since this touch allows the once blind girl to realize the Tramp is her benefactor.

Now it is Cherrill's turn to be shocked. "You?" she hesitantly asks. Giving her a humiliated smile, Charlie answers with a nod.

Still finding the scene hard to comprehend, the Tramp has to ask via a title, "You can see now?"

Responding as if in a stupor, yet looking directly into Charlie's sad eyes, she dully states, by way of a title, "Yes, I can see now."

After a series of close-ups between the two, the camera ultimately stays on the Tramp. The haunting image of this face is the picture of pathos — the difficult smile that somehow acknowledges that this romance is certainly at an end. As Agee wrote, "It is enough to shrivel the heart...."

Over a quarter century later Chaplin told an interviewer that take after take of this scene had resulted in being "overdone, overacted, overfelt." The winning result was a product of metaphorically taking himself out of the scene, playing it as the compassionate director:

> This time I was looking more at her [Cherrill], interested to see that she didn't make any mistakes. It was a beautiful sensation of not acting, of standing outside of myself. The key was exactly right — slightly embarrassed ... apologetic without getting emotional about it. He was watching and wondering what she was thinking ... without any effort. It's one of the purest inserts — I call them inserts, close-ups — that I've ever done. One of the purest.[27]

Before departing from arguably cinema's greatest scene, one must address a frequently neglected final facet to *City Lights*' conclusion. For the longest time Chaplin was celebrated as a great comedian despite what was seen as his technical limitations. It required André Bazin's milestone essay, "The Virtues and Limitations of Montage" (1958) to make it clear that Chaplin's decision to film in long shot and long take was wise technically and represented the comedian's production awareness of the most effective form of presentation for his comedy art.[28] This is realism at its most magical — Chaplin's ability to transform inanimate objects into a litany of other things. Sophisticated editing would only have distracted from Chaplin's magician-like abili-

Chaplin in the poignant conclusion of *City Lights*, with the fragility of the moment accented by his flower.

ties. Beyond this use of long take and long shot, another crucial component of cinema realism is ambiguity — multiple meanings to a given scene, as in life. Thus, despite the apparent feelings of Cherrill's character at the picture's close, the ambiguous, open-ended quality of the conclusion makes *City Lights* all the more attractive to a realist.

A comparable modern movie conclusion would be the beguiling close to writer-director Sofia Coppola's *Lost in Translation* (2003). The wistful, almost romantic relationship between two bungling Americans in Tokyo (Bill Murray and Scarlett Johansson) is most certainly over. But Murray's whispering of an undisclosed something in Johansson's ear, as time expires, also gives the picture's ending a touch of ambiguity. Of course, besides appealing to realists, this element of hope is also alluring to romantics. And it avoids the overtly sentimental closing action of a picture like Chaplin's *The Vagabond* (1916), a movie in other ways very similar to *City Lights*. Again, Charlie plays caretaker to another vulnerable young heroine (Purviance), whom he rescues from gypsies. But with her then falling for a handsome artist and being reunited with family, Charlie is on the romantic outside looking in. However, Chaplin tacks on an eleventh hour romantic wake-up call for Purviance, who suddenly realizes the importance of Charlie and orchestrates their reconciliation. Ambiguity is better.

Despite the uniqueness of *City Lights'* conclusion, there are several other signature sequences in the film that give it a creative run for its money. The most notable is the picture's opening, which works on three hilarious creative levels. To set the scene, city officials and a large crowd have gathered for the unveiling of a three-figure monument entitled "Peace and Prosperity." But first these local dignitaries, a rotund mayoral type (played by longtime Chaplin regular Henry Bergman) and a stereotypical pompous clubwoman, must proceed with the standard boring civic-political chatter associated with these events. What Chaplin does next is brilliant. He uses the synchronized distorted sounds of a saxophone to double as this typical public-spirited prattle. In this one simple act, the comedian produces a double satirical whammy — undercutting both the mind-numbing political event *and* the poor sound quality of early talkies. Had *City Lights* showcased little more than this one-two punch beginning, period critics would still have lionized the movie. For example, *The Hollywood Reporter* observed, "Chaplin has opened his picture with a knockout blow. The first gag is the best and takes an awful sock at the talkies."[29] The *New York Sun* described the scene as a "devastating gag showing Mr. Chaplin's opinion of the talkies as a succession of impressionistic noises," while the *New York Herald Tribune* called it "a grand bit of fooling."[30]

The beauty of this unfolding satirical situation is that Chaplin has not yet revealed his comic coup de grace. This arrives with the unveiling of the three-figure statue configuration: a seated maiden perhaps symbolic of justice, with two standing males — one implying peace by way of an extended hand, the other a defensive warrior brandishing a sword. Where's the satirical joke? Charlie is asleep in the motherly lap of justice! As film historian Gerald Mast has amusingly noted, the iconoclastic Charlie "doesn't break the idol, but he does sit on it."[31] In fact, one of the ironies of Chaplin is that he is both icon and iconoclast, whose Charlie persona is an equally paradoxical everyman — not like any one figure but rather a composite of them all.

Chaplin effectively milks this comic send-up of officialdom by falling back on more realism — poor Charlie simply tries to get out of the spotlight, but everything he does is a further inspired affront to the dignity of the situation, from planting his keister against the feminine nose of justice, to sitting on justice's extended hand. He even manages to get those Charlie-defining baggy pants skewered by the warrior's sword, which manages to hang him up briefly, like a flag. The analogy is also one that no doubt would have appealed to Chaplin, since he tops Charlie's comic attempts to extricate himself from this dilemma by introducing "The Star-Spangled Banner" on the soundtrack — a fitting number for a civic unveiling. Yet, it wonderfully interjects what comedy theorist Henri Bergson has famously described as "mechanical inelasticity," that funny phenomenon where other actions are called for but prior conditioning cause one to respond in the most predictable of ways.[32] Consequently, though Charlie should continue to work at getting his trousers loose from said sword, the national anthem has him attempting to come to attention while he quite literally dangles in the wind. Knee-jerk "patriotism" has never been funnier. It also represents a safeguard for Charlie. Chaplin's use of more distorted sound effects has made it clear that the unveiling audience has been less than pleased by the Tramp's derailing of a serious ceremony. But since they, too, are comic victims to mechanical inelasticity, "The Star-Spangled Banner" manages to momentarily defuse their anger until Charlie can finally manage an escape.

(A year after *City Lights*, the mechanical inelasticity application of "The Star-Spangled Banner" was used as a comic safeguard by Laurel and Hardy at the close of their Academy Award–winning short subject *The Music Box*, 1932.)

Like the aforementioned André Bazin, Siegfried Kracauer is another realist theorist especially taken with the Tramp. However, like Chaplin, he is a realist hesitant about the use of sound. In a section of Kracauer's theory text entitled "Speech undetermined from within," he praises the opening of *City Lights* and the distorted sound which Chaplin substitutes for the speech of the pompous civic leaders.[33] Kracauer is afraid of a "theatrical" situation, in which dialogue would displace the visual. Sound for Kracauer should reinforce the visual, which is just what the Chaplin example does.

If *City Lights'* conclusion is the height of pathos, and its opening is the most brilliant of double-edged satirical thrusts, the movie's boxing sequence is the most laugh-out-loud scene. *Variety* went so far as to claim:

> Perhaps the [film's] high spot is a burlesque prize fight which in rehearsal time alone must have taken weeks to shoot. Chaplin's feat is making this passage not only stand up but stand out behind recent features which have had some pretty funny ring fight stuff themselves.[34]

The *New York Times'* verdict on this scene was equally stellar—"the stretch [of the movie] that caused most merriment."[35] Charlie has accepted a boxing match which is to be fixed, with the Tramp to receive a guaranteed split of the purse. But his sure thing opponent is suddenly called away, and Charlie must face a legitimate tough guy (Hank Mann) with a winner-take-all attitude. Determined to obtain funding for the blind girl's operation, the antiheroic Charlie reluctantly enters the ring. What follows is more of a choreographed dance than a typical boxing sequence. One is reminded of a jealous W.C. Fields' left-handed compliment about his comic rival, "He's the world's greatest ballet dancer, and if I ever meet the son of a bitch I'll murder him!"[36]

There are numerous delightful facets to the boxing scene, from Charlie's comically coward clinches, to the ring bell rope becoming attached to his body, which results in a momentary rescue when smacked — the pull of his body ringing the bell. But as in a comic nightmare for the Tramp, when he moves towards his corner the bell is again rung, and a new fighting round begins. While the rapid succession of rings which follow means a nonstop revolving door–like situation of danger-reprieve-danger-reprieve, the pivotal boxing material involves Chaplin's orchestration of not only himself and fellow pugilist Mann but also the referee (Eddie Baker). The manner in which their movements are comically synchronized is a treat to behold, from first using the referee like a shield, to a choreography eventually so elaborate that Charlie manages to play at being the referee while Baker and Mann go at it.

Not surprisingly, the *Variety* critic who felt the ring routine must have taken weeks to perfect was correct. Chaplin spent thirty days rehearsing the elaborate choreography with his referee and ring opponent.[37] The comedian's attention to detail here is reminiscent of his imaginatively staged scene in the early classic *Easy Street* (1917), where the movements of Charlie's potential neighborhood antagonists are closely synchronized with his every step. Regardless, Charlie's *City Lights* ring misadventure ultimately takes a predictably antiheroic route (a loss), and he must continue to look for other ways to obtain cash for the blind girl's operation.

As a sidebar: The comedian was hardly a stranger to cinematic ring material. He had played a comic referee in Mack Sennett's *The Knockout* (1914), hitting the canvas more frequently than the picture's nominal boxing star, Fatty Arbuckle. This short subject might have been the catalyst for *City Lights'* inclusion of the referee in the physical shtick. And in Essanay's *The Champion* (1915) Charlie plays a long-shot pugilist who pulls out a victory by putting a horseshoe in his boxing glove! Film historian David Robinson has noted that "Chaplin at this time loved boxing — going to prizefights with members of his staff was his favorite leisure occupation...."[38] The boxing promoter in Los Angeles at the time was Thomas McCarey, the father of later acclaimed film comedy director Leo McCarey. The elder McCarey's most famous staged fight, the Wolgast-Rivers lightweight championship (July 4, 1912), was the real-life source material for a comic twist in *City Lights'* ring sequence, in which Chaplin and his opponent simultaneously flatten each other. This formerly unheard of development actually occurred in the McCarey bout: "The two fighters connected with simultaneous punches and both went down, apparently knocked out."[39] Though Chaplin did not witness the event, he

The Tramp (Chaplin) and the inebriated millionaire (Harry Myers) along the *City Lights* river.

was so enamored of raconteur Thomas McCarey's later rendition of this unbelievable incident that he included a variation of it in *City Lights*.⁴⁰ (Leo McCarey would also work a similar salute to this double whammy into his boxing picture, *The Milky Way*, 1936.)

Since Charlie's *City Lights* boxing produces no cash, the forgetful alcoholic millionaire (Harry Myers) will eventually have to produce the needed funds. Though none of the Tramp's scenes with Myers are quite on a par with the three pantheon sequences already highlighted, they are all consistently funny. The most elaborate is the attempted river suicide which got Myers' predecessor Henry Clive fired (the dispute over heating the studio pool). With the millionaire's life being dependent upon Charlie having saved him, which nearly resulted in the comic drowning of the Tramp, Myers is the most supportive friend ... when he has been drinking.

More than a comedy teammate for Charlie, the millionaire provides an upper class environment in which the Tramp can play at being a rich man. Probably the most incongruously comic scene along these lines has Charlie driving his millionaire friend's Rolls Royce ... in search of discarded cigarettes. But the topper for the sequence is the look of surprise on the face of a fellow hobo, after Charlie bolts from the most ritzy of cars and beats him to a cigarette butt.

The millionaire also provides a backdrop for Chaplin's love of visual puns — mistaking one look-alike object for another. For instance, after Myers' character takes the Tramp to a nightclub, Charlie gets so involved eating his spaghetti that he mistakes a party streamer for one of his noodles and nearly gobbles his way to the ceiling. Later, at a party at the millionaire's mansion, the Tramp mistakes a guest's bald head for a melon being served during the festivities. When this apparent culinary treat turns out to be someone's noggin, Charlie has the most surreal of moments.

Though these visual puns are brief throwaway scenes of comic exaggeration, much of *City Lights* (despite its war on talk) is given over to *realistic* slices of life: Charlie trying not to look at the nude statue in a store window, or Chaplin defusing a potentially overly sentimental sequence (a smitten Charlie staring longingly at the blind girl) by merely having her rinse a flower container and unknowingly pitch the water directly into his face. Such bits and pieces are so memorable in and of themselves that they have inspired comparable other scenes and whole movies by a host of Chaplin aficionado filmmakers. Examples might range from Roberto Rossellini recycling the naughty fascination of a nude statue by a priest in *Open City* (1945), to Woody Allen grafting a sighted variation of *City Lights*' conclusion onto *Manhattan* (1979). But for a metaphorical impact on a complete picture, one has only to view Federico Fellini's *La Strada* (*The Road*, 1954) and the bewitching performance of Giulietta Masina (Fellini's wife) as Gelsomina, the clown-like servant to Anthony Quinn's strongman, to appreciate the depth of Chaplin's influence on Fellini. The film's mixing of comedy and pathos, Masina's delightful mimicry, even the title—*The Road*—all suggest the world of Charlie. More specifically, one could define the character of Gelsomina, the lightheartedly loyal but ill-used servant, as a somber variation on the equally lightheartedly loyal Charlie of *City Lights*. Though Charlie is neither so mentally simple as Gelsomina, nor so defeated (Gelsomina's eventual hurt destroys her will to live), both beautifully portray first the humor of complete devotion, and then the pain of rejection when that love is not returned. Appropriately, Fellini called *City Lights* a "masterpiece among the silents."⁴¹

City Lights' impact on *La Strada* is even more significant, since Fellini considered the work his "most representative film," as well as the one in which he feels closest to the characters.⁴² Yet there is no shortage of other Chaplin-flavored Fellini films, from *Nights of Cabiria* (1956), with Masina's touchingly comic streetwalker who longs for love, to *The Clowns* (1970), which often evokes individual scenes from Chaplin movies, as well as including Victoria Chaplin in the cast, as a tribute to her dad.

One would need, of course, several additional chapters to chronicle all the footnotes to Chaplin in the works of other artists. But a final example merits noting, with regard to *City Lights*. France's greatest director is arguably Jean Renoir, son of the equally acclaimed Impressionist painter, Pierre-Auguste Renoir, and this filmmaker was profoundly influenced by Chaplin. Renoir pays constant tribute to the creator of Charlie, whether it is the story of an iconoclastic Tramp in *Boudu Saved from Drowning* (1932), or the *Modern Times*–ish conclusion of *The Lower Depths* (1936). In his unforgettable *Rules of the Game* (1939) Renoir makes direct reference to Chaplin's *The Count* (1916) by the manner in which it replicates that short subject's high society chase and confusion of identities. But for all this homage, the most poignant and pathos-oriented Chaplin connection occurs in the Renoir masterpiece *Grand Illusion* (1937). Erich von Stroheim plays the refined German commandant of a World War I prisoner of war camp. In this drab stone-gray fortress he allows his cultured sensitivity to manifest itself through both a friendship with a similarly well-bred prisoner (Pierre Fresnay) and the cultivation of a single flower. But when each of these duty-driven men play out their obligation — creating a diversion for an escape, and thwarting such an escape — Fresnay's character dies at the hand of his friend, von Stroheim. Though both men accept and respect these developments (Fresnay suffers a lingering death), one last sees von Stroheim cutting the flower.

Unlike some film classics not fully appreciated until years later, such as Buster Keaton's *The General* (1927) or the Marx Brothers' *Duck Soup* (1933), *City Lights* was acclaimed from day one. The New York premiere (February 6, 1931) produced kudos where the optimum word was *genius*. The *New York Sun* stated, "The genius of the Garbos and [Jack] Oakies may be disputed, but the genius of Chaplin is admitted — now that *City Lights* ... has opened in our town at the Cohan [Theatre]."⁴³ The *New York Post* added:

> For once again Chaplin's consummate artistry is put forth with that earthy simplicity which is the touchstone of his genius, so that it is impossible not to share keenly in the tribulations which beset the friendly figure in the shabby hat and baggy trousers.⁴⁴

The term "genius" was not good enough for the *New York World*, who preferred the description "cosmic rightness"!⁴⁵ Even the sedate *New York Times* produced a mini-headline for its review of "cosmic rightness" proportions — "Pathos Is Mingled With Mirth in a Production of Admirable Artistry."⁴⁶ The *New York Herald Tribune* had no such restraint. Critic Richard Watts, Jr., opened his critique with the suggestion that if *City Lights* did not result in "dancing in the streets, ringing of bells and awarding of the city's keys ... then something has gone wrong with New York's powers of appreciation."⁴⁷ (When the film opened in London, no less an artist than George Bernard Shaw said, "The little fellow is a genius whom none of us has properly appreciated."⁴⁸)

An interesting corollary to all these hosannas was the previous Chaplin quality barometer film to which period critics compared *City Lights*. Without question today, the only rival for the movie's supremacy in the Chaplin canon would be *The Gold Rush*. Yet, in none of these aforementioned reviews, nor any other one consulted, is that watershed movie mentioned. Surprisingly, the most frequent 1931 comparison keynote picture was Chaplin's *The Pilgrim* (1923).[49] A perfectly charming film and even somewhat controversial in 1921 (Chaplin's free-spirited impersonation of a clergyman got the movie banned in Pennsylvania), it now seems an odd choice against all the inspired moments in *The Gold Rush*.

Maybe these earlier critics made a flower and ambiguity connection between *City Lights* and *The Pilgrim*. Minister Charlie, an escaped convict, has been arrested at the end of *The Pilgrim*. But a benevolent Western sheriff takes Charlie to the Mexican border and gives him a chance to escape by suggesting the Tramp go pick some *wild* flowers across the line in Mexico. But as Charlie attempts to do that, the antiheroic component kicks in and some banditos come shooting by. Consequently, as the Tramp attempts to run for freedom, this new danger factor necessitates that he straddle the border between the two countries — not quite safe, not quite free.

Besides this affinity for *The Pilgrim*, New York critics also donated a great deal of print space to Chaplin's visit to the city. Prime topics ranged from the artist's views on talkies to the fact that Albert Einstein had accompanied Chaplin to the Los Angeles premiere of *City Lights*. (Chaplin's escort had been his *Gold Rush* heroine Georgia Hale, who had nearly replaced Cherrill as the blind girl.) Chaplin shared a provocative perspective on how he might one day handle sound with an unnamed *New York American* journalist:

> If I do go into the talkies, it will be in a different character. I shall change my makeup. My own medium is pantomime. I don't think of myself in terms of speech. The talkies are stiff, too restricted. They lack flow. They're easier to make than silent pictures, but they can't be molded in the creative process. They lack beauty for me.[50]

His comments on a "different character" and a new makeup anticipate his Parisian Bluebeard in the groundbreaking dark comedy *Monsieur Verdoux* (1947). But ironically, these 1931 Chaplin comments appear in an article whose run-on title suggests the transition will occur shortly —"Old Chaplin Dead? Say It's Not True, Charlie: Cane, Derby and Mustache Doomed If He Enters Talkies." The same essay shared, "Einstein rollicked at a [Los Angeles] showing of *City Lights*, nudged Charlie until Chaplin's ribs were sore."[51] Shortly after the comedian's arrival in New York he had shared with another reporter his thoughts on a pre-screening dinner with Einstein, "I'm afraid I did all the talking, and [I] talked only about pictures. But we could not very well talk about the Einstein theory; I don't understand a thing about it."[52] (In a comic footnote to Einstein's 1931 visit to Los Angeles — he received various offers to sign a film contract! But he declined.[53]) In Chaplin's later autobiography he added these concluding thoughts on the Los Angeles premiere of *City Lights*, as it pertained to his special guest: "During the final scene I noticed Einstein wiping his eyes — further evidence that scientists are incurable sentimentalists."[54]

Though the New York opening boasted no one of Einstein's stature, there were some prominent guests, too. Chaplin was accompanied by the wife of media power-broker William Randolph Hearst, and famed American editor and drama critic George Jean Nathan. Other eminent first nighters included film censorship czar Will Hays and writer Anita Loos, best known for her comic novel, *Gentlemen Prefer Blondes* (1925). With regard to Chaplin, Loos' satirical scripts had originally helped solidify the career of the comedian's best friend, Douglas Fairbanks.

Of course, with a Depression era premiere ticket price of eleven dollars a seat, a "crowd of about fifteen hundred gathered outside the theater, [and] temporarily blocked traffic at Times Square between 42nd and 43rd Streets...."[55] *New York American* movie critic Regina Crewe undoubtedly spoke for most 1931 fans when she wrote, "If Charlie wants to continue making silent films, no one will find fault with him ... The only thing we clamor for is Chaplin pictures — sound or silent. He should make more — one in two years is not sufficient."[56] But *New York Evening Journal* film critic Rose Pelswick probably offered the most comically practical take on Chaplin's provocative decision to remain cinematically silent, "*City Lights* has no dialogue. And it's just as well, because if the picture had had words, the laughs and applause of last evening's audience would have drowned them out."[57]

Chaplin's 1931 feelings about keeping the Tramp silent were so strong that he turned down an amazing offer of $650,000 to do a series of radio broadcasts. As reported in the *New York Times*, "the comedian intended at all costs to preserve the 'mystery' and 'illusion' of the character he had created on the screen."[58] Of course, Chaplin's idealism here was possibly bolstered by the record earnings *City Lights* was beginning to generate. For example, even before the movie opened, he received a $2,000,000 advance for the United Kingdom — "the largest individual deal ever known in the British film industry."[59] And his tour of Europe with the picture was one command performance after another. Chaplin was so fêted that his travel took on a comic tone. "The French capital is not to be outdone by London, where the comedian was the guest of the Prime Minister. Tomorrow Mr. Chaplin has a luncheon engagement with Foreign Minister Briand."[60] (And he would subsequently be the first foreign film actor to be decorated with France's Legion of Honor medal.[61]) Paradoxically, the only bad European press Chaplin received was when he did *not* visit a country, such as neglecting to honor Prague with a visit![62]

Like all great art, the angles of vision one might apply to *City Lights* are endless. But for closing comments it seems most appropriate to return to the picture's haunting finale. Beyond its mix of comedy and pathos, it is a moving exercise in secular humanism — trying to make sense of life's emotional and/or intellectual experiences. Gerald Mast went so far as to suggest the movie was never about any potential future between Charlie and the flower girl — "Its real subject is what sorts of human actions make human existence possible."[63] For the Tramp, the key human action is sacrifice, even when that means losing the love of one's life. But that sacrifice never plays as a lesson. Maybe this is Chaplin's greatest gift — what the later *New Yorker* critic Anthony Lane called the challenge the comedian most relished, "How do you make an adventure out of a sermon?"[64]

Despite the baggy pants and those "east-and-west feet," Charlie remains a humanism tutorial, asserting human dignity and worth in the most challenging of situations — not a bad foundation for cinema's still reigning king of comedy.

CHAPTER 2

Eddie Cantor's
The Kid from Spain (1932)

> When the masquerading as a Mexican Eddie Cantor is asked how he wants to die by a tough guy rival in *The Kid from Spain*, he says, "I think I'd like to die from eating strawberries." Informed there won't be any strawberries for five months, he answers, "That's okay, I wait."

While Eddie Cantor (1892–1964) is probably the least well-known comedian of those addressed in this text, he was an American entertainment *giant* in the early 1930s. Film historian David Thomson observed, "Al Jolson may have been America's biggest [stage] star in the early decades of the twentieth century, but Eddie Cantor wasn't far behind — and in certain fields surpassed him."[1] Two of those fields were radio and the movies. *The Eddie Cantor Show* was the top-rated program on radio in its first season (1931–32).[2] The next two seasons he would not only repeat that distinction, his program would pull in "over 50 per cent of the listening public," a staggering number.[3] While a radio staple for the rest of the decade, his occasional forays into film were also very successful. In 1933 he even made Hollywood's most coveted list — the annual top ten box office stars, impressively finishing ahead of Wallace Beery, Jean Harlow, Clark Gable, Mae West, Norma Shearer, and Joan Crawford.[4] What made this especially notable was that during Cantor's 1930s heyday he never made more than a single film a year. Top ten box office numbers for most stars were based upon several movies per year. (Interestingly enough, Cantor's banner 1933 grosses can be credited to *The Kid from Spain*, a late 1932 release. His only 1933 movie, *Roman Scandals*, did not open until December of that year.)

So how does one characterize the Cantor persona? Recycling film critic Janet Maslin's 1992 pocket definition of Robin Williams would be a start—"More of an energy source than an actor."[5] A description of Cantor as a Jewish leprechaun also comes to mind. Like today's late night talk show host Conan O'Brien, Cantor was all about nervous animation. Indeed, just as O'Brien cannot do his opening monologue without moving in and out of the camera frame, Cantor's hand-clapping and skipping about the stage (often while singing novelty songs like "If You Knew Susie Like I Know Susie") was a microphone problem for early radio. Of course, O'Brien's bobbing style purposely plays with the television format, *à la* Ernie Kovacs, while Cantor's comic dance shtick problem with early radio was corrected only with a portable mike.

Most enduring screen comedians, however, have a face and/or body which doubles as a comedy mask. This produces a head start on humor — they literally look funny before they say something laughable. Comedy historian Henry Jenkins even provocatively suggests that the antisocial tendencies synonymous with cinema clowns are "marked directly onto their bodies":

> The clowns display abnormally large eyes (Eddie Cantor, Hugh Herbert) and mouths (Winnie Lightner, Joe E. Brown), bulbous noses (W.C. Fields, Jimmy Durante), angular and contorted physiques (Groucho Marx, Bert Wheeler), and unkempt hair (Harpo Marx, Ed Wynn).[6]

Now whether one buys these goofy appearances as iconoclastic DNA markings, or simply the standard shtick for comedians, no one would contest that looking funny is a pivotal part of being funny.

Cantor amusingly maximized the visual potential of his undersized antihero with the owl eyes. That is, he could register little-boy comic fear by making those already large peepers banjo-sized. Steve Allen called this Cantor's "frightened-rabbit

One gets a sense of Eddie Cantor's expressive eyes in this *Kid from Spain* scene, with Robert Young (right).

expression."⁷ But on the flip side, the comedian could turn the most innocent of remarks into sexual innuendo with a roll of those popeyes. Historian Jenkins has whimsically described this latter phenomenon as Cantor's "eye-rolling double entendres."⁸ Thus, while the old proverb might credit the eyes as being the window to the soul, Cantor rerouted them to the funny bone.

Thinking of Cantor, I am reminded of the *Fargo* (1996) witness' description of character actor Steve Buscemi, who also has bulgy, saucer-sized, sad eyes: "The little guy was kinda funny-lookin' ... Funny-lookin' more than most people, even." One should hasten to add, though, that unlike the minimalist restraint of the typically dark comedy Buscemi performance, Cantor was a hopping, bubbling, make 'em laugh force of comedy, from an era when performers seemed committed to both entertaining *and* being loved.

Cantor's signature movement had actually been born of self-defense. Comedy historian and show business personality Joe Franklin, who knew and idolized the comedian, later stated, "Cantor's fast moving, bobbing style of entertaining was a hangover from his tomato-ducking days in vaudeville when he had to move fast or suffer the consequences."⁹ Fittingly, self-preservation has long helped mold the personae of comedians. For example, both Groucho Marx and Robin Williams developed their propensity for machine gun patter to avert the potential anger of hard-to-please audiences. Saturation comedy was the best antidote for a joke which misfired: Follow it up with something else ... quickly.

Cantor, the performer who so dominated show business at the start of the Great Depression, had been born (1892) during America's last major depression. His humble entertainment roots were in New York amateur nights and burlesque. He worked as a singing waiter in Brooklyn and played Coney Island cabarets. Cantor was also part of comedy teams, first with Sammy Kessler, and later with Al Lee. He graduated to quality vaudeville during the World War I era (1914–18). But Cantor's show business validation came in 1917 when he first joined the *Ziegfeld Follies*, New York's most razzle dazzle entertainment showplace.

Theatrical producer Florenz Ziegfeld helped create what is known as the revue in his *Follies of 1907*. This evolved into an annual production known as the *Ziegfeld Follies*— a mix of elegantly gowned long-legged showgirls in ritzy tableaux, and America's greatest comedians. Cantor would be a fixture in the *Follies* in 1917, 1918, and 1919, enabling him to work with such legendary laugh makers as Will Rogers, W.C. Fields, Bert Williams, and Fanny Brice. Cantor became close to all these clowns, and many more, including Jimmy Durante, who was the piano player in the saloon where Banjo Eyes was a singing waiter.

Probably the most significant of the group, however, with regard to Cantor, was W.C. Fields. Cantor had been orphaned at two and raised in New York's Lower East Side by his maternal grandmother, known to all as "Esther." It was a tough hand-to-mouth existence, and school definitely received short shrift. "Professor" Fields became Cantor's college. They would room together when a "pre-season" edition of the *Follies* would go on the road to prepare for the revue's New York opening. And while the older comedian gave Cantor entertainment tips, especially as they pertained to pantomime (Fields' act was then still silent), the key thrust of their relationship was about literature. Fields traveled everywhere with three large steamer trunks ... two of which were filled with books! Like Charlie Chaplin, Fields was a self-taught, bookish sort who most admired Charles Dickens. Starting with *Oliver Twist*, Fields would quiz Cantor nightly on various classic novels and offer extended tutorials on the world according to W.C. Fields. These bonus insights often keyed upon culinary subjects and fine wines. For the alcoholic Fields, drinking rivaled his love of comedy. At times he even combined the two. For instance, when asked if he had ever had DTs, Fields replied, "I don't know. It's hard to tell where Hollywood ends and the DTs begin."[10] Cantor recalled that when the 1917 *Follies* went on tour and opened big in Boston, after the show Fields ordered several bottles of champagne at the hotel. He told Cantor, "Here you are, son. Let's drink to your health." Cantor later added, "We kept drinking to my health till we damn near ruined it."[11]

During the 1920s, Cantor and Fields simultaneously graduated to major Broadway stage successes. From 1923–26 Cantor would have a huge hit with *Kid Boots*, while mentor Fields also had a triumph in *Poppy* (1923–24). Though it is hard today to imagine Cantor and Fields in *silent* films, both of these signature theatrical productions (with their stars in tow) resurfaced as motion pictures. Under the direction of D. W. Griffith, *Poppy* became *Sally of the Sawdust* (1925). *Kid Boots* retained its original title and opened in film theaters the following year.

At the end of the decade, Cantor would score his greatest stage hit in the Ziegfeld-produced Broadway musical comedy *Whoopee!* (1928–29). But when this play was adapted to the screen (1930), sound had just come to the movies, and Cantor was all the better for it. Between his comic patter and such hit songs as "Making Whoopee" and "My Baby Just Cares for Me," this tale of a hyper-hypochondriac firmly established Cantor as a screen star. Independently produced by the now legendary film pioneer Samuel Goldwyn (1879–1974), the film had Ziegfeld as a technical adviser. Goldwyn had long admired Ziegfeld's showmanship, from the elaborate sets and costumes to the beautiful women. Thus, it was a natural for Goldwyn to make a Ziegfeld production into a film.

Now flash forward to the Goldwyn-produced, Cantor-starring *The Kid from Spain*. Again one has lavish Ziegfeld-like spectacle, complemented by the musical number staging of Busby Berkeley, who had also choreographed the production numbers in the film version of *Whoopee!* But the real auteur on *Spain* was the brilliant young director Leo McCarey (1898–1969), who had been a major creative comic force behind Hal Roach in the silent era, and whose sound film classics would range from the Marx Brothers in *Duck Soup* (1933, see chapter 4), to the populism of the multiple Oscar-winning *Going My Way* (1944).

Since Goldwyn was a producer who thought he was a director, his attempts to influence the production were an ongoing creative thorn in McCarey's side. For example, like most 1930s producers, Goldwyn believed in a Hollywood caste system, or, as McCarey later described it, "a director was a director, a writer a writer ... So if you tried to intrude in someone else's province, he'd say ... 'That's not your department. Stay out of it'"[12] Consequently, McCarey had to keep his rewriting contributions, always a given on a Leo production, secret. Cantor, who later described McCarey as an "individualist with a tremendous comedy sense ... [who'd] rewrite a script done by Paddy

Chayefsky or Eugene O'Neill," chronicled one such secret session in his memoir *Take My Life*:

> One Saturday morning we got to a scene that didn't play funny. "Why don't you get sick, Eddie?" McCarey said. "We'll go to Santa Barbara [Leo's beach house], rewrite the thing, and shoot Monday morning."
> "I'm not only sick, I'm almost blind." I cried and went into a sick-headache routine. An hour later we were en route to Santa Barbara. Monday we shot one of the best scenes of the picture. Goldwyn, seeing the rushes, was amused and baffled. He couldn't figure out where the scene had come from.[13]

To Goldwyn's credit, he always bankrolled a first-class production. Indeed, the mere fact that the picture had a million-dollar budget at the height of the Great Depression was news itself. Regardless, *Spain*'s pool of behind-the-screen talent included the song- and sometimes script-writing team of Bert Kalmar and Harry Ruby (now forever associated with the Marx Brothers, such as Groucho's theme song "Hooray for Captain Spaulding"), choreography by the aforementioned Busby "Overhead Shot" Berkeley, cinematography by Gregg Toland (later creator of deep-focus in *Citizen Kane*, 1941), and director McCarey — arguably on the eve of being the greatest comedy auteur in the history of cinema.[14] Couple all this, of course, with America's new personality comedian sensation (Cantor), and the movie's beautiful "Goldwyn Girls" for background window dressing, with two of their number (Betty Grable and Paulette Goddard) earmarked for future stardom, and *Spain* became one of the top box office hits of the year.

Given all these accolades, the *Spain* storyline is rather thin, but such is often the case in the world of personality comedy. At its most basic, the plot turns upon a case of mistaken identity. Eddie Williams (Cantor) has gone to Mexico on the lam, wrongly accused of a crime. But this is a mythical Mexico, as only a 1930s Hollywood could produce. Early in the decade the film capital specialized in comedies set in zany foreign lands, especially small fictitious European countries. Cantor's picture was sandwiched in the midst of this mini-movement. Prior to *Spain*, *Cracked Nuts* (1931) had the team of Bert Wheeler and Robert Woolsey in the land of El Dorania — which the latter had won in a crap game! Later that year Sylvania was the equally imaginary setting for Will Rogers' title character in *Ambassador Bill* (1931). Shortly after *Spain*, *Million Dollar Legs* (1932) had W.C. Fields as the President of Klopstokia, a nutty country obsessed with the Olympics (an event which had just been hosted by Los Angeles). And *Duck Soup* featured Groucho as the cocky dictator of Freedonia, while brothers Harpo and Chico were spies for the equally fabricated Sylvania — without a trace of Will Rogers' Ambassador Bill.

Cantor's story also might have gone with another comically counterfeit country, but the thin plot had a legitimate reason for using a real country (Mexico), albeit the most goofy Mexico imaginable. Given Eddie's fugitive status, he is under constant comedy surveillance by the law. His cover is to pretend to be Don Sebastian the Second, the son of a famous Spanish bullfighter — thus the title, *The Kid from Spain*. Naturally, Cantor's character will eventually have to get into the bullfighting arena — which represents the picture's comic finale.

As with most 1930s personality comedies, *Spain* has the genre's standard romantic subplot involving Eddie's Mexican college roommate Ricardo (a miscast Robert Young) and Anita (Ruth Hall), the daughter of a wealthy landowner. Young was at the beginning of a lengthy journeyman film career which would be usurped by his later television stardom as the title characters in *Father Knows Best* (1954–63) and *Marcus Welby, M. D.* (1969–76). Young's *Spain* casting as a Mexican could only occur in that zany early 1930s Hollywood mindset about foreign lands. But he is a good straight man for Cantor, and Young's character provides the comedian with a south-of-the-border home base.

Spain was not without other prominent performers in support, such as character actor Noah Beery playing Hall's father. But Cantor is best complemented by the sexy eccentricity of Lydia Roberti (1906–38), who plays the comedian's uninhibited love interest, Rosalie. Roberti's previous film outing had been in the aforementioned and equally loopy *Million Dollar Legs*. The Cantor-Roberti teaming in *Spain* was a perfect fit for several reasons. First, her man-chasing character was just what Cantor's wannabe Romeo needed. Second, Roberti's background as a former trapeze artist and daughter of a circus clown allowed her to gracefully match any physical shtick opportunities Cantor threw her way, such as repeatedly using a shapely naked leg (from behind a dressing curtain) to point Eddie towards her clothes. Third, just as it was later said that Ginger Rogers gave Fred Astaire sex appeal, the sensual Roberti's comic interest in Eddie made him appear, if not sexy, at least owl-eyed desirable. Fourth, the fact that platinum-blonde Roberti was playing Ruth Hall's *Mexican* best friend was yet another absurdist Hollywood take on life south of the border — a world where a little Jewish comic (Cantor) could be mistaken for a great matador.

Cantor's scenes with Roberti are the most entertaining of the film, beginning with their first encounter. Eddie has entered Rosalie's bedroom on a mistaken rescue mission. She tells him, "Don't look at me, I'm half undressed." He replies, "That's okay, I keep one eye closed." Naturally, that other attentive banjo-sized eye follows her every move. But Rosalie is not the shy type. When it soon becomes apparent that Eddie has kidnapped the wrong girl, he moans, "What have I done?" She invitingly answers, "Nothing yet. But I'm waiting." Rosalie hides the key to the car down her front, stranding them until she gets a passionate kiss. After Eddie gifts her with said smooch, he goes limp, and one can practically see smoke coming from his ears. When Cantor's character recovers, she gives him back the key, but he puts it back down her front so they can ardently go at it again. Then, after a third amorous kiss (each of which has involved bending Rosalie over, with Eddie's back to the camera), she gets all weak-kneed. Roberti's character goes to return the key but he casually shows her that he has it already. A surprised but happy smile of naughty recognition comes over her and she pursues him anew. However, even a pre–Code picture can only go so far. Consequently, they next go into a musical number, "Look What You've Done," which entertainingly includes Roberti singing the lyric, "What did you want to make those eyes for?" as Cantor rolls his signature peepers.

Since song was always a central part of his stage persona, there are two other pivotal Cantor numbers. The first is entitled "In the Moonlight," which segues into a comic historical perspective on love. The other seminal number, "What a Perfect Combination," is the highlight of the nightclub scene, late in the picture. Once again, Eddie must avoid detection, so he disguises himself in blackface. This being a Mexico only of the movies, Cantor suddenly becomes the floorshow and sings, "What a Perfect Combination," complete with his skipping gait and clapping hands. Though blackface now raises all kinds of politically incorrect red flags, it was a standard part of that era's entertainment world. Moreover, film historian David Thomson calls Cantor's use of the technique "neither politically correct nor incorrect" because "this blackface is purely cosmetic: there's not the slightest suggestion of imitating or patronizing or colonizing blacks, not a touch of [Al] Jolsonish minstrelsy; this is just a Cantor trademark that works for him (and for us)."[15]

Regardless, when Cantor reprises "What a Perfect Combination" as a duet with Roberti at the picture's close, it is without the blackface. And the scene plays just as effectively, though maybe that can simply be credited to what a period critic called, "The bouncing, attractive Lyda Roberti."[16]

Spain's huge commercial success was no doubt also fueled by Cantor's non-stop plugging of the movie on his popular radio program, as well as in his stage work. The latter activity involved a six-month vaudeville tour that opened Thanksgiving week 1932, coinciding with the opening of *Spain* in most American markets.[17] Since big-time

Eddie Cantor (center) plays hard to get with sexy man-chasing Lyda Roberti in *The Kid from Spain*, with Robert Young (right).

vaudeville had evolved by the early 1930s into stage support of first-run movies, many Cantor fans then had the opportunity for a double dip of their favorite comedian. Even today, with those expressive rolling eyes or his signature comic song shtick of skipping gait and clapping hands, the Cantor energy level still makes *Spain* a very entertaining picture.

Period critics were almost unanimously of the same opinion. For instance, the *New York Post* observed, "Eddie Cantor contributes some excruciatingly funny moments, and they aggregate considerably more and better comedy than is to be found in the usual humorous picture."[18] But then, reviewers seemed to like everything about the movie, starting with megaphone man McCarey. The *Hollywood Reporter* said, "Leo McCarey's directions should land this fellow right on his feet in the front ranks of the present-day hit directors, for he has certainly done tricks with his handling of this production."[19]

The *New York Daily News* rave review lead also made note of another factor in the film's favor: "Eddie Cantor's *Kid from Spain* is a merry mixture of slapstick, song and that daring sport known as bull-fighting."[20] The matador subplot was the most fortuitous of developments for two reasons. First, just prior to the release of the film, Ernest Hemingway's book-length tribute to the sport, *Death in the Afternoon*, had been published to great critical acclaim and best seller status.[21] Second, one of Hemingway's highlighted matadors, the Brooklyn-born Sidney Franklin, was also featured in the film. Thus, here was a pop culture production whose eventual blockbuster status even received a boost from the tony world of literature. Rare was the review that did not devote considerable space to this provocation connection. For example, the *New York American* stated:

> Sidney Franklin, called by Mr. Death-in-the-Afternoon Hemingway, the sixth dam' best caballero in all Espagne, or words to that effect ... gives us, perhaps, the first authentic glimpse of the national Spanish sport as she should be played. And while it may seem less intriguing to Americans than a tied score with a minute play, still the bull fight has its points. And we don't mean on the horns of the bull.[22]

Leave it to the sports-conscious McCarey to even *score points* with the national pastime ... of another country! But he was probably also thinking about the added comedy potential for his star, or as the *New York Times* critic declared, "It is amusing enough just to think of Mr. Cantor undertaking the part of a matador."[23] Indeed, the merry mix of Hollywood and Hemingway even had film critics playing at being comics. To illustrate, the *New York Sun* reviewer said, "Mr. Franklin, at close range, swishes his cape or shawl — page Mr. Hemingway, I have forgotten what it is called."[24]

As might be expected, *Spain*'s comic highlight for many was Cantor's funny finale as a bullfighter. Even forty-five years later McCarey was very enthusiastic about the scene:

> In *The Kid from Spain* there is the most extraordinary *corrida* [single bullfight] that was ever filmed. And this is not only my opinion but that of the critics ... There was much humor and much emotion ... For five days we tried to shoot that sequence and we had multiple annoyances. When we wanted the bull to charge he didn't want to budge. And when the cameras weren't running, he tried to kill us all.[25]

Ironically, some of the most gripping footage from this bullfight was caught *after* a frustrated McCarey had left the arena. Thanks to a persistent cameraman (Toland) and Cantor's stunt double, a pivotal action sequence, to be intercut with film of the actor as a matador, was obtained. But it came at a cost — Cantor's double was hospitalized with several broken ribs. When the director visited him, the young man said, "Senor,

The comic incongruity of Cantor as a brave bullfighter in *The Kid from Spain*.

I had taken off my protective clothing! But I knew how much you needed that scene, so I did it anyhow."[26]

Though Cantor's time in the arena seldom put him at risk, he later confessed in his autobiography, "I've never been so scared in my life as I was during the bullfight sequence."[27] The gag idea for the scene was that the bull would respond to a certain code word. All Cantor's character had to say was, "Popocatepetl," and the animal would lie down. But as *comic* luck would have it, the bulls are switched, and the new animal does not respond to the term. (Ultimately, Cantor's comic matador subdues the thundering beast with a cloth of chloroform!)

As noted earlier by McCarey, period critics found the best part of this much praised picture to be Cantor's bullfighting finale. To illustrate, *Variety* opined, "The bullfight scene climaxes the funning, being properly pitched for a riotous top-off."[28] And the *New York Evening Journal*'s review opened with the claim, "An amusing sequence in which Eddie Cantor is chased around the arena by a bull is the highlight of the saucer-eyed star's new picture."[29] Of course, for Hollywood insiders, the "highlight" of the picture was the shooting of Sidney Franklin's serious clinic on bullfighting, included in the film to heighten Cantor's later spoofing of the sport. Many of the movie capital's great stars came out to watch Franklin perform at the special bull ring constructed on the United Artists lot. The film royalty included three of the studio's founders, Charlie Chaplin, Douglas Fairbanks, Sr., and Mary Pickford. In Franklin's later autobiography, the amusingly entitled *Bullfighter from Brooklyn*, this real matador was moved by Chaplin's and Fairbanks' concern for his safety.[30] But this was just bullfighting business as usual for the Brooklynite.

A close reading of *Spain*'s reviews reveals only a single occasional negative, one that had nothing to do with storyline, or stars. Several critics, despite their praise for the picture, were upset over Goldwyn's initial road show release policy — which meant *Spain*'s opening would be limited to a few select cities at a then high individual ticket price of $2.[31] While Goldwyn was no doubt out to get a quick return on his million dollar budget before going into general release, neither McCarey nor Cantor was pleased about this less than egalitarian pricing. In fact, their opposing view was sometimes cited in reviews. The most high-profile example occurred in *Variety*'s critique, which quoted Cantor: "A guy making a small salary must give up 10% of his [weekly] income to see me in a picture. That's too tough nowadays."[32] (The average price of a ticket at this time was just under a quarter.[33])

McCarey's differences with Goldwyn had, however, hardly been limited to ticket prices. The producer was forever getting into Leo's face if there were production delays. For instance, it took days to get a bull to jump a fence and chase matador Cantor down a corridor. While McCarey was the picture of patience, Goldwyn exploded:

> "Leo, why doesn't that bull jump?"
> "I'm trying to get him to jump."
> "Well, you're the director, aren't you?"
> "Yes, but the bull isn't a member of the Screen Actors Guild.
>   You're the boss, Sam, you tell him."[34]

Comic comebacks such as these did not go over well with the autocratic producer, and Goldwyn even made noises about replacing McCarey. But the director's overall orchestration of *Spain* could not be faulted, and the Irishman stayed.

Ironically, while Leo's personal wit was not yet known outside the film community, Goldwyn's comic bouts with the English language were known everywhere Hollywood columns were read. As a Polish Jew born in Warsaw, the producer's English malapropisms were almost as famous as his films. Bad weather was the catalyst for a McCarey-related example during the making of *Spain*. Goldwyn was widely reported to have told his director, "Tomorrow we shoot, whether it rains, whether it snows, whether it stinks."[35] McCarey would later joke that Goldwyn's fractured English helped prepare him for the world of the Marx Brothers, where verbal slapstick was also the standard currency.

Between the comedy collaboration of Cantor and McCarey, and the Goldwyn-driven showmanship, one had an inspired personality comedy film successfully integrated with the eye candy spectacle of the *Ziegfeld Follies*. What more welcome escapist entertainment could one ask for at the height of the Depression? It might not match Charlie Chaplin's ability to take low comedy to high art levels (*á la* the previous year's *City Lights*), but then no one else has matched that artistry either — then, or now. What is more, after all these years, *The Kid from Spain* still manages to be a *tour de silly*. One can ask little more from comedy.

CHAPTER 3

Mae West's
She Done Him Wrong (1933)

> When women go wrong, men go right after them.
> — Mae West in *She Done Him Wrong*

Who or what was Mae West (1893–1980)? She most resembled a female impersonator ... with the verbal wit of Oscar Wilde. Armed with this repartee, West somehow transformed a small, pleasantly plump, over-forty physical form (through platform shoes and padded 1890s gowns of hourglass proportions) into an inspired parody of sex. (She could transform an appearance into a performance.) Like many of her 1930s screen contemporaries, from Will Rogers to the Marx Brothers, she came to sound films with an established persona, honed from years of stage work. Also like many of these funnymen, especially Groucho and W.C. Fields, her older, cynical, worldly-wise screen character matched the harsher climate of the Depression. This was in marked contrast to the youthfully innocent and/or naïve screen clowns of the silent era, such as Harry Langdon, Harold Lloyd, and Buster Keaton.

Like film comedians of all eras, however, her persona began with an iconically comic physical presence. A steamy, or was that seamy, figure poured into that hourglass gown, she accented all the "merchandise" with the most come hither shimmying strut since Eve. But her sashay was provocatively slow, which paralleled the message of her merriment — savor the sensual, be it the West walk, or the sex act itself. After all, one of her defining songs featured in *She Done Him Wrong* heavily praises "A Guy What Takes His Time." (Along related but paradoxical lines, for a sensual spoofer of all things sexual, her elaborate period gowns made her the most covered of provocative performers.)

West's deliberately dainty style, moreover, further accented the sexual parody heart of her act — a titillating tease to a pay-off that 1930s censorship laws would never allow. This slowly methodical pacing also differentiates West from most of her comedy contemporaries. For example, the nervous antiheroic persona of Eddie Cantor was complemented by his helter-skelter dance steps whenever he sang one of his novelty songs. Groucho's bent-over, loping gait was always done in a fast-forward mode, as if to accent his driven nature to comically dominate. Of West's fellow 1930s comedy legends, only

W.C. Fields, her later *My Little Chickadee* (1940) co-star, matched Mae's drawn-out deliberate style. In fact, like West, Fields' leisurely lingering nature was often about the language. But whereas she pushed her speech towards sexual innuendo, Fields' overstated verbiage was an end in itself. That is, a primary part of his entertainment shtick was a drawling *verbal slapstick* dripping with the comically overstated language of the nineteenth-century romantic novel. (Appropriately, his favorite literary character was the like-minded Micawber of Charles Dickens' *David Copperfield*, a part he also played in MGM's 1935 adaptation of the novel.)

West's application of a slower pacing also fit with her propensity to set her screen stories during the 1890s, a seemingly more languid era. Of course, in all honesty, every era is probably equally hectic for its participants. But the looking-backwards filter of time often creates a nostalgic mindset that invariably pronounces this to have been a simpler period. Though there had been an initial reluctance on her home studio's (Paramount) part for West to use the 1890s setting for *She Done Him Wrong* (over the fear that this would not be attractive to younger audiences), this era was a good fit for three reasons. First, *Wrong* is based upon West's signature stage role of the 1920s — *Diamond Lil*, which originally opened in New York on April 9, 1928 (running 176 performances). In her autobiography *Goodness Had Nothing to Do with It* (1959), she confessed that the character of Lil best defined her: "I'm her and she's me and we're each other."[1] Also the 1890s period is central to how West both defined Lil (as playwright and star), and then closely recycled the figure as Lady Lou of *Wrong*. Second, for a 1930s production there was an appropriateness to an 1890s setting, since this was the last decade in which America had suffered through a depression. Third, despite Paramount's surprising initial reluctance about the marketability of an 1890s story, this was an era which had been rediscovered in the decade prior to *Wrong*:

> By the mid-twenties, the country was in the midst of a gay-nineties revival. Several turn-of-the-century productions enjoyed new runs on Broadway. Books about the period sold well. Images of the 1890s appeared throughout American culture.[2]

One could argue that with the exception of Charlie Chaplin, who dominated every aspect of his productions (writing, directing, producing, and even composing the music, as well as starring), West creatively dominated her film productions more than any other 1930s comedy star. Now granted, all the funnymen highlighted in this text had such an excellent handle on their personae that they each acted as chief arbitrator for what comic business best suited their screen characters. But that being said, they were often greatly assisted by other artists. For instance, the Marx Brothers' best picture was their collaboration with director Leo McCarey, *Duck Soup* (1933, see chapter 4). Along similar lines, Will Rogers' unmatched movies were those directed by John Ford, especially *Judge Priest* (1934, see chapter 6).

Such was not the case with West. Naturally, she benefited from competent craftsmen, and probably her best film after the creation of the censorship code (1934), *Belle of the Nineties* (1934), was megaphoned by the talented McCarey. Still, during West's 1930s heyday she was largely a product of her own scripts, which in turn were often drawn from plays she had written in the 1920s, such as *Diamond Lil.* Besides Chaplin and West, the only other major screen comedian of that era who even occasionally provided the original story and/or script for his feature films was W.C. Fields. But Fields' personae, fluctuating between hucksters and antiheroes, were assisted greatly by the authors of two 1920s stage productions — Dorothy Donnelly's Broadway play *Poppy* (1923, with Fields starring as the title character con man), and J. P. McEvoy's antiheroic musical comedy revue *The Comic Supplement* (1925, in which Fields starred as part of the *Ziegfeld Follies*).

While West's entertainment roots dated from early in the twentieth century, she came into her own by authoring the following series of controversial stage productions: *Sex* (1926), *The Drag* (1927), *The Wicked Age* (1927), *Diamond Lil* (1928), *Pleasure Man* (1928), and *The Constant Sinner* (1931). Addressing such then-provocative material as intercourse, homosexuality, drag queens, and prostitution, these eye-opening properties not only got the author-actress noted, an obscenity charge even resulted in a short West jail term for *Sex*. But as she observed in 1927, after threats of censorship by the normally free-spirited New York Mayor James J. Walker forced *The Drag* to close out of town, "Every knock is a boost. It makes me better known."[3] West was definitely a student of the old axiom, "There is no bad publicity, as long as they spell your name correctly." Though she would largely anchor her screen persona upon the title character of *Diamond Lil*, the sexually contentious aura which surrounded the multitasking Mae was initially fueled by all these properties. Thus, by the time she entered film she was already something of a legend. For example, critic John Mason Brown's *New York Post* review of *Wrong* compared the actress to tall tale figure Paul Bunyan.[4] Along equally impressed lines, the *New York Evening Journal*'s Rose Pelswick affectionately complained in her critique of *Wrong*:

> It's almost impossible to put Mae West into print. You can't write down the drawling way in which she talks and the undulating manner in which she walks. Her knowing mannerisms refuse to be reduced to adjectives. Confronted with the task of translating her unique personality into cold type, this column can only throw up its hands ... and tell you not to miss Mae West in *She Done Him Wrong*....[5]

What makes such comments doubly impressive — underscoring West's already mythic nature — is that *Wrong* was her *first* starring movie, and only her second overall, after the George Raft vehicle with its own provocative title *Night After Night* (1932).

Surprisingly, given the sexual spoofing nature of West's persona, past commentators have missed a more sophisticated parody component to her work. That is, beyond the broad spoofing style of a Bob Hope in the 1940s and 1950s, or Mel Brooks in the 1970s, is a more subtle form of the genre sometimes referred to as "parodies of reaffirmation."[6] Like the stereotypical gambler, who plays everything "close to the vest," this approach to parody is so similar to its comedy target that it is often confused with the genre being undercut. An excellent example of this is director John Landis' *An American Werewolf in London* (1981), in which broad parody (such as the ironically comic use of songs such as "Bad Moon Rising" and several versions of "Blue Moon") alternates with shocking horror (graphic violence and painfully realistic werewolf transformations). This produces a fascinating tension between genre expectations (in this case, horror—to be scared) and a parody that is comic without deflating the characters involved.

This is opposed to the more traditional horror parody of a *Young Frankenstein* (1974), in which, for instance, Marty Feldman's Igor, with his bulging eyes and a roving hump on his back, can never be taken seriously. Consequently, the reaffirmation approach can add a poignancy not normally associated with over-the-top parody. One is truly saddened by the death of the American werewolf (David Naughton). The closing deaths of the central heroes in the reaffirmation parody classics *Bonnie and Clyde* (1967) and *Butch Cassidy and the Sundance Kid* (1969) elicit even more deep-felt emotions. Yet for many, *Bonnie and Clyde* is merely a violent offbeat gangster film, and *Butch Cassidy and the Sundance Kid* is no more than another 1960s revisionist look at the Western. But as with the later *American Werewolf in London*, both these films maintain a mesmerizing disquiet between genre expectations (the crime and violence of gangster and Western outlaws) and an endearing sense of parody that encourages viewer identification. Consequently, Butch and Sundance are bumbling outlaws who make their living by comically *avoiding* shoot-outs. Butch shows genuine concern for their victims, is not particularly good with a gun, and has everyone wanting to protect him from the law. Indeed, my correspondence with the film's screenwriter (William Goldman, who won an Oscar for Best Original Screenplay) revealed that these things were what really fascinated him about the story:

> Here was this incredibly charming man, uncatchable (he just rode into farmhouses and said, "Hello, my name is Butch Cassidy, the law's on my tail, mind if I hide in your basement?" and they'd say, "Sure") ... People *adored* Cassidy; he was just that amiable ... Couple that fact with his job as head of the biggest most successful gang in Western history and he wasn't good at any of the things gang members were good at; well, I think that's interesting.[7]

Along similar lines, the title characters of *Bonnie and Clyde* are outlaws who manage to exist quite nicely outside the gangster norm of the predatory — asphalt jungle — city at night, frequently behaving like Mack Sennett's Keystone Cops in their slapstick, broad daylight rural chases with accompanying upbeat banjo soundtrack music. A revisionist might also be moved to call *Bonnie and Clyde* a dark comedy, with its juxtaposing of random violence with personality comedian–like slapstick.

It is not necessary, however, to limit oneself to modern (after 1960) cinema for examples of the more complex reaffirmation parodies. Though neither as obvious nor as prevalent as the traditional spoof movie, they, too, have always been there. Buster Keaton, silent film comedy's only rival to Charlie Chaplin, often used this method. Appropriately, Keaton's greatest and now most acclaimed film, *The General* (1927), applies this approach, with the comedian having a Civil War backdrop of epic realistic proportions. Befitting the emotional range of this genre, one might best showcase the scene where Buster demonstrates basic clown comedy physical shtick via his awkwardness with a saber. But the ending of the segment, where the blade comically detaches from its handle and flies off (as Buster attempts a dramatic flourish with said weapon), has the most somber close — the movie cuts to an impaled enemy soldier lying dead.

This surprisingly dark comedy conclusion returns the viewer to the traditional meaning one would gather from a straight rendition of a Civil War story — people die, often in the most haphazard of ways.

Unfortunately for Keaton, period critics and audiences did not appreciate this more subtle approach to parody, and *The General* was a critical and commercial failure. This is the downside to reaffirmation spoofing — the less-than-discerning viewer does not get it. And since comedy, especially with personality comedians, is usually about accenting the obvious, this artful, more edgy form of parody often goes unnoticed.

While *She Done Him Wrong* was a huge critical and commercial success, the reviews frequently revealed a telltale sign of reaffirmation parodies: The picture was often discussed in non-comedic terms. Since *Wrong* is a balance between melodrama (dealing with prostitution, prison, murder, unrequited love, and attempted suicide) and skewering those subjects, critiques sometimes sounded more like a straight examination of a soap opera. The *London Times* was the most derailed along these lines — praising *Wrong* yet warning, "The film is not a pleasant one — the reek of the [crime] underworld is in every foot of it...."[8] The *New York World Telegram* discussed its "old-fashioned melodramatics," while the *Brooklyn Daily Eagle* lauded the picture despite the "rowdy, coarsely written melodrama" of its script.[9]

Thornton Delehanty, a second reviewer for the *New York Post*, managed a more entertainingly balanced look at *Wrong*'s mix of soap opera and silliness: "It is enough for you to know that here is a resurrected Fourteenth Street [New York] melodrama that deals with crooks and flowing beer and hot intrigue, and that the warmth is supplied by Miss West's own central heating plant."[10] But *Vanity Fair* critic Pare Lorentz, who would later be acclaimed for his documentary films, came the closest in the 1930s to a reaffirmation parody statement on West's film: "*She Done Him Wrong* is played straight, and to the hilt, and as a result it is good fun ... [and *Diamond Lil* co-adapter] John Bright kept a good melodramatic pace in the manuscript."[11]

One should keep in mind that *Wrong*, as a reaffirmation parody, is the only featured film in this text, besides Bob Hope's like-minded spoof *The Cat and the Canary* (1939, see chapter 12), in which the reviewers are regularly distracted from what should be the front and center topic — comedy. Regardless, this reaffirmation "reading" of West puts her wit on an edgier level, since the aforementioned litany of melodramatic subjects was hardly a standard backdrop for any sort of comedy in the 1930s. For example, West's former lover (Owen Moore) in *Wrong* is serving hard time for trying to keep her in diamonds. While he poignantly continues to obsess about her, she has moved on to another diamond provider (Noah Beery). The closest she comes to any compassion for Moore's character is to deadpan, "I wish he'd forget me, but the guy is a memory expert." But another darkly comic comment of hers from the picture might have been applied here, or in several comparable reaffirmation moments: "Diamonds is my career."

An additional non-traditional but equally compelling take on West here (beyond reaffirmation parody), is to see her as a new age, sexy, crackerbarrel philosopher. Though no one would confuse her for Will Rogers, a veritable poster boy for the crackerbarrel phenomenon, the West analogy is not without a period precedent. In 1934 George Kent did a *Photoplay* piece drawing parallels between the two comedians.[12] Granted, the article could be labeled "studio damage control," since West was then being attacked by various conservative groups. Film fan magazines at that time, like *Photoplay*, are sometimes seen today as an innocent extension of the various studio publicity departments. How true such a claim might be would undoubtedly vary from subject to subject. But a key point in favor of using such period pieces is that their emphasis invariably seems more focused upon being informatively interesting than on a pitching a polemic. It also does not hurt that these publications often boasted quality writing staffs, including such later acclaimed authors as Theodore Dreiser and Robert E. Sherwood.

Regardless of one's take on the nature of 1930s film fan magazines (years before they were usurped by scandal sheets in the 1950s), the case for seeing West as a crackerbarrel philosopher works on several levels. First, as is the case with most of these blue-collar oracles, her screen character regularly dispenses worldly wisdom — though it is usually of a sexually provocative nature. For instance, in *Wrong* she comforts a victimized woman by noting, "You know, it takes two to get one in trouble." Second, as is the norm for crackerbarrel types, West's insights are gleaned from a lifetime of people-related professions. This point is inherent even in the term "crackerbarrel philosopher"— someone who ran a general store and jawed over the issues of the day with a cross-section of customers, amidst the barrels of crackers and assorted merchandise. West's people-profession in *Wrong* and assorted other stories, is that of a saloon girl–singer. One has a precedent of sorts in the beloved crackerbarrel figure "Mr. Dooley," writer Finley Peter Dunne's Irish bartender who dispensed both spirits and wisdom —"All th' wurruld loves a lover — except sometimes th' wan that's all th' wurruld to him."[13] Fittingly, like West's Diamond Lil character (*Wrong*'s Lady Lou), Mr. Dooley is associated with the 1890s, too, though Dunne's popular creation continued to comically comment on current events well into the 1920s.

Of course, a more X-rated slant on Mae's people profession is that saloon girls were essentially prostitutes. Moreover, West never shied away from that implication. For instance, when a *Wrong* friend says, "Ah Lady Lou, you're a fine gal, a fine woman," she responds, "One of the finest that ever walked the streets." When she visits a former beau in prison, seemingly every convict on the cell block *knows* her; all toss off terms of endearment as she goes into her celebrated Mae West strut. Two of West's landmark songs from *Wrong* even have direct links to prostitution. "Easy Rider" is a slang reference for a pimp, and the legendary folk number, "Frankie and Johnny," is really a true blues tale about a St. Louis prostitute (Frankie Baker) who killed an unfaithful lover. And there is always West's public savoring of sex. When Cary Grant's Salvation Army captain in *Wrong* asks her, "Haven't you ever met a man who could make you happy?" her Lady Lou answers, "Sure, lots of times."

Third, though Mae is hardly the standard outreach example of a crackerbarrel type, *à la* Will Rogers, she does have a proclivity to help fellow misfits, such as the suicidal girl at the beginning of *Wrong*. West's sensitivity to the underdog was also reflected in the actress' real-life kinship with African-American culture, which she often dovetailed into her films. Both of the aforementioned songs owe their origin to this ethnic group, which is also reflected in the blues nature of West's singing. *Wrong* also showcases a more progressive interaction between West and her black maid (Louise Beavers) than was the norm for that time. West is still definitely in charge, but it is more the banter of friends instead of separate classes. One of their most entertaining conversations discusses how Lady Lou was not always rich, tipped off with West's confession, "I was once so poor I didn't know where my next husband was coming from."

Any connection between West and sensitivity, however, comes with a warning — her *me first* persona could not pay lip service to assistance. Indeed, she would seemingly talk it down. For example, Lady Lou tells Grant's captain that his mission charges are not worth saving, and adds, "If you hang around 'em long enough, you'll get that way yourself." Yet, West later secretly buys the mission building when she hears Grant is about to be evicted. Does she do this out of compassion, or a sexual fascination with the handsome Grant? I suggest it is a combination of the two. No less a humanist than director Leo McCarey would describe West as a kindred spirit in his 1935 article, "Mae West Can Play Anything."[14]

An advocacy for the disenfranchised reveals an underlying sense of populism (the home genre for crackerbarrel philosophers). Put another way — to know and care about the battered underside of society is to be a compassionate, non-judgmental person. Ironically, this can bring one back to the non-traditional people profession of prostitution. Pivotal populist director John Ford originally had his title character (Will Rogers) from *Judge Priest* (1934, see chapter 6) walk in a funeral procession for the town madam. Though period censors forced the deletion of the segment, Ford returned the scene to his later remake of the picture, *The Sun Shines Bright* (1953). Along related lines, the most sensitive populist characters in Ford's watershed Western, *Stagecoach* (1939), are the prostitute (Claire Trevor) and the alcoholic doctor (Thomas Mitchell, in an Oscar-winning performance). For all West's fascination with diamonds, one senses that stereotypical "harlot with a heart of gold" sensitivity.

As with most personality comedies, the character-driven *Wrong* is thin on plot. After a colorfully checkered past, her Lady Lou seems to be the kept woman of the Bowery saloon owner and local powerbroker Gus Jordan (Noah Beery). Beery was the older half-brother of the Oscar-winning Wallace Beery, who, coincidently, also played an 1890s Bowery saloon keeper that same year in *The Bowery* (1933). Noah Beery funds his *Wrong* operation through both a counterfeiting ring and selling victims into white slavery (prostitution), to which Mae's character is oblivious. Given Lady Lou's otherwise worldly nature, this seems like a modest flaw in the proceedings. But it does complement that inherent well-intentioned honesty of West's aforementioned populist base. This innocent factor, if that factor can ever be applied to her, also ultimately allows Lady Lou to avoid any jail time with regard to both her Beery character involvement and the self-defense killing of Jordan's partner, Russian Rita (Rafaela Ottiano).

West's persona was about dominating men — beating them at their own power games. Even her matter-of-fact nature about sexuality is often perceived as masculine in nature, which is why she was often likened to a female impersonator. This was merely an extension of the real West, who confessed in a 1933 interview: "I can take 'em [men] or leave 'em. I'm just like a man with my romances — here today and gone tomorrow. Men are conveniences to me, nothing more. If they can help me in any way, socially or financially, I can be nice to 'em...."[15]

Given this mindset, the casts of West's movies often feature actors with less than a strong presence. Having said this, though, a key strength to *Wrong* is that her leading men here are more forceful, from the gruff Beery, to the smooth-talking Grant. Of course, this does not stop Lady Lou from dominating them, but it makes their interactions appear to start on a level playing field. But West can turn the anti-male tables quickly. Consequently, shortly after she gives Grant her famous line from *Wrong*, "Why don't you come up sometime 'n' see me?" she coldly tells him, "You can be had...."

Interestingly enough, West's autobiography all but claims she discovered Grant, suggesting *Wrong* was his first film.[16] In point of fact, this was his eighth feature. Naturally, Grant resented this and enjoyed pointing out that the director of *Wrong*, Lowell Sherman, had been a fan of Grant's performance opposite another legendary leading lady, Marlene Dietrich, in *Blonde Venus* (1932).[17] Regardless, West's main criterion in casting Grant was right on target — a great-looking young man. And while he had not yet orchestrated the suave Cary Grant persona (which came together under the direction of Leo McCarey in *The Awful Truth*, 1937), the actor was an excellent romantic foil for West. Fittingly, she would again cast him as her leading man in the follow-up picture, *I'm No Angel* (1933).

Anchored in the clout of West's defining characterization, Diamond Lil, *Wrong* was a huge critical and commercial success. The movie's producer, William LeBaron, who worked so effectively with both West and W.C. Fields, "credited the film with saving Paramount Pictures [during the Depression] from bankruptcy."[18] This was the

Mae West, in her *She Done Him Wrong* diamonds, with Cary Grant.

general consensus in the industry, too. The picture's domestic gross was a staggering $2 million, an amazing amount, considering the average price of a movie ticket in 1933 was 23 cents.[19] (The production cost for *Wrong* was approximately only $250,000.)

The reviews were almost uniformingly stellar. For instance, *The New Yorker* said, "*She Done Him Wrong* is one of the great comedy pictures of the current year. And God knows the year needs all the laughs one can squeeze out of it."[20] *New York Herald Tribune* critic Richard Watts, Jr., both praised the picture, "a hearty, hilarious and handsomely rowdy motion picture," and defended it against bluenose conservatives:

> It is one of the grandest things about Miss West's robust comedy that she is so frankly and heroically proud of her roughness that there never is anything leering or underhanded about it. She is always friendly and healthy and it supplies the film with just the touch of comic honesty that it needs.[21]

In contrast, *Vanity Fair* acknowledged *Wrong*'s racy nature and still celebrated both its pathos and showmanship: "[T]his picture is not just smutty, and ... although definitely a burlesque show, it has a certain Beery poignancy and, above all, a gusto about it which makes it a good show."[22]

The *New York Evening Journal* said, "[T]he picture is guaranteed to keep you hugely amused from the moment it starts until the moment it ends."[23] Other glowing notices ranged from a *New York Post* thank you — "[I]t is not only a relief but a pleasure to escape with Miss West into the didoes [mischievous "reading"] of a bygone day"— to the *London Time*'s reverence towards West's persona:

> Miss West has amazing vitality and an air of self-conscious insolence which, in combination, are extremely effective and which build up a picture of a definite personality. [Lady] Lou is, in fact, a character seen "in the round" [realistically full-blown], and such characters are all too rare on the screen.[24]

Such acclaim for this cinematic version of West's Diamond Lil character would hardly have been surprising to a period fan. In fact, as early as Stark Young's 1928 *New Republic* theater review of the Broadway *Diamond Lil*, the critic credited West with having "created a sort of Lillian Russell-gay-nineties-bad-good-diamond-girl myth or figure, heightened and typified, that is becoming as distinct as Charlie [Chaplin's Tramp]."[25] Such character-driven kudos seemed to strike a responsive chord with West. In a 1934 *Los Angeles Times* interview, the actress would draw parallels between how both her persona and that of Chaplin's parodied sexuality.[26] In this same interview, West also underlined how firmly entrenched she was in the Diamond Lil character ... even before films: "When I came here [Hollywood] I was a finished product [persona]. That's why I had the success which I did ... I was really ready-made."[27]

An amusing bonus to some of the positive *Wrong* notices were critics who peppered their reviews with comedy of their own. Sometimes, this simply amounted to an understated aside, such as the *New York Post*'s John Mason Brown's comment, "There is nothing of the nun about Miss West."[28] Or, the critic might play at comic irony, given film censorship attacks on the picture. The *New York Herald Tribune*'s Richard Watts, Jr., stated, with tongue firmly-in-cheek: "Miss Mae West, that lyric immaculate ingénue,

3. Mae West's *She Done Him Wrong* (1933)　　　　　　　　　　47

brings her characteristic sweetness and light to the Hollywood version of her stage predecessor to 'Alice in Wonderland,' which originally was known as 'Diamond Lil.'"²⁹

For all this praise, comic, or otherwise, conservative moralists of the time were outraged by the sexual innuendo of West's *Wrong*. For example, the censor-happy Catholic priest with the most imposing of names, Father Daniel Lord, who had helped

Here is the whole Mae West *She Done Him Wrong* sexually spoofing package transforming an appearance into a performance.

create Hollywood's Production Code of 1930, said of *Wrong*, "[E]veryone knows [it] is the filthy *Diamond Lil* slipping by under a new name."[30] But this could be expected from a Catholic colleague of Joseph "Hollywood Hitler" Breen, who would join the Hays [censorship] Office in 1934 as chief of the Production Code Administration (PCA). More disturbing was the mixed message a normally liberal publication, such as *The Hollywood Reporter*, could send. On one hand, the trade newspaper honored *Wrong*'s bravery over bucking the official puritanical policy of Will "the Presbyterian pope of Hollywood" Hays:

> It is so much funnier than it is filthy, so atmospherically perfect and so well acted and directed that its repugnant yarn never becomes offensive, that one must not only forgive, but congratulate [the home studio of] Paramount for wholeheartedly thumbing its nose at Haysiana and going ahead with *Diamond Lil* [*Wrong*]....[31]

Paradoxically, the same *Hollywood Reporter* review also said, "Our advice ... to exhibs [exhibitors] who book this picture, is to ban the kiddies and invite the adults (pure or polluted) to come in and have a swell time. You could hardly blame the Women's Clubs for not wanting their young to 'learn about women' from Mae West."[32]

Of course, for today's viewer any sense of controversy connected to *Wrong* seems unbelievable. The sexual innuendo remains amusing but hardly censorable. Coupled with the modern viewer's surprise over this 1930s hullabaloo is the aforementioned paradox that this sex symbol was not traditionally sexy, or as film comedy historian Gerald Weales suggested, "[S]he is the avatar [goddess] of sex in the head. Her best lines — like those of Groucho Marx and W.C. Fields — are widely quoted ... usually in an approximation of her own suggestive delivery...."[33] Cary Grant added with wry insight, "Her [comic] personality is so dominant that everyone with her becomes just a feeder [someone who sets up her lines]."[34] Certainly, as with many personality comedians, one sometimes remembers moments over movies. But West so peppers this picture with her signature lines that *Wrong* is an exception to that tendency, such as her provocative reply to Grant's comment that an army of men would have been safer if she had been born in handcuffs: "I don't know ... hands ain't everything."

Though conservative America was offended by West in *Wrong*, the film industry got it, as well as appreciated her Depression era boost to a sagging box office: The film received an Academy Award nomination for Best Picture. Though *Wrong*'s controversial success would help fuel the reinvention of the American censorship code in 1934, which attempted to homogenize West, the enlightened left continued to celebrate her comic artistry throughout the 1930s. Thus, after the actress' heavily censored movie *Belle of the Nineties* (1934), there were numerous critical defenses of West. Andre Sennwald, the brilliant but now sadly neglected film critic for *The New York Times*, authored one of the more spirited articles. He counseled, with comic common sense, that there were too few world-class comediennes "to let Mae West be cast into the pit to make a reformer's holiday." But he soon turned insightfully serious: "In a single cynical phrase like her characteristic line ... '[K]eep cool and collect' [from *Belle*], she casts acid ridicule upon the sulphurous sex dramas of the Dietrichs and Garbos.... West comes like a cleansing wind ... with candid sentiments."[35] *New Republic* reviewer Otis Ferguson, arguably America's greatest film critic prior to James Agee, had an equally entertaining defense-celebration of West in *Belle*:

> She not only gives more and better publicity to the chief erogenous zones than any five Godwin [*sic*] authors: she has moments in this picture of clear loveliness. She has the most honest and outrageous and lovable vulgarity that ever was seen on the screen.[36]

Late in the 1930s, pioneering cinema historian Lewis Jacobs even championed in his watershed work, *The Rise of the American Film: A Critical History*, an early argument for a feminist defense of the actress along sexual lines:

> Mae West averred that women get just as much pleasure out of sexual contact as men ... [and] that the female can reverse the old custom and cajole the male ... Mae West eyed a man from head to foot. All the time you knew she was evaluating him in terms of virility, as James Cagney eyed a woman. Neither had any use or time for camouflage ... Both knew what they were after, let you know it, and were intent in their playfulness.[37]

Jacobs' feminist point is well taken, and the comparison with Cagney is especially fitting, given his association with the gangster genre. The actor's career was established with the controversial classic *The Public Enemy* (1931), part of the pivotal modern gangster film movement which also included such seminal works as *Little Caesar* (1930, with Edward G. Robinson) and *Scarface* (1932, with Paul Muni). How does this tie in with West? The catalyst for the 1934 establishment of the aforementioned censorship-related PCA is usually credited to both the provocative West and this violent new take on the crime picture. But what period historian Jacobs reminds the modern student of movies is that while these and other gangster films were usually first criticized for their violence, the pictures were also pushing the sexual card (*à la* West). For instance, when Cagney's *Public Enemy* character first spots the sexy Jean Harlow, his "evaluating" of her leaves little to the imagination.

West's movies helped usher in a more comically edgy portrayal of the relationship between men and women. Just how radical this was is best encapsulated in a story from the most iconic female star of the previous (silent) era, Mary Pickford. After the release of West's *Wrong*, Pickford shared the following anecdote with the *Motion Picture Herald*:

> I passed the door of my young niece's room — she's only about 17 and has been raised, oh so carefully — and I heard her singing bits from that song from *Diamond Lil* [the screen adaptation, *Wrong*] — I say "that song" ["A Guy What Takes His Time"] just because I'd blush to quote the title line even here.[38]

If the original "America's Sweetheart" was mildly scandalized by West, one can assume a sizable portion of the country was, also. When West was not upsetting a Hollywood legend, she was redefining a legendary symbol of America — *Belle of the Nineties* showcases her in a skintight costume as the Statue of Liberty. Magazine editor and drama critic George Jean Nathan later comically likened her Liberty pose to the "Statue of Libido."[39]

Early in *Wrong*, an admirer of West's Lady Lou was so happy to meet her, he gushed, "I am delighted. I have heard so much about you." Lady Lou's dryly comic reply redefined this praise, "Yeah, but you can't prove it." Today West no longer needs to prove anything. This quintessentially American original invariably turns up on any list of pantheon screen comedians. Like Chaplin, the iconoclastic West has become an icon.

CHAPTER 4

The Marx Brothers' *Duck Soup* (1933)

> Forget? You ask me to forget? A firefly never forgets. Why, my ancestors would rise from their graves and I would only have to bury them again. Nothing doing. I'm going back to clean the crackers out of my bed. I'm expecting company.
>
> — Groucho in *Duck Soup*

America's own peculiar brand of "Marxism" can be traced to 1887 — the birth year of Leonard Marx, the oldest of the Marx Brothers.[1] Leonard, who later (and forevermore) would be re-christened "Chico" for vaudeville audiences, was followed in order by Adolph (1888, "Harpo"), Julius (1890, "Groucho"), Milton (1893, "Gummo"), and Herbert (1901, "Zeppo"). For the sake of familiarity and simplicity, the brothers will be referred to by their stage names throughout this text. It is also a tradition both Groucho and Harpo turned to when they became team biographers, as did other chroniclers from their family.

While all five were at some time part of the team (although never simultaneously), the best Marx Brothers "cast" listing is analytical biographer Joe Adamson's tongue-in-cheek title: *Groucho, Harpo, Chico and Sometimes Zeppo.*[2] Gummo was only part of the early stage act before entering the armed forces in World War I. Zeppo replaced Gummo and was with the team on Broadway and through its first five commercially released films — all for Paramount. (Frequent co-star and satirical target Margaret Dumont was sometimes also later referred to as the fifth Marx "Brother.")

At the time of *Duck Soup* (which was originally called *Cracked Ice*), the Marxes were a microcosm of movie comedy. Groucho represented the fast-talking twentieth century huckster — timely for both the Depression and sound cinema. Groucho's shyster had a saturation comedy tongue that spewed out words and assorted puns at the speed of comic sound. In a Groucho world, the message was that nothing was as it seems, and this was especially true of his language. And as if to compensate for this Groucho verbal monopoly, one brother, Harpo, spoke not a word. Harpo was simply otherworldly, from his silence or that trademark "Gookie" expression (like crossed eyes painted on an over-inflated balloon), to his sorcerer's pockets from which he drew so many odd items. Harpo was especially popular with period critics and intellectuals as a homage to both the recently past silent comedians, and a mainstream application of such topical subjects as surrealism. (Salvador Dalí proved to be one of Harpo's greatest fans.[3]) As with Groucho's verbal slapstick, Harpo's surrealistic visual comedy suggested that nothing was as it seems.

Chico's entertainingly theatrical Italian accent designated him as the team's dialect comedian, a comedy shtick once very popular in America's immigrant-rich early twentieth century entertainment. In fact, during the evolution of the Marx Brothers act, Groucho once used a German "Dutch" persona, while Harpo briefly struggled with an Irish dialect! But of equal significance for Chico's character is that he is a throwback to the old-fashioned flim-flam tradition. Though Brother Groucho is a funny/frightening modern big-time con artist, Chico's ongoing reversion to an old school street huckster invariably gets the best of the mustached one. This is consistent with the hoary maxim of humor being leery of authority. Yes, we enjoy Groucho because he often pricks the high and the mighty but when he battles Chico it is Groucho who usually occupies the vulnerable authority position. Moreover, as French film critic Louis Chavance wrote in 1932, Chico is the "smiling accomplice of the public."[4] His is the everyman promise of the small-change nineteenth-century scam artist out to transfer a personal "Manifest Destiny" into the individual profit column.

Zeppo, the youngest and last brother to join the family act, never received an

The Marxes (left to right), Chico, Zeppo, Groucho, and Harpo, in *Duck Soup*'s antiwar conclusion.

opportunity to fully flesh out his persona. But when given half a chance, Zeppo represented the new leading man of sound comedy — a handsome Arrow Shirt type willing to play the comic, too. Movies in the 1930s often had a sappy romantic subplot, a narrative device frequently true of Marx pictures. But it always seemed more palatable if Zeppo was part of the assignment. The irony of this missed potential (Zeppo retired from the screen after *Duck Soup*) was that within the family he was considered the really funny one. Indeed, Zeppo's confidently breezy real-life personality was sometimes likened to Groucho's movie character.

When studying and savoring the inventiveness of the Marxes, their comedy is often about the teams within the team, such as Groucho and Chico, or Harpo and Chico. Though Chico's popularity as a character has been eclipsed by Groucho and Harpo, the dialect one was "much more of an essential ingredient [to the team] than most people ever realized."[5] From being Harpo's frequent screen interpreter (for Groucho and assorted other comedy nemeses), to out-conning the mustached one, Chico was the proverbial glue that held the team together.

Interestingly enough, Groucho's interactions with Chico and Harpo allowed his persona to be more comically multifaceted. While Groucho did not fluctuate between huckster and antiheroic roles as did W.C. Fields, the otherwise dominating Groucho forever played antihero to his brothers. One sees the normally comic "King Leer" in continuous funny defeat. A prime example for Chico would be the tootsie-fruitsie ice cream scene in *A Day at the Races* (1937), where he sells Groucho a "library" of unnecessary betting books. But the most other-worldly illustration, however, appropriately draws upon eccentric Harpo. In *Duck Soup*'s classic mirror scene (which will be examined in detail shortly), Harpo, comically disguised as Groucho in his nightgown and cap, magically passes as his brother's reflection. It is funny and somehow fitting that the normally invincible huckster Groucho should be vulnerable only to his brothers — like a "superman" comedian who is just one of the boys among the Kryptonite crowd. The screen Groucho is the ultimate example of how one can never get too self-important among family.

In the Marxes' early years their stage-door-mother Minnie was the dominant force in the family — creating and managing their act. Part of her clout with the boys, beyond the stereotypical strong-arm immigrant mother image, came from the show-business success of her younger brother Al Shean (changed from Schoenberg). At the beginning of the 1890s Shean had both organized and starred in the influential vaudeville comedy and musical act the Manhattan Comedy Four (which naturally sends one thinking of the later four Marx Brothers, especially since Uncle Al's comedy writing for his nephews helped elevate them to big-time entertainment). Today Shean is best known as part of the later vaudeville team of Gallagher and Shean, whose signature musical refrain was "Absolutely, Mr. Gallagher?" "Positively, Mr. Shean." Gallagher and Shean was one of America's favorite comedy teams early in the twentieth century.

For *Minnie's Boys* (the name of a later Broadway play about the Marxes) the monthly visits of their funny and famous uncle was like a holiday. Shean's arrival generated a party storm of Minnie-directed activity, as her boys were sent to buy Uncle Al's favorite food and drink. Groucho's regular assignment was to purchase Kümmel cheese; Harpo bought the huckleberry cake; and Chico (being the oldest) picked up the beer.

Another plus for the relatively poor Marx boys was the financial side to their uncle's visits. As he prepared to leave he gave each one a silver coin. (Memories of the amount later varied, from Harpo recalling a top amount of a quarter, to Groucho placing the figure at a dollar.) Regardless, any figure would have been a major windfall for these youngsters.

There was another entertaining factor associated with Shean's visits, beyond the easy silver and party atmosphere. Uncle Al, in Groucho's own words, was a "handsome dog" (which period photos document), whose sexual conquests were legend in the family and something he enjoyed elaborating on during each visit. Boys being boys, this was a fascinating new slant to show business for the young Marxes. And in later years the team would be legendary skirt-chasers, especially Chico — whose nickname was derived from an obsession with "chicks" (women). But more to the comedy point, with the exception of Mae West, no other Depression comics so focused upon sexual suggestion as the Marxes, from their lecherous leader (Groucho), to Harpo's screen propensity to show no restraint around a pretty girl.

W.C. Fields once said of the Marx Brothers' vaudeville act: "[I] never saw so much nepotism [a brother act, written by an uncle, managed by the mother] or such hilarious laughter in one act in my life. In Columbus I told the manager I broke my wrist [he had a juggling routine] and quit."[6] While no record seems to have been left of Groucho's views on Fields' vaudeville act, the mustached one's son (more nepotism!) said in *Life with Groucho* that his father later considered Fields "one of the all-time great comedians" as well as "one of the few people who's ever been able to make Father laugh out loud."[7]

When one judges the considerable merit of *Duck Soup*, however, it goes beyond a Groucho-Fields mutual admiration society, or Marx family nepotism. This is the team's most inspired film because for the first and only time they had a great director — Leo McCarey. Not only does *Duck Soup* have signature McCarey routines throughout, it is now recognized as one of the definitive clown films of all time. No less an artist than Woody Allen calls it "probably the best talking comedy ever made," and the American Film Institute cites it as one of the five funniest American movies (joining *Some Like It Hot*, 1959, *Tootsie*, 1982, *Dr. Strangelove, Or: How I Learned to Stop Worrying and Love the Bomb*, 1964, and *Annie Hall*, 1977).[8] Plus, *Duck Soup* can also be classified as a groundbreaking dark comedy, with Groucho's political paranoia as the president of a small European country (Freedonia) anticipating the fanatical general Jack Ripper (Sterling Hayden) in *Dr. Strangelove*.[9] But Groucho's outrageously dark comedy antics are peppered throughout the picture, from declaring war on a whim to appointing a peanut vendor (Chico) to his cabinet. Beyond *Duck Soup*'s most basic genre attractions (personality comedy and black humor), the film also is an affectionate parody of the musical — the most pervasive movie type in the early 1930s, given the then-recent introduction of sound to cinema.

At the picture's most provocative best, *Duck Soup* manages to sell all three genres simultaneously. For instance, when the Marxes sing and dance "This Country's Going to War," with all the peppy enthusiasm synonymous to a sappy period musical, they spoof a genre as well as indict a society that can so naively send the young off to die. Woody Allen, *Duck Soup*'s greatest advocate, even chose to showcase the "This

Country's Going to War" sequence in a pivotal point of his own much praised movie *Hannah and Her Sisters* (1986, where Allen's hypochondriac character decides against suicide after viewing the film).

For someone universally celebrated in later years as the only director to put a personal stamp on a Marx Brothers picture, McCarey did his best to avoid megaphoning what became *Duck Soup*. The director then most famous for teaming and molding Laurel and Hardy during the late 1920s (and a later multiple Oscar winner for *The Awful Truth*, 1937, and *Going My Way*, 1944), had no desire to accept an assignment that involved the *four* manic Marxes. (Within the industry, the team was famous for being hard to direct.) The often freelancing McCarey felt so strongly about avoiding the Marxes that he skipped re-signing a lucrative multiyear contract with Paramount (the brothers' home studio), knowing the team was anxious to work with him. But on March 9, 1933, the Marxes broke with Paramount. The *New York Times* had the team "serving notice on the studio executives that they considered their contract breached because of assorted non-payment of certain [substantial] sums of money, as well as the transfer of their contract from one corporation [Paramount] to another."[10] The Depression had come to Hollywood, and Paramount was in financial trouble.

In April the team received their incorporation permit (as the Marx Brothers, Inc.) and continued to plan to produce their next picture. The projected first film was to be an adaptation of George S. Kaufman and Morrie Ryskind's Pulitzer Prize–winning play *Of Thee I Sing*. With the Marxes taking these independent initiatives, McCarey signed up again with Paramount. But one should never assume anything with the Marxes. When adequate funding was not forthcoming on *Of Thee I Sing*, the team patched up their differences with Paramount and re-signed with the studio. Like it or not, McCarey was about to direct a Marx Brothers film.

With today's 20/20 hindsight, much of McCarey's pre–*Duck Soup* career would seem to point toward the Marxes. For example, as film historian Richard Barrios has noted in his watershed work, *A Song in the Dark: The Birth of the Musical Film* (1995), *Let's Go Native* (1930) "was sheer [joyful] malarkey, played with bounce and directed by Leo McCarey with some of the affinity toward musical anarchy he later brought to *Duck Soup*."[11] Moreover, *Native* had opened simultaneously with the Marxes' *Animal Crackers* (1930), and been favorably compared by period critics with this pioneering zany team classic.[12]

If *Native* had caught the Marxes' attention, the critical and commercial success of the McCarey-directed *The Kid from Spain* (1932, with Eddie Cantor) probably sealed the deal with America's most surreal comedy team. And like *Native* and the forthcoming *Duck Soup*, *Spain* had showcased more mythical "malarkey" — a fictional Mexico only Hollywood could create. Had the Marxes been students of silent film, they would have been further buoyed by McCarey's *Long Fliv the King* (1926), the short subject that features Charley Chase as the leader of another mythical kingdom, Thermosa. Watching the comic bravado of Chase as the new king, such as casually discarding a cigarette into the gloved hand of a palace guard, one is reminded of Groucho's cocky dictator in *Duck Soup*, who leads Freedonia into war.

Of course, while the celebrated Bert Kalmar and Harry Ruby were the principal credited writers for *Duck Soup* (as they had been on *Spain*), by the end of rehearsals in summer 1933, "McCarey shared the viewpoint that a script for the Marx Brothers was about as definite as a treaty for the Indians."[13] The team became very familiar with Leo's beach house, as the improvisational director decided to rework a host of his earlier, largely silent routines.

McCarey's Laurel and Hardy period proved to be an especially rich comedy source for *Duck Soup*. This is best demonstrated by the extended tit-for-tat routine Leo created in the film for peanut vendors Chico and Harpo versus the lemonade stand seller Edgar Kennedy (the Irish actor who had once been a regular nemesis for Laurel and Hardy). The beauty of this conflict, which stretches over two major scenes and involves much take-your-turn comic violence, is how McCarey manages to lace this tit-for-tat situation with additional inspired elements. Comedy historian Allen Eyles has likened Harpo's routine-ending dance in Kennedy's large glass cauldron of lemonade as nothing short of a medieval Puck "whose delights included dancing in the butter churns."[14] Even more impressive is McCarey's ability to work in yet one more classic hat routine (*à la* his films with Laurel and Hardy), as Chico and Harpo manage to drive Kennedy to comic distraction by a nonstop switching of each other's headgear — topped off by Harpo doing yet another face-distorted signature "Gookie."

Kennedy also surfaces in Harpo's *Duck Soup* homage to Paul Revere, where, with comic irony, McCarey has the silent Marx Brother trying to alert people that war has been declared. (The original script for this film about a comically unbalanced dictator, Groucho, also had the Marxes appearing in an operetta within the picture. The Revere segment is a remnant of this side story.) Harpo's oversexed Revolutionary War character stops during his "midnight ride" of warning at the house of a beautiful woman he sees undressing. (In the Marx Brothers world a pretty girl would *always* take precedence over a national emergency!) Unfortunately for Harpo, his potential dalliance is interrupted by the arrival of the woman's husband (Kennedy). Unmoved by either war or a sexy wife, Edgar opts for a bath. And as film critic and archivist Charles Silver reminds us, "Kennedy's bathtub [scene] recalls the famous shot of the sadly neglected silent comedian Max Davidson sitting nude in a three-sided tub in [McCarey's *Call of the Cuckoos*, 1927, which also featured Laurel and Hardy]."[15] But whereas Davidson's bath is ruined by a collapsing tub, Kennedy must cope with a bugle-blowing Harpo somehow rising out of his bathwater, like a surrealistic figure from the Salvador Dalí painting of your choice. Ultimately, Harpo's Revere gets home and beds down with his wife and trusty ... horse, as a tracking shot first reveals the discarded shoes of Harpo and his wife and four horseshoes! The situation is not unlike Laurel and Hardy's *Angora Love* (1929, from a McCarey story), where the duo keep a goat under their bed. (Fittingly, the comic heavy in *Angora Love* is Edgar Kennedy as the landlord.)

McCarey's later film editor, Edward Dmytryk, who would go on to be a successful director and author, insightfully observed of his boss and friend, "Leo had tremendous comedic inventiveness coupled with superior recall. He remembered every funny thing that had ever been said or done in his presence. And he was always pulling something out of his mental attic to see if it fit."[16] Dmytryk also wrote of McCarey, "Insecurity was his middle name."[17] Or, as Leo himself once admitted, "No matter how a director times a screen scene, there are always a bunch of little mental gremlins, whispering in his ear that maybe the scene is too long ... maybe the tempo is too swift, maybe ..."¹⁸ But this was merely an extension of an artist whose personal life was every bit as antiheroic as his movies. Author Sidney Carroll later entertainingly chronicled the director's propensity for comic self-destruction in an *Esquire* article that brilliantly summarized the phenomenon in a witty longwinded title, "Everything Happens to McCarey: During those sparse times when he isn't breaking his valuable neck, Leo McCarey does direct some extraordinary pictures."¹⁹

McCarey's greatest contribution to *Duck Soup* was the celebrated "mirror scene," where Harpo doubles as Groucho's nightgown-attired reflection. The catalyst for the sequence came from Leo's Charley Chase short subject, *Mum's the Word* (1926), a discovery I made while researching a biography of McCarey.²⁰ In doing two earlier books on the Marx Brothers, I was aware that previous attempts at a sort of comedy etymology for the mirror sequence are scarce to nonexistent, though occasionally vague references to vaudeville are mentioned.²¹ Given that McCarey was a great student of Chaplin's, one could also argue that a semblance of the idea was drawn from the acclaimed comedian's short subject *The Floorwalker* (1916). Chaplin's "Tramp" figure, Charlie, briefly parrots the movements of another character in the picture's department store setting. One might also footnote pioneering French screen comedian Max Linder's *Seven Years Bad Luck* (1921), where his in-film servant plays at being his reflection. But unlike *The Floorwalker*, Linder's picture was unfortunately a little-seen commercial failure.

That being said, it is difficult to deny the significance of the scene from *Mum's the*

Chico (left) and Groucho relax on the *Duck Soup* set (director McCarey always had a piano), with the mustached one in his nightgown for the mirror sequence.

Word. The opening of this bedroom farce finds Chase visiting his mother in her bedroom. But when his new, jealousy-prone stepfather (who still thinks Charley is merely the valet) comes to the door, the young man goes out the window onto a second-story deck. As the suspicious husband then paces back and forth in his wife's bedroom, he thinks he sees the outside shadow of someone on the window shade (which had been pulled down with Chase's hasty exit). Yet the shadow had matched the movement of the stepfather (Charley was pacing, too). Consequently, the older man varies his image as he passes in front of the shade — placing one hand pensively at his mouth. But the shadow mirrors his moving image exactly.

Perplexed, the husband makes another pass in front of the shade — moving at a sprinter's pace. Yet the shadow remains in sync with his impromptu acceleration. Doubly puzzled now, Chase's stepfather crosses in front of the shade one final time. And given the sequence's apparent link to the later Groucho-Harpo "mirror scene" of *Duck Soup*, the jealous husband's last pass assumes a most ironic pose — he walks in the crouched-over gait that is now synonymous with Groucho! Again, the shadow mirrors this unlikely movement. Only when the older man attempts to light a cigarette does the shadow fail to keep up. Comically, however, when the stepfather then throws up the shade, Chase has his lighter in readiness for the man — the ever dutiful servant.

At the expense of a pun (a comic device much favored by both McCarey and the Marxes), this ingenious routine obviously *foreshadows* the "mirror scene" from *Duck Soup*. Groucho, just like Anders Randolf's jealous husband, will comically attempt to fool what purports to be an extension of himself (Harpo as a reflection, whereas Chase plays at being a shadow). Making this link between the two scenes is significant for four reasons. First, it further underlines the artistry of McCarey on *Duck Soup*. One can now undoubtedly say he was the inspiration behind the sequence the aforementioned critic Allen Eyles calls "Harpo's tour de force" in besting his brother.[22] Second, comparing the two scenes allows the student of comedy to better understand how McCarey elevated a charming routine into one of the acclaimed scenes of cinema. Third, this sketch idea is a hallmark of McCarey's "do it visually" philosophy. While this might seem like stating the obvious for the silent film *Mum's the Word*, think about the uniqueness of *Duck Soup*'s mirror sequence, a *silent*, unforgettable visual routine starring cinema's greatest *talker* — Groucho Marx. Four, this McCarey touch underlines all the more why *Duck Soup* is the team's most comically visual picture. For once, Harpo was granted screen parity with the loquacious Groucho and Chico. It was easy for McCarey to play a favorite. The director later confessed, "As my experience in silent films had very much influenced me, it was Harpo that I preferred."[23] Favorites or not, all the Marxes recognized the comedy genius of McCarey. For instance, Groucho later affectionately reminisced about the mirror sequence:

> McCarey added a lot of stuff to the film. He had an important influence on the picture. Like that mirror scene, I remember we did it one Saturday morning. We rehearsed it in that one morning. It was all McCarey's idea.... It wasn't terribly hard to shoot that scene although it looks very difficult because ... our movements were synchronized ... McCarey knew what he was doing and knew his way around a camera. He was the best director we ever had.[24]

So what constituted the McCarey-Marx mirror sequence? First, Groucho and Harpo (made up like his brother) simply peer at each other in what appears to be a large entryway (doubling as a mirror); then they walk away and stop. Next, they turn and look back twice, the second time quickly. Third, they each bend over (all these movements are perfectly synchronized), and then comically shake their rumps. Fourth, the duo comes back to a close peering distance, and follows this by walking off to the side. Fifth, with Harpo briefly out of sight, we see Groucho move his glasses down his nose and slowly lean into the doorway — which is exactly matched by Harpo. Sixth, Groucho decides to fool this suspect "reflection" by getting down on his hands and knees and again leaning into the entryway. But Harpo mirrors these movements, too. Seventh, Groucho does a goofy little run past the entryway, and Harpo imitates it again. Next, Groucho goes past the entryway in the opposite direction ... hopping like an oversized bunny. But there is no denying the mimicking Marx — Harpo. Eight, Groucho makes yet another doorway pass performing a silly goose step, yet Harpo matches it. Ninth, Groucho faces his "reflection" and launches into a crazed dance routine with a big finish — spinning around and throwing his arms out. Harpo is with him until the spin, and it briefly looks like Groucho has finally fooled him. But Harpo anticipates his brother's hands-out close (and since Groucho's spin negates checking a similar movement by Harpo), the silent "reflection" wins again. This is the high point of an inspired routine, with my college students invariably breaking into spontaneous applause and/or laughter at this moment. The sketch has a few more twists but Groucho and Harpo soon break the "mirror" plane and switch sides in the entryway. While the remainder of the routine is funny, the magic of the "mirror" effect is now past. Still, this tour de silly sketch is not officially over until Chico (also made up as Groucho) appears, and suddenly Groucho has two "reflections"! Lewis Carroll's Alice had nothing on McCarey's Marxes. While she merely went through a mirror, they were capable of creating their own reflection ... times two.

As an addendum to the mirror sequence connection between *Mum's the Word* and *Duck Soup*, the lead-in to the Marx Brothers sequence also has a tie to McCarey's Charley Chase picture. *Word* mixes clown comedy with bedroom farce, and just prior to *Duck Soup*'s mirror routine, Chico, Harpo, and Groucho (all made up as the mustached Marx) stage their own bedroom farce (one comic at a time) in Dumont's boudoir. Besides constantly catching her in comically compromising situations, they drive their favorite straight woman to the point of distraction, as Dumont frequently thinks she is alone only to find one of the brothers lurking about. When she tells Chico, "But I saw you [leave] with my own eyes," the Marxes' designated dialect comedian responds with the team's standard illogic, "Well, who you gonna believe, me or your own eyes?" As comedy historian Gerald Weales once noted, poor Dumont "moves through the Marxian world as though courtesy and reason were possible."[25]

Sandwiched between the farcical goings-on in Dumont's bedroom and the mirror sequence is another "highlight reel" scene featuring McCarey's favored Marx — Harpo. The silent one has the combination to Dumont's safe, which holds the plans for the forthcoming war. Spies Chico and Harpo have broken into the mansion to steal those blueprints. But as an excited Harpo works the numbers on what he thinks is the safe dial, it turns out to be a radio! Suddenly blaring music (a John Philip Sousa march, no less!) announces Harpo's presence. Then, to comically compound this twist, there is a series of Harpo attempts to quiet this 1930s *boom* box. From spraying the radio with seltzer water, to smashing it with a fireplace iron, nothing seems to stop the music. Finally, Harpo finds blessed comedy quiet by tossing the discombobulated radio remains out the window. McCarey liked the scene enough to use a variation of it in his later celebrated screwball comedy, *The Awful Truth*. But in this latter case, a sexy Irene Dunne purposely "loses" a car radio dial for some musical chaos (*à la* the Marxes) with Cary Grant.

Just as McCarey had creatively quieted the machine gun patter of Groucho in the brilliant mirror sequence, the director imaginatively showcased the normally chattering Chico in an entertaining silent spot with Harpo outside Dumont's *Duck Soup* mansion. As undercover types, the two Marxes are trying to break into the estate, where Groucho is spending the night. But Chico and Harpo get involved in an elaborate battle of wits with the butler. They ring the doorbell and hide behind a hedge. The servant comes out to check, and Harpo manages to get in but closes the door on Chico. The bell is then rung by Chico. When Harpo comes out, Chico briefly gets in, but eventually the butler returns to lock both Marxes out! This musical chairs approach to the front door is foreshadowed in two earlier McCarey short subject — *Fighting Fluid* (1925, with Charley Chase) and *Early to Bed* (1928, with Laurel and Hardy). Though neither precursor is as elaborately choreographed as *Duck Soup*, all exhibit that mischievous McCarey oeuvre — where butlers have a sense of humor, too.

Probably Leo's most ongoingly inventive *Duck Soup* visual suggestion for his preferred Harpo was having him take scissors to everything and anything, from Chico's hot dog to Edgar Kennedy's wardrobe. Fittingly, given McCarey's penchant for hat humor, Harpo is especially adept at destroying headgear, such as snipping the decorative helmet plume off each passing soldier during the antiwar "The Country's Going to War" number. Leo even applies his talent for using off-screen space to this scissors-happy hooligan, and it comically benefits the traditionally underused Zeppo. Harpo has done a screen left exit, after an audience with Groucho. Zeppo immediately enters from the left, with a disgruntled look on his face. He takes his hat off, and disgustedly throws it aside — revealing only then that half his hat has been cut away. Harpo strikes again!

Despite creating a universally accepted classic, McCarey confessed that this "wasn't the ideal film for me ... [T]hey were the four battiest people I ever met, which didn't stop me from taking great pleasure in the shooting of several [improvised] scenes in the film."[26] His bugaboos with the team included difficulties keeping them together on the set, their inability to match his passion for comedy (except for Harpo), and a Marx contract that protected them from starting a new scene after six o'clock. The latter point was especially bothersome for Leo, since his improvisational tendencies were obviously impervious to the clock — a fact his family-like crews accepted. But this was not the case with the Marxes, whose off-screen leader tended to be Chico, the oldest brother. His cue for a team exit fluctuated from the comical, "It's after quitting time in New York" to the bald, "Read my contract."

Still, McCarey moxie and sheer comic genius made the team respect him all the more. There were, of course, additional reasons for the Marxes' partiality to Leo besides his gift for comedy. Groucho's earthy memories of McCarey sound rather like the womanizing Marxes. But his respect for Leo was still predicated upon ability: "I know [McCarey] liked fucking and drinking and I don't mind a guy fucking or drinking if he's got talent."[27] And Groucho biographer Hector Arce felt Chico's affection for Leo was that of "a kindred [gambling] soul," which Arce based on comments by the comedian shortly after the release of *Duck Soup*:

> I had lost a lot of bets to him, so I decided to fix him. I came in one day with a bag of walnuts. "How far do you think you can throw a walnut?" I said. "Further than you, I bet," he said, rising to the bait. "I bet you a hundred," said I. "Done," says he. He threw the first walnut and it went about a hundred feet. I threw a walnut and it went off into the blue. Looked like a half mile.... He didn't know that my walnut was filled with lead.[28]

Years later Groucho would describe the McCarey-Chico connection succinctly: "He [Leo] was a funny man and he liked to shoot craps with Chico."[29]

Being victimized by Chico fits the antiheroic mold in which Leo forever saw himself, even if this particular time he was unaware of Chico's betting trickery. Regardless, the biggest bet now associated with the movie was where that nonsensical title, *Duck Soup*, came from. The popular notion is that McCarey recycled the moniker from his Laurel and Hardy days, when he supervised Stan and Ollie in a 1927 short subject of the same name. Whether true or not, *Duck Soup* fits the animal-related titles associated with the Marxes' other Paramount pictures — *Animal Crackers* (1930), *Monkey Business* (1931), and *Horse Feathers* (1932). Animals are without ethics and so, goes one explanation, are the Marxes. Given the surrealistic tendencies of the Marxes, one could also argue that the team's animal-related titles might have been inspired by Luis Buñuel and Salvador Dalí's *Andalusian Dog* (1928). These two controversial artists were especially pleased that they had coined a title for their groundbreaking surrealistic movie which had nothing to do with the picture's content, as would be the case with the later Marxes movies. Regardless, in 1930s slang, "duck soup" also meant something was really easy. But punster Groucho preferred to provide a truly "Marxist" reason/recipe for *Duck Soup*: "Take two turkeys, one goose, four cabbages, but no duck, and mix them together. After one taste, you'll duck soup the rest of your life."[30]

Amusingly, this most memorable of movies, like Buster Keaton's now celebrated *The General* (1927), was a box office disappointment during its initial release. A solid explanation for why the Marxes' often nihilistic attack on the absurdity of government did not connect with the public comes down to its overly dark comic approach to a then vulnerable establishment. Sociological film historian (and now gifted screenwriter and director) Andrew Bergman insightfully expands upon this unfortunate timing: "After a year of [President Franklin] Roosevelt's energy and activism [e.g., the flurry of New Deal legislation], government, no matter what else it might be, was no absurdity."[31] The Bergman perspective is further bolstered by historian Robert S. McElvaine's suggestion — "Had *Duck Soup* been released a year earlier, while the [floundering] Herbert Hoover was still in the White House, it probably would have enjoyed a much friendlier reception."[32] As in all things comic, it was a matter of *timing*.

Several years ago I was a featured scholar on an A & E *Biography* segment on

Groucho in which Bergman's perspective was noted. Another guest, television personality Dick Cavett, condescendingly suggested that no one leaves a theater early on account of skewering the government. But he missed the point. To punningly paraphrase a Groucho line from *Duck Soup*, Bergman was not suggesting the Marxes made viewers "leave in a huff." The historian simply implied the movie's political content, at that time, kept patrons from even going to the theater. Moreover, by 1933, the release date of *Duck Soup*, the formerly "Depression-proof" movies were experiencing a drop in attendance figures.

Duck Soup's box office numbers undoubtedly also suffered from the plethora of pictures 1930s Hollywood had already turned out about zany foreign lands, especially comedies about small fictitious European countries (see chapter 2). Even *Duck Soup*'s working title, *Cracked Ice*, was reminiscent of comedy team Wheeler and Woolsey's *Cracked Nuts* (1931), in which the comics vie for leadership of the mythical European kingdom of El Dorania. More specifically, over six months prior to *Duck Soup*, another Wheeler and Woolsey film with parallels to the later Marx movie opened—*Diplomaniacs* (1933). Indeed, at one point Paramount even accused *Diplomaniacs*' RKO studio of lifting material from the still-in-production *Duck Soup*.[33] Though not in a league with the Marxes' film, *Diplomaniacs* (co-scripted by Joseph L. Mankiewicz!) is an amusingly strong Wheeler and Woolsey outing, with the duo as Indian reservation barbers turned delegates to a Geneva peace conference ... which naturally leads to war.

What makes the *Diplomaniacs–Duck Soup* links most intriguing is that the entertaining villain pushing for war in both pictures is played by Louis Calhern. Now best known for his later serious character roles, such as the criminal mastermind in *The Asphalt Jungle* (1950), Calhern is a wonderful straight man to Chico and Harpo in *Duck Soup*. Though period critics neglected to note his masterful support of the Marxes, Calhern often stole the *Diplomaniacs* reviews from Wheeler and Woolsey. For instance, the *New York Post* stated, "The most amusing sequences in the film are contributed by Louis Calhern, a charming villain, who is less strenuous than Wheeler and Woolsey, and generally funnier."[34] And the *New York American* credited his satirical representative of a bullet manufacturing company as the actor who "easily captures the [comic] honors in the current insanity."[35] Given Calhern and other story parallels between *Duck Soup* and the earlier released box office hit *Diplomaniacs*, the superior Marxes movie was probably hurt again by the timing of its release.

The public's period apathy over *Duck Soup* is anticipated in the *New York Herald Tribune*'s review: "[I]t is my fear that American experts at satirical farce are not at their best when mocking the frailties of dictatorship."[36] The only thing misleading about this perspective, which has unfortunately often been echoed through the years, is that the Marxes were mediocre satirists—given that the team did not offer the genre's standard alternative perspective. But this is yet another reason why the Marxes are best placed in the black comedy pigeonhole—dark humor is beyond satire. The message with black comedy is that there is no message.[37] And this perfectly captures the anarchistic spirit of the Marxes. Chaos is the background music of their world. As Groucho sings in *Horse Feathers*, "Whatever It Is, I'm Against It." Of course, for all that darkly comic outrageousness, the modern viewer also relates to the Marxes because their take on anarchy

4. The Marx Brothers' *Duck Soup* (1933) 63

The catalyst for Groucho's political paranoia in *Duck Soup* is gifted straight man Louis Calhern (right), with Chico (left) and Harpo (center).

often sounds like the world of today. As the acclaimed writer Jim Knipfel wrote in his memoir *Slackjaw*:

> I keep returning to that simple mantra of mine [when life gets difficult], Deal With It, while recognizing that life has become one long slapstick routine—like living a Marx Brothers movie, except without quite so many musical numbers.[38]

The Marx Brothers came by their own dark comedy perspective on life quite naturally. In Harpo's autobiography he wrote with simple eloquence:

> When I was a kid there really was no future. Struggling through one twenty-four-hour span was rough enough without brooding about the next one. You could laugh about the past, because you'd been lucky enough to survive it. But mainly there was only a present to worry about.[39]

It was a period (early twentieth century) when American literature was discovering "naturalism" (muckraking realism), with subject matter often focused on the plight of this country's more recent immigrants. While the Marx family was not straight out of Upton Sinclair's *The Jungle*, times were not easy; and Harpo's autobiography sometimes has a

The ultimate Marx Bros. take on chaos: The team (left to right), Harpo, Chico, Groucho, and Zeppo, casually play cards during an apocalyptic scene deleted from *Duck Soup*.

matter-of-fact naturalism about it that can be shocking. For example, his description of what might be labeled the East River breast-stroke — the "pushing away" motion of your hands — was "the only way you could keep the sewage and garbage out of your face" when swimming.[40]

For the young Marxes, even traveling around New York City was like entering a war zone. The brothers often fell back on several different huckster techniques. These ranged from the most bold of cons — assuming the ethnic dialect of the gang whose space had been violated — to carrying some expendable trinkets with which to bribe one's way out of trouble. Just as their children-of-immigrants status had taught them that language and customs were not always what they seemed, their youthful ongoing misadventures around New York further fueled their later black comedy.

Because of *Duck Soup*'s less than stellar performance at the box office, the film has sometimes been wrongly labeled a critical flop, too. Such was not the case. While not without its naysayers, the majority of the reviews were positive. *Variety's* critique even opened with a positive prediction: "Practically everybody wants a good laugh right now and *Duck Soup* should make practically everyone laugh."[41] And the *New York Daily News*' punning superlatives favored a funny recipe:

> If you like duck soup try the hot and spicy dish which the Rivoli [theatre] introduced to Broadway yesterday.... Four different kinds of nuts [Groucho, Chico, Harpo, Zeppo] give it its special and peculiar flavor ... [I]f this dish doesn't make your mouth water it will your eyes, because the gags make it smart. It is ... the funniest of the Marx Brothers' productions.[42]

Along similar lines, *Newsweek* opined, "*Duck Soup* is just the dish for those desiring a minimum of sense and a maximum of madness in their films."[43]

Not surprisingly, director McCarey was often at the center of this praise. *The Hollywood Reporter*, especially taken with the mirror sequence, said, "Leo McCarey's direction shows up well, and his knowledge of building up comedy routines with the camera stood him in good stead more than once."[44] And the *Daily News* added, "McCarey ... juggles his clowns around with skill. He keeps things happening and never lets the procedure drag."[45] While the director's fast pace is praised here, this seemingly modern saturation technique might also have contributed to the picture's so-so box office in 1933. Normal audience expectations for comedy during the 1930s favored a fragmented, variety show–like presentation. Morrie Ryskind, frequent screenwriter for the Marxes, both before and after *Duck Soup*, later observed:

> You'd have a very funny scene ... so you couldn't follow that with another funny scene. You have to have a break and a change of pace. So the two lovers would get up and sing a song ... then you were ready for another [comic] scene. You didn't have ice cream [comedy] all the way through![46]

Today's viewers, however, enjoy "ice cream" throughout, which explains why audiences now prefer the nonstop comedy of *Duck Soup* over those Marx Brothers pictures that are frequently derailed by romantic subplots. Along related lines, McCarey so streamlined the movie that he even eliminated another popular variety show factor in Marx

Brothers films — the musical solos by Chico (piano) and Harpo (harp). Though not without a certain charm, especially since they still involve the Marxes (as opposed to supporting players in the romantic subplots), the solos would completely stop the story, too.

Of course, one could argue that this McCarey streamlining of *Duck Soup* was simply being true to a basic Marx family axiom. That is, Harpo would later write, "The only tradition in our family was our lack of tradition."[47] However one cuts it, *Duck Soup* remains a unique film, even for the Marx Brothers.

CHAPTER 5

Laurel and Hardy's *Sons of the Desert* (1933)

HARDY: "To catch a Hardy, they've got to get up very early in the morning."
LAUREL: "What time?"
— From *Sons of the Desert*

Film comedy historian Gerald Mast once stated, "The starting point of every Laurel and Hardy film is that they are overgrown children."[1] While this rings true, it is less insightful than it appears—*all* comedians are essentially overgrown children. But in Mast's favor, Laurel and Hardy are more childlike than most. Coupled to this is an inherent goodness that helps explain why the duo are arguably the most beloved of all funnymen. Dark comedy novelist Kurt Vonnegut addressed this latter point in the prologue to his appropriately named book *Slapstick*, which was also dedicated to the team. For Vonnegut, this very loosely autobiographical novel has Stan Laurel and Oliver Hardy ties because their *slapstick* films are "what life *feels* like to me. There are all these tests of my limited agility and intelligence. They go on and on."[2] With Vonnegut, the team's "fundamental joke" is that they try their hardest at every test, always in "good faith" that this time will be different. Even though this is why Vonnegut, or the viewer in general, finds Laurel and Hardy funny, there is also a certain "common decency" about their patient methodical persistence in the face of life's constant frustrations.

What else is there about the team that makes even their mere caricatures so popular? First, and most basic beyond their obvious ties to comedy, Laurel and Hardy quite literally look funny. Theirs is the most fundamental of comic contrasts—the interaction between a fat person and a skinny one. They further accent the difference in various comic ways. For instance, Stan's scarecrow dry hair is often seemingly combed straight up, as if he had just had an electrical shock, while Ollie's hair is invariably slicked down close to his head. More subtly, when Stan is confused or frightened, he goes into his elongated, vacuous facial expression (tears optional), vertically culminated by his reaching up and scratching the top of his head (like a comic El Greco, if the master of lengthened figures had done clowns). In equally subtle contrast, Ollie's most memorable comic "mask" (expression) occurs when he broadens his face in disgruntlement over another boner by Stan, tilting Hardy's head slightly downward and allowing his many chins to pile up onto his chest. Unlike Laurel's elongated hand motion to the top of the head, Ollie's corresponding trademark gesture happens during times of shyness, when he plays with his tie, thus breaking its perpendicular lines.

Of course, instead of inferring humor, one might also translate the meaning of these fat-skinny contrasts into metaphor, such as unconventional symbols for feast and famine. Granted this is a rather outlandish suggestion. But in the spirit of "Ripley's Believe It or Not," such a correlation occurred at a remote shrine in 1930s China, where their picture was used on an altar for just that reason.[3] This is not an invitation to dust off one's knees and begin worshipping the duo. It does, however, underline the worldwide pervasiveness of the duo even in the 1930s, as well as the almost primal contrast in their body shapes.

The second factor behind the universality of their personae as icons (after simply looking funny) is that they represent the ultimate symbol of comic frustration. Naturally, rare is the humor figure that does not know some degree of laughable letdown. But Laurel and Hardy established new highs for comic lows as they participated in the evolution of the comic antihero in mainstream American humor. While comedy genius director Leo McCarey's teaming and molding of Laurel and Hardy did not invent the comic antihero, their phenomenal late–1920s rise to prominence in that comic guise paralleled the center stage emergence of the character on the national scene.[4] Because of the gifted McCarey, the early Laurel and Hardy belong in an antihero pantheon with the comic literary legends James Thurber and Robert Benchley.

So what components constitute the antihero? Five distinctive characteristics emerge from extensive study of the subject: his constant frustration, his childlike naiveté, his abundant leisure time, his apolitical nature, and his life in the city.[5] Each characteristic also constitutes a break with what had formerly been the dominant character type in American humor—the capable, crackerbarrel philosopher.

The core characteristic here, of course, is frustration. Stan and Ollie succeed at very little. Any attempts to deal with an irrational world in a rational matter are generally doomed from the beginning. Their only parallel with the capable crackerbarrel is that they do manage, as the Benchley comic antihero does, to be persistent (which they complement with slow thinking). The following brief Laurel and Hardy overview demonstrates the comic richness of their antiheroic appeal. The examples are drawn from their early McCarey short subjects in order to parallel the time when the comic misfit was moving to the center stage of American humor. (Consistent with this, the team's *Sons of the Desert* draws heavily from the 1928 McCarey-authored and -directed *We Faw Down*, which will be expanded upon shortly.)

First, Stan and Ollie's frustration is based on conflict with both wives and machines. Their wives dominate them, though Hardy generally finds himself to be the most comically misused (as was the case with Thurber's "battle of the sexes"). Still, even when the story seems to overlook the woman, there exists a foreboding tension just beyond the screen. For example, the opening title of *Should Married Men Go Home?* (1928, McCarey co-authored story) asks the question: "What is the surest way to keep a husband home? Answer: Break both his legs."

The domestic "front" provides the team with one of its most popular settings for a pivotal Laurel and Hardy theme—escape. They are often trying to sneak away from the restrictions of marriage, if only for an evening. (A getaway from the wives is at the heart of *Sons of the Desert*.) These matrimonial "jail breaks" also provide a more logical understanding of what might first seem an illogical Stan and Ollie setting — their propensity to turn up in real prisons, too, with the expectation that a comic escape will be attempted. Yet for this team, marriage and prison are two comic extremes of what the boys symbolically are always trying to escape — the debilitating restrictiveness of modern life itself. This subjugation, real or imagined, also includes an irony befitting an antiheroic world view. That is, an extended escape by the duo is not only rare, it is probably not in their best interest. Domination by prison guards and wives might be viewed as supervision for truly childlike antiheroes. Regardless, the price of their security is suppression, especially when we see the increased incompetency on their own.

The other primary source of frustration for the antihero is his dealings with the mechanical. For Stan and Ollie (especially Ollie), mastering a mechanical device is another way to assert their shaky hold on manhood. But unlike the escape attempts, this play for technological dexterity represents not so much proving manhood (necessitating secrecy from one's wife) but rather playing it out before her and/or for her benefit. In *Hog Wild* (1930, McCarey story) Laurel & Hardy systematically destroy a house in order to get a radio antenna on the roof. Granted, Ollie's wife has set him to the task, but it is a matter of male pride for him to accomplish it. Thus, when he comes crashing down the chimney, like some out-of-season Santa in civvies (after several other unplanned exits off the roof), Hardy's wife tells him maybe he ought to call it off. Ollie refuses, with a resounding, "I'll put it on the roof if it's the last thing I do!" (Had the film been produced in today's more black comedy–friendly world, Ollie just might have received his wish!)

The second commonality between the antihero and Laurel and Hardy is their childlike nature. Several of their films begin with Stan just dropping in at Ollie's home, as if to say, "Can you come out and play?" Certainly the relationships with their wives are more that of parent and child than of husband and wife. There is seemingly no sexual bond, and the mothers/wives make the decisions. Moreover, the periodic escape attempts by the "boys" might best be equated with that nearly universal childhood dream (invariably pondered if not always acted upon) of running away from home, even for only a short adventure. And such key comedy components as Stan's crying routine and Ollie bashfully playing with his tie are direct links to the insecurities of childhood.

In *Brats* (1930, McCarey story), Laurel and Hardy literally double as both fathers and sons. The dual-focus narrative convincingly illustrates that the Stan and Ollie adults are no different from the Stan and Ollie children. While the twosomes play at separate games (checkers and pool or blocks and boxing), both pairs tend to fight and to be comically destructive. Appropriately, while the earlier activities of the fathers and sons were usually reciprocal, the finale is something of a shared experience. Their children have left water running in the bathtub from the beginning of the film, and when little Ollie asks for a bedtime drink, his father unleashes a tidal wave by merely opening the door.

A third shared trait between the team and the comic antihero is their quantity of leisure time. While there are exceptions to this, Laurel and Hardy still seem to have a preponderance of free or play time, which also reinforces one's image of them as children. Historically, this reflects a period (1920s) when increased leisure time for the masses was fast becoming a reality. It also demonstrates, as noted by comedy historian Hamlin Hill, a retreat from the ever more complex and dangerous modern world. That is, the antihero deals with this frightening outside realm by not dealing with it at all. Instead, he focuses "microscopically upon the individual unit ... that interior reality — or hysteria ... In consequence, modern humor deals significantly with frustrating trivia."[6] (Ironically, the television series *Seinfeld* is sometimes considered groundbreaking along these lines — "the sitcom about nothing" — yet antihero pioneers like Benchley, Thurber, and McCarey's Laurel and Hardy were doing this seventy years earlier.) An excellent example of Laurel and Hardy leisure-time activity occurs in *A Perfect Day* (1929, McCarey co-authored story), a film that also complements some of the antiheroic points examined thus far. As the title indicates, it was just the right sort of day for a picnic. Stan and Ollie, their wives, Uncle Edgar (Edgar Kennedy, with a bandaged gouty foot), and the family dog prepare for a carefree day.

Laurel and Hardy make the sandwiches while their wives attend to other details. Just when the sandwiches have been arranged on a tray being held by Ollie, the kitchen's swinging door shoots Stan into Ollie and the sandwiches are broadcast all over the room. The two fight, make up, and eventually rearrange the sandwiches. But all the mayhem has encouraged the dog to attack Uncle Edgar's bad foot. When Hardy tries to tear the family pet off Edgar's foot, he again scatters the sandwiches.

Eventually all is ready and the car is packed. Neighbors yell goodbye and the trip begins, almost. A tire hits a nail in the driveway and now there is a flat to fix. As Ollie fixes the tire, Stan accidentally assumes the dog's role of attacking poor Edgar Kennedy's foot. He manages to sit on the foot, step on it, slam it in the car door and, in the grand finale, drop a tire jack on it. Eventually the tire is fixed, but numerous other comic frustrations deny the bunch their picnic. So much for the fate of antiheroes, even on a "perfect day."

There is more to Stan and Ollie's free time, however, than just the domestic scene. They play golf in *Should Married Men Go Home?* (1928, McCarey co-author of story and supervisor), while their original plan in the McCarey-orchestrated *We Faw Down* was a night of poker with the boys. But their non-domestic leisure time more often found them in a nightclub, such as with unplanned dates in *Their Purple Moment* (1928, McCarey supervisor); the team's misadventure at the Pink Pup Club in *That's My Wife* (1929, McCarey story and supervisor), with Stan in drag as Ollie's wife); and *Blotto* (1930, McCarey story), where they somehow manage to get drunk on a nonalcoholic beverage!

The fourth common characteristic linking Laurel and Hardy to the comic antihero is a nonpolitical nature. The closest they come is probably one of their prison or police films. Still, there are no real issues at stake. The comic interactions are more a game of hide-and-go-seek between overgrown kids. Gerald Mast, while comparing law enforcement characterizations in the films of Charlie Chaplin and Mack Sennett, makes a comment pertinent to the world of Stan and Ollie: "The prison cops in [Chaplin's] *The Adventurer* (1917) ... shoot rifles at the escaping Charlie, and their bullets, unlike the bullets in Sennett comedies, look as though they could kill."[7] Like Sennett's cops, Laurel and Hardy's men in uniform are harmless. Indeed, the Stan and Ollie cop is often given enough personality (something generally lacking in Sennett films) to make him likable. For instance, Laurel and Hardy stock player Tiny Sandford has a small but endearingly memorable cop role at the close of *Big Business* (McCarey story and supervisor). He runs through a roller coaster of comic emotions as he first incredulously observes a classic tit-for-tat confrontation, and later tearfully commiserates with the boys as they momentarily feel remorse for their violent actions.

The utter incompetency of the comic antihero encourages the nonpolitical stance. He is constantly buffeted by the day-to-day frustrations of an irrational world. This figure is hardly capable of planning his leisure time, let alone becoming political. Crucial issues for Laurel and Hardy included things like keeping their derbies on or safely lighting a gas stove.

Just to play a comic devil's advocate, one might still wonder: If a political event were thrust upon an antihero, would he respond? No. Even then he would probably miss it because of vacuity reminiscent of Laurel and Hardy, which fittingly might be called the "derby disease." That is, pioneer antiheroic writer Robert Benchley, with his best spoofingly professorial style, made an alleged well-documented study of news photographs taken of "cataclysmic events" and found that:

> If you want to get a good perspective on history in the making, just skim through a collection of news-photographs which have been snapped at those very moments when cataclysmic events were taking place throughout the world. In almost every picture you can discover one [antihero] guy in a derby hat who is looking in exactly the opposite direction from the excitement, totally oblivious to the fact that the world is shaking beneath his feet. That would be me, or at any rate, my agent [such as Stan and Ollie] in that particular part of the world in which the event is taking place.[8]

Non-controversial comedy has long been a major selling point for Laurel and Hardy audiences, just as it has no doubt contributed to the fact that most critics now take the duo seriously. Appropriately, one period critic who did recognize the team's significance, novelist Graham Greene, also praised the importance of their nonpolitical stance. His 1940 review of the team's *A Chump at Oxford* ranked it ...

> ... with their best pictures — which to one heretic [Greene] are more agreeable than [the often political] Chaplin's; their clowning is purer; they aren't out to better an unbetterable world [later that year Chaplin released his black comedy on Hitler, *The Great Dictator*]; they've never wanted to play Hamlet [an unrealized Chaplin project, as well as a frequently cited serious role when a comedian starts to go somberly self-reflective].[9]

The fifth and final connection between Laurel and Hardy and the comic antihero is that they are citizens (read: victims) of the city. Born of a period that for the first time found America's urban population outnumbering rural residents, the team's classic films often presented the masses comically running amok, be it the epic pie fight of *The Battle of the Century* (1927, McCarey story and supervisor), or the cartoon-like traffic jam-demolition derby called *Two Tars* (1928, McCarey story and supervisor). Even in the seemingly more subdued California suburbs, those rows upon rows of identical white bungalows represent a bottled humanity just waiting for an excuse to explode comically, such as the team's greatest tit-for-tat encounter with stock company regular James Finlayson in *Big Business*. This particular exercise in "reciprocal destruction" has the team systematically destroying Finlayson's house, while he puts the kibosh to their car.[10] But as with all Laurel and Hardy tit-for-tat scenes, the participants politely take turns as they wreak organized chaos ... at Christmas time!

As noted earlier, the McCarey-orchestrated *We Faw Down* was a precursor to *Sons of the Desert*, a fact noted by some period critics.[11] *Down* opens with a patented McCarey axiom which might have graced *Desert*: "This story is based upon the assumption that, somewhere in the world, there are husbands who do not tell their wives everything." Film comedy theorist Alan Dale has labeled McCarey's earlier "marital woes" comedies with comedian Charley Chase a "combination of slapstick and melodrama."[12] This certainly also applied to both *Down* and *Desert*, though a better moniker might be "clown comedy meets a farcical spoof of melodrama." *Down* is such a quintessential example of this phenomenon, that besides being the blueprint for Laurel and Hardy's greatest feature, *Desert* (after their amicable split with McCarey), the short subject also provides an opening foundation for arguably McCarey's best film — *The Awful Truth* (1937, for which he won his first directing Oscar). Coming full circle here, *Truth* is also a watershed example of screwball comedy, a farcical genre that often mixes slapstick with a healthy spoof of marital melodrama.

Regardless, here is the essential background for McCarey's *Down*. Stan and Ollie hatch a plan to slip out on their wives for a night of poker with the boys. The team's cover is an alleged meeting with their boss at Los Angeles' Orpheum Theatre, McCarey's old childhood stomping ground. But naturally Stan and Ollie's plans go awry, and they spend some compromising time with two party girl types they meet on the way to the theater. However, their wives have reason for concern because the Orpheum burns down while the boys are gone. After reading about the fire in a late edition of the newspaper, the women head downtown to check on the fate of Stan and Ollie. But as luck (or the lack thereof) would have it, their spouses spot them leaving the apartment, via a window, of their new friends. More damning still, the duo are in the process of hurriedly getting dressed. Of course, it is not what it seems. The boys' clothes had gotten wet while they attempted to assist their new acquaintances, and naturally the girls invited them home to dry their wardrobe. But what wife would believe that? (The catalyst for the window exit came when a boyfriend suddenly appeared and misread the situation, too.)

Naturally, Ollie's later bumbling cover-up story gets a most chilly reception, with the bottom dropping out when one of the girlfriends (Vera White) turns up at the door with Hardy's forgotten vest! At this point, comic melodrama cuts straight to slapstick when Ollie's wife (Vivien Oakland, a fixture in McCarey's Charley Chase pictures) gets a shotgun and pursues the scampering boys outside. She fires as Laurel and Hardy run between two apartment buildings. The report of the gun is the sudden cause for countless seemingly cheating men to jump out of innumerable apartment windows (up to and including the third floor) in varied states of undress. This brilliant close was recycled for the conclusion of Laurel and Hardy's *Block-Heads* (1938), the team's last great feature.

While *We Faw Down* acts as a diagram for *Sons of the Desert*, the latter film achieves its unique status in three ways. First, without exactly recycling specific celebrated Stan and Ollie routines, it is the one feature that comes closest to the spirit of their classic early McCarey-influenced antiheroic short subjects. Pivotal to the whimsical world of Laurel and Hardy is McCarey's central theory of comedy — what he often called the "could-be quality." The sometimes scholarly director would even later write an article on the subject, noting:

> [G]ood comedy, whether it's pie-in-the-face, or fluff-on-the-fancy, starts with a believable premise ... [W]ithout ... [this,] the far-fetched scenes used by everyone in comedy would be utterly incredible, therefore valueless. But if they can start with a fact which can be accepted, laughs can then cover up any deficiency in logic in ensuing development. Just keep a string tied to fact.[13]

Thus, *Sons of the Desert*, based on the most "could-be quality" of stories (hoodwinking husbands), makes this the most comically grounded film included in this text, with the possible exception of chapter 7's *It's a Gift* (1934, with W.C. Fields as another antiheroic husband).

The spirit of earlier Laurel and Hardy work is best demonstrated in *Desert* by the antiheroic battle of the sexes. Particularly memorable is pots and pans–throwing Mae Busch as Mrs. Hardy (Busch appeared in fourteen Laurel and Hardy films). And because of this particular role, as well as her equally lethal Mrs. Hardy in *Their First Mistake* (1932), she represents to me the definitive domineering Ollie spouse, just as Fields' most comically frightening screen spouse is Kathleen Howard (see especially *It's a Gift*). But Busch also played a wide range of parts in other Laurel and Hardy films (besides Ollie's shrewish wife), from the murdering widow of *Oliver the Eighth* (1934) to the boys' accidental drinking partner in *Them Thar Hills* (1934).

Desert's Dorothy Christie, as Mrs. Laurel, is also a most memorable antiheroic wife, frequently seen here with her hunting rifle, reminiscent of *Down*'s shotgun-toting Vivien Oakland. One could even credit Christie's role, especially her initial home-from-the-hunt appearance (carrying her rifle and a string of ducks, and nicely decked out in hunting attire) as a possible inspiration for Jane Fonda's big game hunter fantasy sequence in *9 to 5* (1980), where she is tracking chauvinist boss Dabney Coleman. Of course, the comic twist in *Desert*, as it sometimes is in other Laurel and Hardy films focusing on the domestic scene, is that Stan is eventually babied by Christie because he tearfully tells the truth like a good little boy. In comic contrast, the Hardy wife seldom shows such mercy. Here, Ollie has been so routed by Busch (the viewer has heard the comic off-screen violence while honest Stan has been pampered on screen), that the rotund one is moved to close the film by throwing a pot at Stan.

Even Laurel's weakness for the occasional bit of fantasy (though always anchored in a realistic story) is kept consistent with his antiheroic, slow-witted screen persona. The scene in question finds Stan waiting for Ollie and helping himself to an apple ... a *wax* apple from the Hardys' purely decorative bowl of wax fruit. Now, while most conscious people would not make this mistake, at least beyond the first bite, Stan proceeds happily to munch away. While unlikely, it is a veritable showcase of neorealism compared to that *Way Out West* bit of fantasy where Stan has the igniting thumb.

Moreover, unlike the latter example, which goes against type, the wax fruit routine reinforces the comic stupidity of this clown. And like most good comedy, it also comes complete with a topper. After Ollie brings the mistake to Stan's attention, Busch matter-of-factly observes, "That's the third apple I've missed this week."

A second reason for the significance of *Desert* is that unlike many personality clown feature films, generally including those of Laurel and Hardy (as in *Pardon Us*, 1931), where the plot is merely connecting a helter-skelter line of funny but not necessarily related comedy sketches, *Desert* manages to integrate all the comic actions *without* sacrificing any of the rich characterizations. As film comedy historian Donald W. McCaffrey has observed: "Such simplicity [the attempted deception of their wives] within complexity [all that this entails for two antiheroic husbands] makes the work one of the outstanding comedies of the period."[14] However, it should be emphasized that plot cannot be a tradeoff for humor. That is, the team's generally inferior 1940s features, excluding *A Chump at Oxford* and *Saps at Sea* (both 1940), often ploddingly pushed plot to the complete detriment of Laurel and Hardy–style comedy (the team by then having lost most of its production control).

Another plus for *Desert*, as related to an integrated storyline, is that Laurel and Hardy did not have to share screen time with singing romantic interests as in the comic opera *The Devil's Brother* (1933). Period tastes often dictated that the duo and other comedians, such as the Marx Brothers, blend their comedy with a variety show format, such as including a romantic subplot. Not surprisingly, producer Hal Roach, who enjoyed casting Laurel and Hardy in comic operas (at their best in *Babes In Toyland*, 1934), also had reservations about unadulterated comedy features:

> The greatest comedies that were made by anybody were made in two reels, I don't care who it was. It's a simple damn thing. If you can stop after 20 minutes, you've only got to go up to this peak for your last laugh. But if you've got to go clear to 60 minutes, the last laugh is three times harder. It's that simple. And I don't care how funny a guy is, if you listen to him long enough, you're going to be bored to hell with him.[15]

A third reason for the importance of *Desert* is its ongoing "contemporary" appeal. Besides its display of antiheroic humor, there is its gentle yet complex satirizing of man's need for belonging to fraternal organizations. In this case, it is the Shriner-like "Sons of the Desert" from which the film receives its name. In order to attend their Chicago convention, the boys (fittingly from "Oasis 13" of Los Angeles) attempt to do the impossible — put one over on their wives. (Their cover is an alleged ocean voyage for Hardy's health.)

This affectionate send-up of fraternal associations is accomplished in three imaginatively broad strokes. First, there is the team's late arrival at the lodge's self-important, seemingly sacred gathering. Everyone wears uniform sashes and tasseled hats and listens closely to their "Exalted Ruler"—everyone, that is, except tardy Stan and Ollie, whose inability to enter quietly and find seats at this solemn occasion is decidedly funny and innocently rebellious. While the Marx Brothers would have openly broken up the meeting with their anarchic style and W.C. Fields would have peppered the air with fifth-columnist asides, Stan and Ollie's incompetent but accidental disruption is

5. Laurel and Hardy's *Sons of the Desert* (1933)

Charley Chase (center) plays against type in Laurel (right) and Hardy's mild take-off of fraternal organizations in *Sons of the Desert*.

ultimately the most comically damning, because these two knuckleheads are actually accepted members of this organization!

The second fraternal jab is dependent upon an excellent but unusual cameo appearance by Charley Chase, *the* Roach comedian after Laurel and Hardy but a talent yet to be fully recognized. Chase's role here, however, is atypical; instead of his normally likable screen persona, he plays a comically abrasive practical joker at the convention. Obviously, this is another legitimate liability of fraternal gatherings everywhere, as well as most national conventions. But it is equally obvious that such behavior was out of character for Stan and Ollie. It is thus farmed out to a supporting character (Chase) but narratively integrated by having the duo be the ones victimized. Moreover, Chase's negative nature is made all the more appropriate when he turns out to be the brother of Ollie's strong-arm wife.

The third side-swiping of fraternal organizations finally implicates Stan and Ollie in another stereotypical activity of such groups — the fun-loving silliness of their public parades, again reminiscent of the Shriners. In this case one follows a "Sons of the Desert" parade as it merrily winds through the streets of Chicago, with Stan and Ollie being two of its most enthusiastic participants — quite literally dancing along in the streets with the amusing progression.

Such childlike fraternal silliness is one characteristic that is an easy yet endearing target for comedy. It is reminiscent of those real parades where miniature cars (frequently piloted by Shriners) produce comic surprise by periodically rearing up on their back wheels and scooting about in the most non-traditional manner. And who better than Stan and Ollie personify the highs and lows of childhood, whether the "stand by me" loyalty of their friendship or its accompanying antiheroic frustrations — so often peppered with comic violence.

Unfortunately for Stan and Ollie, they ham it up for Chicago newsreel cameramen covering the parade — film footage their wives will later see at their local Los Angeles theater. Worse yet, the Honolulu ocean liner on which the boys were to have arrived home was, according to the in-film newspaper headline (more echoes of *Down*), "FOUNDERING IN TYPHOON." Consequently, just as with *Down*, Hardy, acting as the duo's spokesman, does not have a chance as he comically attempts to lie his way through the eventual showdown with the wives. As usual, Stan only makes things worse. For instance, when Ollie begins talking about their alleged shipwreck, Stan interjects, "Just as the boat was going down for the third time...."

Laurel and Hardy's gentle 1930s satire of a Shriner-like organization in *Sons of the Desert* anticipates a lampooning lithography by celebrated American Regionalist artist Grant Wood (1892–1942). Most famous for his pitchfork-toting couple in *American Gothic* (1930), Wood's 1939 work, *Shrine Quartet*, affectionately kids fraternal organizations by keying upon four members in their jester-like hats and protruding ears. But unlike the similarly arranged senile old women of a more biting Wood satire of another fraternal affiliation, *Daughters of Revolution* (1932), there is also a Laurel and Hardy–like affection for his subjects in *Shrine Quartet*, especially with the pyramids in the background. The difference was probably based in the fact that while Wood was not a fan of the Daughters of the American Revolution, the artist was a Shriner. Interestingly enough, Stan Laurel lived long enough to be in on the inception of the still very active Laurel and Hardy fan club — the "Sons of the Desert." In the spirit of the film from which the title is taken, the club is a gentle satire of fraternal orders.

Satire or not, the comic artistry of the film *Desert* was also not hurt by the inclusion of the soon-to-be hit song "Honolulu Baby," composed by Hal Roach's talented musical director T. Marvin Hatley, who had written the team's delightful "Dance of the Cuckoos" theme song. (Laurel and Hardy literature bounds with title and spelling variations of this song, but "Dance of the Cuckoos" appears to be the most official.) Interestingly enough, the *New York Post*'s review of *Desert* felt the "hummable tune entitled 'Honolulu Baby'" was the best thing about the picture.[16] Though the song is introduced in a Chicago nightclub segment, while Laurel and Hardy are in their Shriner-like, at-play mode, Stan begins to sing "Honolulu Baby" at the close, also. With a more forgiving wife, he is in a happy mood, while Hardy has just weathered (barely) an onslaught of glassware (Ollie is wearing a pot, as if it were an army helmet). Thus, Stan's rendition of a tune synonymous with a fake Honolulu trip for which he has just been "busted" is too much. The picture ends with Hardy taking his sidekick out by way of a well-thrown pot. Though not on a par with McCarey's shotgun close to *Down*, one so identifies with the put-upon Ollie that flattening Stan here is comically cathartic.

Before addressing the generally positive critical notices for *Desert*, one should note a unique commercial achievement for the picture. *Desert* is the only Laurel and Hardy feature to rank among the annual top moneymaking films, according to the records of such industry publications as the *Motion Picture Herald, Motion Picture Daily,* and *Film Daily*.[17] Other personality comedian pictures on this 1934 box office list were *Belle of the Nineties* (Mae West), *Judge Priest* (Will Rogers, see chapter 6), *Kentucky Kernels* (Wheeler and Woolsey), and *Roman Scandals* (Eddie Cantor).

Praise for the picture began with an early West Coast review in *The Hollywood Reporter*. Critiquing it on November 10, 1933 (the movie's major East Coast opening was not until January of 1935), the *Reporter* comically observed, the film "has nothing at all to do with the desert but plenty to do with real genuine laughter ... Laurel and Hardy are grand in this film."[18] The *New York Times*' Andre Sennwald was especially strong with his superlatives, to the point of waxing metaphorically poetic:

> Let it be said at once that the new Laurel and Hardy enterprise has achieved feature length without benefit of the usual distressing formulae of padding and stretching. It is funny all the way through. The mournful and witless Mr. Laurel and the frustrated Mr. Hardy are just as unfitted for the grim realities as they have ever been. A Quixote and Panza in a [comic] nightmare world.[19]

Newsweek credited the duo with having "done themselves proud," while the *New York American* stated, "*Desert* is one of the best entertainments created by the comedy combine ... [which adheres] to the Laurel-Hardy formula, establishing the funny fellows as the martyr husbands of ... Christy and Busch."[20]

As with the *Hollywood Reporter* critic, reviewers often had fun with the movie's title. The *New York Sun*'s John S. Cohen, Jr., was the most ambitious along these lines, feeling it might be a "lampoon of sheiks, Riffs, the Foreign Legion or other such figures that the movies have romanticized...."[21] Paradoxically, Cohen neither segued his review to *Desert*'s real lampooning of Shriner-like institutes, nor even a positive recommendation. He was one of those aforementioned period enemies of unadulterated comedy features. He much preferred Laurel and Hardy in *The Devil's Brother* (1933, also known as *Fra Diavola*), with the duo as assistants to the romantic musical lead Dennis King.

There were also, of course, those left-handed critical compliments that all personality comedians sometimes face, such as the *New York Daily News*' closing comment on *Desert*: "If you enjoy this team you will enjoy their antics in this farce."[22] *Liberty Magazine*'s review started along these lines, "Whether or not you like this one will depend on whether or not you like Laurel and Hardy...."[23] But they then immediately put a positive spin on being a fan of the duo by noting the various pseudonyms by which Laurel and Hardy were famous around the globe. The other distinctive quality to the *Liberty* piece was the almost equal space allotted to supporting player Charley Chase, who was credited with receiving "more fan mail than any other comedian in [1934] Hollywood."[24] Moreover, for students of comedy fascinated by Leo McCarey's ongoing influence on *Desert* (via *We Faw Down*), Chase's presence in the cast brings to mind his inspired collaborations with McCarey.

Today, Laurel and Hardy and *Desert* live on in countless ways, from the film being the team's best feature-length showcase of their basic comedy shtick, to the picture's

A Laurel and Hardy *Sons of the Desert* still which almost invites the lampooning of Shriner-like institutes.

full title, *Sons of the Desert*, now doubling as the name of their world-wide fan club. Naturally, Stan and Ollie fans also include countless artists in other media (and with radically different target audiences). Two of the most diverse examples are Nobel Prize–winning playwright Samuel Beckett's existential *Waiting for Godot* (1957), and award-winning children's author–illustrator Maurice Sendak's *In the Night Kitchen* (1970), a special favorite of my daughters.

Beckett, sometimes considered the most important of the post–World War II playwrights, draws strongly on Stan and Ollie for the derby-wearing characters Vladimir and Estragon in *Godot*. Along related lines, the three cooks of Sendak's book are identical clones of Ollie. While it is hardly recommended procedure to compare existential plays and children's literature, if a general connection (besides Laurel and Hardy) were made between the two works, it would be in their dark comedy natures.

Granted, there is a world of difference between examples, especially with a play sometimes unofficially referred to as *Waiting for God*. Still, a key point here is how the ongoing comedy relevance of Laurel and Hardy is maintained, at least in part, by the team's anticipation of today's ever-popular dark humor. In fact, I am reminded of when renowned black-comedy cartoonist Gary Larson "starred" Stan and Ollie in one of his "Far Side" cartoon strips. The boys are seen running down a long highway (towards the reader), with an atomic bomb mushroom cloud rising in the background. The Ollie caption simply reads: "Now you've done it!" Larson has merely served up an amusingly pessimistic modern version of Ollie's signature line, "Here's another fine mess...."

One safe bet is that Laurel and Hardy will remain "contemporary" for some time to come. As Richard Pryor, another fan of the team, once observed, "A lie is profanity. A lie is the worst thing in the world. Art is the ability to tell the truth, especially about oneself."[25] Laurel and Hardy, with a gentle assist from McCarey's principle of "could-be quality" comedy, invariably told the metaphorical truth. Stan and Ollie's world is initially not as impressive as the self-conscious pain of the more *serious* artist. But in the final analysis the duo's comic art seems so much more honest and universally pertinent to the individual banalities we all quietly (and sometimes not so quietly) suffer. And by topping it off with a Laurel and Hardy–produced smile of recognition, they gift us with a minor victory we would not otherwise have known.

CHAPTER 6

Will Rogers' *Judge Priest* (1934)

> The first thing I learned in politics is when to say ain't.
> — Will Rogers in *Judge Priest*

> Having defendant Jeff Poindexter (Stepin Fetchit) awakened in his court, Judge Priest (Will Rogers) observes, "If anyone's going to sleep in this court, it's going to be me."

At the time of Will Rogers' (1879–1935) tragic death in a plane crash, he was the most beloved and most influential entertainer in America. He was the proverbial star of stage, screen, and radio. Plus, his syndicated weekly articles and daily telegrams appeared in scores of newspapers coast to coast. Add to this his frequent authoring of best-selling, politically oriented humor books, and one has a figure most Americans perceived as more of an everyman neighbor than a media star. The title of Rogers' 1926 book, *Letters of a Self-Made Diplomat to His President*, perfectly summarizes his comedy shtick, a crackerbarrel populist never far from the political arena.[1] With the possible exception of Bob Hope, Rogers was arguably the twentieth century comedian with the most multi-faceted hold on popular culture America.

While Rogers' writing and *Ziegfeld Follies* work on Broadway had made him a phenomenon by the 1920s, his cinema career only took off with talking pictures. As one reviewer said of Rogers' first sound movie, *They Had to See Paris* (1929), "Will Rogers is the man talkies were invented for."[2] Soon the comedian was a fixture on Hollywood's most coveted list, the annual top ten box office stars. And the hugely successful *Judge Priest* helped make Rogers number one on that list in 1934.[3]

As with many of the personality comedians showcased in this text, Rogers' cinema clown status is predicated, in part, on a close connection with another comedy genre. But whereas the Marx Brothers bathe their laughter in dark comedy and Bob Hope is never far from parody, Rogers' work is invariably anchored in populism. This power-to-the-people genre is about the basic belief that the superior and majority will of the common man is forever threatened by the usurping, elitist few. Other characteristics associated with this classic underdog story which is populism include embracing rural and/or small town life, mythic-like leaders who have risen from the people (reflecting the genre's patriotic nature), an adherence to traditional values and customs (mirroring the movement's strong sense of nostalgia), a faithfulness to honest labor, a general optimism concerning humanity's potential for good, a methodical linear progression, the importance of family (particularly of a paternal nature), the underlining importance of the individual, and a romantically poetic belief in second chances. Historian George McKenna has described populism as "the perennial American 'ism' with its roots extended at least as far back as the American Revolution."[4] Put another way, America was founded upon the populist celebration of the individual making good against amazing odds.

The genre made its first big cinematic noise in the crackerbarrel philosopher movies of Will Rogers during the first half of the 1930s.[5] Herein, the goodness of the common man is borne out in the down-home wisdom of a crackerbarrel representative of the people—Rogers. In other words, Rogers *is* the people. As historian Roger Butterfield noted, the comedian's everyman persona "was the image that many Americans like to make of themselves."[6] While the figure of the comic antihero (best personified by Laurel and Hardy)

This shot of Will Rogers (circa 1933) perfectly captures the humorist's everyman populist appeal.

was fittingly in ascendancy during the Depression (a period when the world was seemingly turned upside down), this topsyturvydom had given the crackerbarrel philosopher some staying power, too, as people searched for fundamental values in difficult times.

The populist crackerbarrel figure is characterized by the key elements capability, employment, fatherly leadership, rural or small town residency, and political involvement. Though not all these components need be present for the populist picture, the genre is best served by utilizing the majority of the points. First, at his most basic, the populist crackerbarrel can take care of himself. Celebrated humor historian Walter Blair called this capability "horse sense," even entitling a book *Horse Sense in American Humor*. The character had ...

> ... learned everything from experience. When he gets into a new situation, he whittles his problem down to its essentials, sees how it compares with situations in his past and how it differs from them, and then he thinks out what he should do—figures out the right answer.[7]

He does not need any "book learnin'." It was a rational universe and life could be planned in a rational manner. Comedy resulted from characters who had trouble planning their existence. But the crackerbarrel figure established positive, rational plans and/or advised others of the correct procedures open to them.

Since a significant part of populist success is the ability to keep track of past experience, the crackerbarrel philosopher is frequently an older man who has grown wise through a lifetime of experience, such as Will Rogers. The most specific example is probably Hosea Biglow's comment on the Civil War: "I'm older 'n you, an' I've seen things an' men, an' *my* experience, tell ye wut it's ben."[8] Film director Frank Capra, so synonymous with populism in later years, often took a young hero and gave him a wise older figure as a model, such as the martyred father of Jefferson Smith (Jimmy Stewart) in *Mr. Smith Goes to Washington* (1939). Will Rogers mentored Capra in the 1920s, so it is fitting that the director seems to footnote his populist ties to Rogers with his pivotal casting and utilization of actor Harry Carey to play the helpful president of the Senate in *Mr. Smith*. Besides bearing a striking physical resemblance to Rogers, Carey's folksy mannerisms are especially reminiscent of the humorist: the slouching posture, a shock of hair falling on the forehead, the half-suppressed smile, hands never quite at rest. Though, on paper, Carey's is a seemingly small part, his largely visual support of the young filibustering Smith is both poignantly entertaining and pivotal to this segment of the film.

In *Judge Priest* Rogers' title figure is the most capable of characters, and "character" is an excellent moniker for him. For example, he often uses his lifetime of experience for purely comic effect. When a fellow Civil War veteran (Charley Grapewin) rehashes his heroic exploits for the umpteenth time, Rogers' judge affectionately calls him to task for some creative embellishments: "Gunboats? Putting them gunboats in there is a new tactic, isn't it, Jimmy?" Rogers' character, befitting the acclaimed nature of humorist Irvin S. Cobb's Judge Priest source stories, is effective at everything he does. These accomplishments range from playing romantic matchmaker for his nephew, to orchestrating the judicial victory of the young man's first courtroom case.

When addressing the crackerbarrel capableness of Rogers, one should note that there are two distinct takes on populism. Of course, all varieties of populism posit the belief that *the people* are inherently good. But the Frank Capra approach is the most idealistic. In his films the genre's salt-of-the-earth types need little prompting to do the right thing. In contrast, the Rogers model suggests that while folks might always have the power of good within them, they frequently need a push in the right direction. In the case of *Judge Priest*, Rogers' character manipulates a deserved not-guilty trial verdict by playing upon the patriotic nature of a jury composed of Confederate veterans. This involves everything from having a key witness (Henry B. Walthall) recap a Civil War battle, to cueing Stepin Fetchit's makeshift band to play "Dixie" just outside the courtroom. However, Rogers' best demonstration of the creative con in *Judge Priest* occurs with his casual quote which opened this chapter, "The first thing I learned in politics is when to say ain't." In other words, play to your audience. And when the typical populist was often a school-of-hard-knocks graduate, a well-placed "ain't" or two was simply good politics.

The second crackerbarrel component with populist underpinnings is gainful employment. As applied to populism, one might label this blue-collar value anti-elitist or a variation on the celebration of the common man. Thus, if the crackerbarrel does not follow the ideal Jeffersonian democracy profession (farming), as do James Russell Lowell's Hosea Biglow or Kevin Costner's Ray Kinsella in *Field of Dreams* (1989), his occupation is the next best thing — the everyday work world, from clock peddler Sam Slick (who first appeared in 1835), to Will Rogers' twentieth-century cowboy and self-made advisor to presidents. Moreover, historian Richard Hofstadter went so far as to claim that the defining characteristic of populist thought is "its willingness to grant the moral legitimacy and political acceptability of anyone who did any kind of honest work."[9]

Even the phrase "crackerbarrel philosopher" is derived from a particular profession — the general store owner who serves up both basic goods and good advice. America's greatest historical crackerbarrel figure came from just such a background: Abraham Lincoln ran a general store before becoming a lawyer and eventually president. Fittingly, the most acclaimed film portrayal of the sixteenth president, director John Ford's populist classic *Young Mr. Lincoln* (1939), defines the man early through his general store experience.

Genuinely passionate about people, these crackerbarrel populists could be said to

Will Rogers, both winking (at left) and standing (white suit), with Henry B. Walthall (foreground, seated) in *Judge Priest*.

have "blue-collar degrees" in counseling. Undoubtedly, the crackerbarrel philosopher with a name most synonymous for these people skills is Judge Priest, especially since much of this figure's time deals with metaphorically "priestly" duties, as well as his comic Solomon shtick. Cobb's coining of such a fortuitous populist name, a marriage of secular wisdom and religious outreach, rivals the importance of the story content itself.

In the world of populism, simply having a profession (keeping busy) also translates into a healthier life, figuratively and literally. One stays in touch with the norm and the normal. In fact, a people-related work ethic could be called a crackerbarrel credo. For instance, at Will Rogers' Oklahoma ranch, there was "a sign up on the barbed wire gate at the section line: 'Nothing Allowed in That Will Interfere With the Work or Scare the Animals.'"[10] Similarly, near the close of *So This Is London* (1930), Rogers' character observes that the "wrong people [are] doing the traveling. They're [the travelers] not the real [to be celebrated] people; they're at home working." Appropriately, in a Fox film press release for *Judge Priest*, the studio underlined the work ethic by noting, "Will Rogers recently declared that he is not happy unless he is busy."[11] The workaholic entertainer was famous for always having a portable typewriter handy so that he could crank out his syndicated newspaper copy whenever he had a free moment in a hectic schedule of filming, radio broadcasts, speaking engagements, and travel (frequently for humanitarian causes). A famous 1930s news photo of Rogers captures the comedian typing away in his favorite studio "office"— the front seat of his LaSalle automobile, with the car door open, the typewriter on Rogers' lap, and his feet resting on the running board.

A third crackerbarrel element central to populism is benefiting from, and often reconnecting with, a strong father figure. This factor is an outgrowth of the significance of family to populism. (The genre is all about second chances, and this phenomenon often begins with family relationships.) In *Judge Priest* Rogers treats his fatherless nephew like a son, protecting him from both an elitist mother and a browbeating first judicial opponent. In addition to his successful matchmaking activities for young Jerome Priest (Tom Brown), the judge also manages to reunite Jerome's love interest, Ellie May (Anita Louise), with the father she has never known (David Landau). This latter revelation is an outgrowth of the movie's most moving back-to-back scenes. Rogers sees the young couple in the moonlight from his bedroom and is reminded of himself and his late wife. He then lights a lamp and a large oval picture of his wife and two children is seen on the wall, with his own face reflected in the tintype. This is the catalyst for a monologue with his wife which poignantly begins, "Been a long way since you and the babies went away [died]."

One senses that this is a regular ritual with Rogers' character. Indeed, he soon takes a small canvas stool to the cemetery, so that he can carry on this "conversation" at her graveside. In populism, the departed continue to impact the living, and similar cemetery scenes surface in other populism pictures, particularly those of John Ford. Memorable later Ford examples would include Abe's (Henry Fonda) visit to the grave of lost love Ann Rutledge in *Young Mr. Lincoln* and Wyatt Earp's (Fonda) sojourn to the marker of his brother in *My Darling Clementine* (1946). John Ford biographer Scott Eyman credits the Rogers cemetery sequence in *Judge Priest* as the first instance of what would become a signature scene in the populist oeuvre of the director.[12] More recently, novelist Mark Spragg effectively utilizes the device in his 2004 populist novel, *An Unfinished Life*, which he and his wife Virginia adapted to the screen in 2005.[13] In this movie, Robert Redford's aging rancher has been struggling for years with the death of his adult son — thus the title, *An Unfinished Life*. Each day Redford's character visits his son's grave and shares his thoughts. But the second-chance healing only begins when he allows himself to reconnect with a granddaughter that suddenly comes into his life. While Rogers' Judge Priest figure is never in the bitter mindset of Redford's rancher, Priest playing father to a needy nephew is undoubtedly a comforting populist second-chance at parenthood.

Regardless, when Rogers' crackerbarrel is at the cemetery, he witnesses David Landau's blacksmith placing flowers on the grave of Ellie's mother, a mysterious stranger to Cobb's town who had died giving birth to the girl. This sketchy background has left a small town dark cloud over Ellie's life, which is why humanist Priest encourages his nephew's love for her — the boy's mother feels the girl is beneath him. The elitist Caroline Priest (Brenda Fowler) had even lectured Rogers' character, "The name of Priest means something in Kentucky," which triggered Rogers' most populist *Judge Priest* comeback, "I never heard it [Priest] meant intolerance." Rogers' courtroom defense of the blacksmith, and the absentee father's reunion with his daughter, are both results of Priest seeing Landau's character that night in the cemetery. Fittingly, for family-focused populism, a graveside scene which began with a celebration of Priest's family ends with the potential for bringing another family together. And to extrapolate a metaphorical "family" connection from the same segment, the collaboration of Rogers, Cobb, and Ford uses unknown people and places to teach us about our own families. Despite the axiom doubling as the title of Thomas Wolfe's 1940 novel, *You Can't Go Home Again*, populism movingly demonstrates how a longing for family — the pull of the past — can bring us *home*.

Interestingly enough, just as father figures are so often central to populist stories, Cobb based the figure of Judge Priest, in part, upon his own father. In his amusing epic of an autobiography, with the darkly comic title, *Exit Laughing* (1941), Cobb stated in his own crackerbarrel manner, "I ... poured about a gill [four ounces] of my father's personality [into every gallon of Priest] ... unlike most opinionated small [physically] men he [the elder Cobb] managed to convey the impression of forcefulness without either strutting or working on his chest expansion."[14] This democratic description of the author's father would not be out of place in a review of Rogers' *Judge Priest* performance.

One must add, of course, that Priest, especially as played by Rogers, reflects more than a little of the beloved crackerbarrel author, Irvin S. Cobb, also. Rogers and Cobb were close friends, and the film star brought the creator of the Priest tales to Hollywood as an advisor on the screen adaptation. The following year Cobb would even co-star with Rogers in *Steamboat Round the Bend* (1935). Make no mistake, however, the single greatest influence upon Rogers' "essaying" of the Priest part was Rogers himself — a variation of the crackerbarrel persona which made him such a beloved figure. But Cobb and Rogers were humorists cut from the same populist cloth, and descriptions of Cobb could double as either applicable to Rogers or the figure of Priest. In fact,

Elizabeth Cobb's characterization of her father, to return to that populism parental component, is reminiscent of historian Roger Butterfield's earlier cited description of Rogers: "He was, both deliberately and instinctively, Mr. Average Citizen. Perhaps that is why so many Americans were so very fond of him. He was themselves, grown famous."[15] But I find her later pocket characterization of her father — "wearing mischief like a halo" — as even more entertainingly appropriate for the populist trinity of Cobb, Rogers, and Priest.[16] That is, beyond creating a charming image, the "mischief" element speaks to that more manipulative approach to populism favored by these crackerbarrel figures, as well as *Judge Priest* director John Ford.

A fourth crackerbarrel trait with links to populism is rural and/or small town residency. The horse sense hero invariably comes from this setting, though he often enters cities and cures their problems, as Seba Smith's pioneering (1830s) Jack Downing or Capra's Jefferson Smith do in Washington, D. C. Moreover, he always longs to return to the country or the small town (just as George Washington and Thomas Jefferson were anxious to lay down the mantle of national duty and return to their beloved countryside).

Populism's ties to the country are an outgrowth of Europe's Enlightenment. This glorification of nature is more specifically an outgrowth of eighteenth century Deism — the belief that to know nature was to know God; therefore, nature was preferable to

Will Rogers (left), Irvin S. Cobb (right) and an unidentified actor in *Steamboat Round the Bend* (1935).

what was man-made. As historian George McKenna has insightfully observed, this is "the doctrinal underpinning for Jefferson's claim that the farmers are God's 'chosen people' and his preference for agriculture over industry."[17] Appropriately for the populist *Judge Priest*, Rogers' title character enjoys nothing more than getting away to nature by way of his favorite fishing haunts. Coupled with this pastoral preference, Priest's humanism also seems to be of a Deist nature, since he ignores organized religion. Yet his unconventional ways are endorsed by the movie's pivotal Reverend Ashby Brand (Henry B. Walthall), who basically tells Rogers' judge that goodness is not based upon church attendance.

The dichotomy between the natural and the man-made is sometimes showcased in the populist crackerbarrel world as country and/or small town versus the city. More to the point, the large urban setting represents temptation and corruption. An excellent example of this populist juxtaposition occurs in a film Rogers did the same year as *Judge Priest*—*David Harum* (1934). Here the laid-back world of small-town banker and title character (Rogers) is contrasted with the complex environment facing him in a large urban setting like New York City. Though the film is an 1890s period piece, roundabout commentary on the Depression is provided, because the time frame is the economic panic of 1893. The message is a familiar one, with Rogers' own patented small-town interpretation of Jeffersonian democracy. In addition, the movie anticipates what would now be seen as Frank Capra populist touches, such as David Harum's democratic interaction with a butler, the significance of Christmas, and the people coming together in a comic community song—"Ta-ra-ra-Boom-de-Ay"—to help Rogers win the trotter race that closes the story.

These Capra parallels notwithstanding, there is a basic difference between the director's populist take on the small town and the Rogers–John Ford position. Just as Capra's brand of populism had younger, more idealistic central heroes with the crackerbarrel mentor in the background, Capra's movie milieu put small town life on a pedestal. In contrast, the front and center crackerbarrel world of Rogers and Ford was not blind to village hypocrisy. Indeed, Rogers and Ford's first collaboration, *Dr. Bull* (1933), in which the humorist's title character is a country doctor fighting illness and small town narrow-mindedness, eventually has Rogers leaving New Winton, Connecticut, because of its gossipy pettiness. But this exit is an extreme act. The more typical Rogers-Ford action would be to simply activate the cajoling nature of their populism—wringing out the inherent goodness of the people through egalitarian-driven manipulation. In *Judge Priest* this involved Rogers' constant playing the Civil War card for a jury composed of Confederate veterans. Suffice it to say that populism's depiction of the village, regardless of the auteur, generally puts a positive spin on the rustic life. But the Rogers-Ford variety will realistically pepper that populism with a few pinched-faced hypocrites, such as Judge Priest's elitist sister-in-law or his pompous political opponent (Berton Churchill).

To emphasize that often idyllic portrayal of the populist village, the genre is often set in the past to reinforce the feel-good nostalgia of a seemingly simpler time. In reality, earlier eras are seldom simpler. For most, the quiet desperation of the typically lived life has been a constant through time. But the beauty of the human condition is a selective memory of the past, often minimizing travail and waxing poetic about the good times. Consequently, by setting the populist picture in the past, as is the case for *Judge Priest*, *David Harum*, and *Steamboat Round the Bend* (all in the 1890s), the small town is bathed in that proverbial "rose-colored glasses."

Certainly, the sleepy Southern village location of *Judge Priest*, loosely and lovingly based upon Cobb's boyhood Paducah, Kentucky, home, matches the bucolic world of an even earlier Tom Sawyer and Huck Finn. Ford's knowing depiction of Americana in *Judge Priest* was justly praised at the time. The *New York Evening Journal* credited the picture as a "heart-warming and genuinely moving story of a sleepy Southern town in the nineties."[18] And the *New York World Telegram* said Ford "manages to catch the homely, numerous, folksy things of life so warmly that you are inclined to grant it more virtues than it inherently possesses."[19]

The only downside to this merry milieu today is a racial question of political correctness. Some might criticize *Judge Priest* for a degree of "Uncle Tom"-ism — the depiction of the happy African-American servant, long freed but still subservient to a white employer. Thus, the film introduced Hattie McDaniel (1895–1952) to moviegoers as the large earth mother actress whom *The New Yorker* would later label "Mammy for the Masses."[20] Today she is best known for her *Gone with the Wind* (1939) Best Supporting Actress Academy Award, the first black performer to win an Oscar statuette. *Judge Priest* also featured Stepin Fetchit (Lincoln Perry, 1902–85), who was then the much bigger black star, as well as the highest paid African American performer in 1930s Hollywood. Ironically, his shiftless shtick, sometimes self-billed as the "laziest man alive," is now the more grating racial stereotype. Yet, recent revisionist black historians have reframed these performances as something positive, given the circumstances. For example, Fetchit biographer Mel Watkins dedicated his book to "all of the early-twentieth-century black comedians who, under the most repressive conditions, satirized and labored to humanize the nation's distorted image of African Americans."[21] Or, as a bemused McDaniel once comically observed of the limited possibilities open to her, in or out of the movies, "I would rather make seven hundred dollars a week playing a maid than be one."[22]

In further defense of Fetchit, who is more prominently featured in *Judge Priest*, he often plays what American humor has called the "wise fool." That is, while his general demeanor might suggest simpleton status, his actions often send another message. For instance, when he is standing trial for theft in Priest's courtroom, the pontificating prosecutor (Churchill) rattles on endlessly. With the rest of the room bored silly (save Rogers, who is reading the comics), Fetchit shows his contempt for Churchill's character by taking a nap. Furthermore, instead of trying to fight the charge, Fetchit introduces a seemingly random fishing hole tip to his testimony. But this dumb-like-a-fox comment qualifies as his "get out of jail free" card. He knows his pal and employer (Rogers' Judge Priest) is an avid fisherman more interested in angling advantages than a few stolen chickens. And true to form, this courtroom scene is followed by the two friends going fishing. Plus, like his populist pal (Rogers), Fetchit is capable of his own special brand of comic axioms. But to take the aforementioned satirical suggestion of Fetchit biographer Watkins, the black comedian's comments often have a nonsense quotient which affectionately mocks Rogers' crackerbarrel wisdom. To illustrate, when Priest asks him why he does not wear the shoes he has tied around his neck, Fetchit says, "Savin' 'em, in case my feet wear out."

Beyond one's ability to appreciate an ethnic persona of the past, the characters played by Fetchit and McDaniel also serve an important symbolic part in the defining of Rogers' title figure. Like many maverick heroes in American popular culture, Priest's metaphorical outsider status is reinforced by his close relationship with these minority societal outsiders. Parallel examples might range from Huck Finn and runaway slave Jim, to the Lone Ranger and his loyal Native American sidekick Tonto. Widower Priest spends most of his free time with the characters played by Fetchit and McDaniel. Besides the aforementioned fishing getaways, Rogers enjoys singing at home with McDaniel as she cleans, or sitting on the porch with Fetchit as his Man Friday plays the harmonica.

In real life the two men were close friends, with Fetchit being especially proud of the screen quality he felt they portrayed: "When people saw me and Will Rogers like brothers, that said something to them."[23] In addition, they had a similar working style. Neither performer liked to memorize lines but preferred to paraphrase the dialogue in their own colloquial manner. While this presented a challenge for some cast members, who naturally desired specific verbal cues, Rogers and Fetchit enjoyed the freshness of their approach. As Fetchit amusingly told a reporter, "Paht of the time he suhprises me. Paht of the time I suhprise him. But mos' of the time we suhprises each other."[24]

Actress Rochelle Hudson, whose *Judge Priest* character also had romantic designs on Rogers' screen nephew, even coined a special phrase for the humorist's proclivity to continually tweak his dialogue—"Rogersized it." By this time a veteran of four films with the comedian (having previously appeared in his *Dr. Bull*, 1933's *Mr. Skitch*, and 1935's *Life Begins at Forty*), she would add, "No author who ever wrote a Rogers script ever recognized his [the humorist's] handiwork in the screen...."[25] The humorist's laid-back approach to dialogue was also reflected in a nonchalant approach to minor continuity questions. Hudson observed that Rogers' "eternal answer to trifling details" was to say, 'Aw, leave it alone, it'll never show on a big screen with loud music."[26] The implication here, which Rogers shared with Charlie Chaplin, is that if the emotional content of a scene does not carry the day over some unimportant continuity error, the film is already lost.

Rogers' casually real approach to acting has generated a great deal of entertaining documentation, with none more pivotal than a 1972 interview with John Ford. Calling *Judge Priest* his "favorite picture of all time," the legendary director shared:

> Nobody could write for Will. He'd read his script and say, "What does that mean?" And I'd say, "Well, that's rather a tough question. I don't know what it means exactly." Then we would finally figure out what it meant, and I'd say to him, "Say it in your own words!" And he'd go away, muttering to himself, getting his lines ready, and when he came back, he'd make his speech in typical Rogers fashion, which was better than any writer for him. Because no writer could write for Will.[27]

An amusing companion piece to this Ford statement comes from a 1935 reminiscence from Cobb, concerning Rogers' affectionate baiting of the director at the production start of *Steamboat Round the Bend*. When Ford asked the two humorists if they had had a chance yet to look at the script, Rogers observed:

Rochelle Hudson with Tom Brown (center) and Will Rogers in the taffy-pull scene from *Judge Priest.*

> Been too busy ropin' calves. Tell you what, John, you sort of generally break the news to us what this sequence is about and I'll think up a line for Cobb to speak and then Cobb'll think up a line for me to speak and that way there won't be no ill-feelin's or heartburnin's and the feller that kin remember after it's all over — if there is any plot by then — gets first prize, which will be a kiss on the forehead from Mister John Ford.[28]

What makes these observations doubly provocative today is that pantheon director Ford is now remembered as the most memorable of martinets — often a creative terror on his sets. His deference here to Rogers suggests a position which will be addressed shortly — that the humorist had a major impact upon Ford's take on populism. But before closing the commentary on the casually real acting approach of Rogers, the insights of the humorist's *Judge Priest* nephew (Tom Brown) merit noting. Years later the actor would still be amazed at the utter naturalness of Rogers:

> He never wore makeup and I don't remember ever seeing them [the makeup staff] comb his hair or doing anything to him. He'd walk on the set and he'd walk off the set; it was as though he wasn't even at work — he was the same. Even though *Judge Priest* was a [period] costume piece, I wasn't even aware that these weren't his clothes — he was that natural.[29]

A fifth and final crackerbarrel component with ties to populism is a political base. While this trait is most synonymous today with the populist world of Capra, from *Mr. Smith Goes to Washington* to *State of the Union* (1948), politics very much defined who Rogers was — both onscreen and off. As the aforementioned "self-made diplomat to his president" statement suggests, politics is just what Rogers did. Indeed, shortly after Rogers' death, Cobb revealed that the humorist had always reminded him of a very political Judge William Bishop, a childhood hero to Cobb that was a model, with his father, for the Judge Priest stories. For Cobb, the central element for Bishop/Priest/Rogers was people politics. Cobb observed:

> [W]hen he [Bishop] went "politician," as he used to say, he talked like the man on the street, in words that the Southerners understood. He was not a judge then, just another citizen. Will Rogers was just another citizen ... he talked the common language, his words touched and humored by his own thoughts.[30]

Crackerbarrel political populism is not just about people skills. These sage folk philosophers are often prophets of the future, too, and these predictions are not of the questionably murky nature of a Nostradamus (1503–66). For example, Seba Smith's pioneering crackerbarrel figure Jack Downing (an apparent later model for America's Uncle Sam figure) had some amazing comments on President Andrew Jackson putting down South Carolina's secession threat twenty-eight years before the Civil War:

> The tops are beat down, but the roots are alive as ever, and spreading under ground wider and wider, and one of these days when they begin to sprout up again there'll be a tougher scramble to keep 'em down than there has been yet.[31]

Along similarly impressive lines, a 1926 Rogers accurately predicted the key role aircraft would play in World War II (1941–45), and even America's future enemy:

> If you think there ain't going to be no Next War you better see some of these Nations drilling and preparing ... The next war you don't want to Look Out; you want to Look Up. When you look up and see a cloud during the next war to end wars, don't be starting to admire its silvery lining till you find out how many [German] Junkers and Fokkers are hiding behind it.[32]

Of course, like many crackerbarrel populists, Rogers' political wisdom was more often associated with short witty axioms, such as these two from a memorable collection published shortly after his untimely death: "We are a nation that runs in spite and not on account of our government," or "I might have gone to West Point but I was too proud to speak to a Congressman."[33] Along these same pithy political lines, again, is the Rogers *Judge Priest* line which opens the chapter.

Not surprisingly, as a beloved populist humorist and the political conscience of the country, American powerbrokers courted Rogers' friendship and support. As Rogers' definitive biographer, Ben Yagoda, has stated, by the late 1920s, "Will had become a figure of real influence in American politics. He was read every day by millions, many of whom uncritically adopted his views as their own ... [something] not lost on politicians...."[34] This was certainly true of then President Franklin D. Roosevelt, whose 1932 election was greatly assisted by Rogers' support. Fittingly, one of the cornerstones of Roosevelt's "New Deal" policy, hiring the unemployed for massive public works projects, was something the humorist had been calling for well before FDR arrives at the White House. But Roosevelt had long had an honest affection for Rogers and what he represented. Even the president's signature name for change, the "New Deal," had a Rogers connection. The phrase was technically drawn from Mark Twain's novel *A Connecticut Yankee in King Arthur's Court* (1889), but Rogers had revitalized both the expression and the book with his hit 1931 screen adaptation of said work — just the year before Roosevelt's election. Thus, shortly after the opening of *Judge Priest*, the president would send the humorist a fan letter, stating, in part, it "is a thoroughly good job and the Civil War pictures [sequences] are very true to life."[35]

As befitted the number one box office star of 1934 (Rogers), *Judge Priest* was also on Hollywood's annual top moneymaking list.[36] Coupled with this were the most superlative of reviews. The *New York Times* said "it shows ... American humor at its best," as well as providing Rogers with "one of the happiest roles of his screen career."[37] *Variety* requested further Priest stories with Rogers, calling it "one of the best performances of his career. He does as well in his serious moments as in his comedy moods, and holds absolute attention."[38] The movie merited two separate raves in the *Los Angeles Times*. The initial sneak preview critique stated, "*Judge Priest* will rank as one of the most distinguished Will Rogers pictures," while a follow-up review, under the headline "Star Scores Screen Hit," added, "Advance reviews of Will Rogers' new picture, *Judge Priest*, unanimously agreed that the comedian gives one of his best, if not the best, performances of his career."[39]

The West Coast preview screening had gone so well that the *Los Angeles Times* was also able to report that *Judge Priest* director Ford was rewarded by being "re-engaged under contract to Fox [studio] ... [and] a story was immediately purchased for him to transform into a film, which he very much liked. This is 'Steamboat Round the Bend'" [which would again also star Rogers]...."[40] (The studio invitations to the Los Angeles preview of this courtroom comedy came in the form of a pretend subpoena![41]) A month later, the East Coast opening was at America's most prestigious movie venue — New York's Radio City Music Hall. And the critics showered Rogers and Ford with nonstop praise.

Beyond the kudos was the ongoing suggestion that this was Rogers' greatest film. The *New York Sun*'s Eileen Creelman called it "Far superior to anything Will Rogers has ever yet tried."[42] The *New York American*'s Regina Crewe said, "Will Rogers outdoes himself in the characterization of the gentle, foxy old judge ... Both script and sets are well-nigh perfect and John Ford's direction is a great attribute."[43] The *New York Evening Journal*'s Rose Pelswick credited *Judge Priest* as "Rogers' best, a heart-warming and genuinely moving story ... [which] provides gentle sobs and chuckling humor...."[44] One should underline here that while Rogers' populist political humor is often associated with a male audiences, these hosannas are all from female critics. Moreover, the power of the picture was such that Rogers was even converting former naysayers. The *New York Herald Tribune*'s Richard Watts, Jr., confessed:

[I cannot] be set down as one of Mr. Rogers' most enthusiastic fans. Nevertheless, it seems to me that in its sentimentally humorous way, *Judge Priest* is a decidedly entertaining motion picture that is easily the best thing the great Jeffersonian Democrat has yet contributed to the screen.[45]

While positive New York reviews continue to be any artist's pivotal scrapbook fare, during the 1930s the most detailed and insightful film criticism was provided by a host of New York–based newspapers. This fact is reflected today in the 1930s clipping files at the Academy of Motion Picture Arts and Sciences' Margaret Herrick Library (Beverly Hills, California). But a specific period documentation of this fact can be tied to a *Hollywood Reporter* policy in the 1930s — phenomenal New York critical successes merited a capsule collage of Gotham City reviews. Appropriately, *Judge Priest* received just such a *Hollywood Reporter* salute, with high praise drawn from eight New York dailies, starting with the *Mirror*: "*Judge Priest* is the best story with which humorist Rogers ever has been provided ... real, down-to-earth drama is ... played superbly by a well-chosen cast. Director Ford made a magnificent job of bringing [Cobb's] Paducah to the screen."[46]

Judge Priest's success was probably also fueled by pre-release publicity courtesy of Rogers' weekly syndicated newspaper articles. In a piece from June 1934, the humorist focused upon what an ongoing Southern historical tutorial was being provided by technical advisor Cobb. Rogers also implied that even during this initial *Priest* production that he would like to revisit the figure: "I hope I don't gum it up, and that this one is good enough that we can at various times keep the character going, for the material is sure there. It's just being able to get the spirit of the character."[47]

The same article revealed a bemused Rogers, pondering a Yankee director (Ford) and a Southern author-advisor (Cobb): the Irish American Ford "can lick the English for you just as entertainingly as Cobb can the Yankees. Funny part [sic] Ford is a Yankee from Maine [megaphoning a movie about Confederate veterans]."[48]

The following month (July) another Rogers syndicated article keyed upon a *Judge Priest* subject which resonates even more today. On the surface the humorist is simply praising Ford for his excellent use of character actors:

> One of the likeable things about Jack [Ford] is, that he remembers. Jack used to direct westerns, and made some great ones with Harry Carey, the most human and natural of the western actors. Well, the other day on a big set, a jury and court room trial, Jack had all his old cowpuncher pals, I had known most of 'em for many many years too, and it sure was good to see 'em again.[49]

Even at this early point in Ford's career he was known for his character actors. A *New York World Telegram* article from the previous year (1933) had Ford sharing his thoughts on why he sought out veteran players, often former stars, for character parts:

> Experience has taught me that a "bit" well done is worth five leading roles ... Their abilities are beyond question. So I preferred them for the small parts they play over others whose work I'm not sure of. These fine actors are courageous people ... They work in small roles others would refuse.[50]

Of course, Ford's signature character actor was the director's older brother and one-time silent star, Francis Ford, whom he often cast in his pictures. Fittingly, Francis, as "Juror No. 12," stole every *Judge Priest* scene in which he appeared. His ongoing bit of comedy shtick was an ability to noisily hit a spittoon with tobacco juice ... whenever the pompous politician-prosecutor (Berton Churchill) was trying to make a verbal point. The continual comic topper for Francis was to keep nailing his target, even though the spittoon was repeatedly moved to harder-to-reach spots.

What reverberates beyond Rogers' basic appreciation of Ford's use of character actors is the humorist's comments about these bit players often coming from the Western genre. One could argue that Rogers had a profound impact on the watershed Westerns Ford would make *after* his collaborations with Rogers. The director would later indirectly suggest this himself when asked what the men of the West were like — "They were like Will Rogers," Ford would reply.[51] Pivotal Ford scholars such as Scott Eyman knowingly draw a direct line between the director's collaborations with Rogers and such pivotal later Ford Westerns as *My Darling Clementine*. Key connections would range from the most methodical of heroes, to such seminal scenes as visiting a loved one's grave, or that "Priest leans back on his porch and puts his feet up (just like Henry Fonda in *My Darling Clementine*)" — a memorable moment that somehow defines Fonda's character.[52]

Rogers' impact upon the Ford Western is also implicit in Ben Yagoda's previously noted biography of the humorist — a fact nicely summarized by *New York Times* critic Margo Jefferson: "As a performer, Rogers pioneered a kind of crafty naturalism that John Ford ... knew would serve Westerns for the next 30 years."[53] And Jefferson's term, "crafty naturalism," is a fortuitous phrase for the more realistic type of populism to which Rogers and Ford were drawn — where the genre's celebrated people have to be maneuvered to morality. Or, as one of the print ads for *Judge Priest* had Rogers observing, "I ain't much on high soundin' language ... just a plain country judge ... hankerin' after the spirit of the law ... not the letter."[54]

One could also push Rogers' influence on the Western beyond the Ford milieu. In critic Jim Kitses' seminal book on the genre, *Horizons West*, much attention is given to the pivotal late 1950s sagebrush cinema collaborations between director Budd Boetticher and iconic cowboy star Randolph Scott. These darkly comic noir Westerns, like the existential film noir private eye pictures of the 1940s, have minimalist Scott speaking in an entertainingly laconic manner, *à la* Will Rogers. In contrast, the typical Boetticher villain is charismatically loquacious. For example, in *Ride Lonesome* (1959), Pernell Roberts' character goes on and on about the stunning sexuality of the heroine (Karen Steele). His comments culminate with the observation, "I guess she's about the best all over good-looking woman I ever seen." To this Scott has the most comically concise comeback, "She ain't ugly." Thus, for critic Kitses, this disciplined character is in the "crackerbarrel tradition," making Scott a "Will Rogers with six-guns."[55] To paraphrase Ford's earlier comment, "The men of the West were like Rogers."

Rogers is arguably America's greatest crackerbarrel philosopher, especially when showcased in a film such as *Judge Priest*— which draws upon the writings of another significant crackerbarrel figure (Cobb), and is directed by an acclaimed populist like John Ford. While both of my previous books upon populism have traced how Frank

Capra's more idealistic take on the genre started under the informal silent era tutelage of Rogers (when both worked for Hal Roach), the humorist's greatest legacy (after his own work) is undoubtedly how his "crafty naturalism" impacted Ford.

Regardless, the uniqueness of Rogers might be likened to the old adage about the magician: while *all* illusionists know where the trap door is, the *magic* is in the personality. And as a 1930s critic wrote, "You feel, somehow, that he [Rogers] has captured the secret of being happy, and that if you watch the screen carefully, this secret may be yours."[56]

CHAPTER 7

W.C. Fields' *It's a Gift* (1934)

When W.C. Fields' *Gift* character is called a drunk he responds, "Yeah, and you're crazy. I'll be sober tomorrow and you'll be crazy for the rest of your life!"

While one normally thinks of a single given persona for every pantheon screen comedian, this is not always the case. For example, Joe E. Brown (see chapter 8) would fluctuate between two small town types — a milquetoast antihero, and a breezy egotistical smart aleck. W.C. Fields (1880–1946) also vacillated between two screen characters — the late-nineteenth-century huckster, and a contemporary small-town, antiheroic, henpecked husband.[1]

Fields' trickster is in the literary tradition of America's nineteenth-century confidence-man golden age. Like the classic pioneering diddlers, who put a *creative* spin on "Yankee ingenuity," the Fields manipulator kept on the move. The *London Times* said of his 1936 *Poppy* characterization, "Like all great showmen he knows to a nicety the moment when the prudent man stops talking and makes hurriedly for open country — preferably on his accuser's horse."[2] Movement protected his sneaky character from the law, from creditors, and from the sucker who has wised up to the comedian's *imaginative* gambling skills. Being forever on the road offered opportunity as well as escape, as humorist Johnson J. Hooper has his notable huckster Simon Suggs observe, "It is good to be shifty in a new country."[3] Like Suggs' diddler of the Old Southwest, Fields' con artist engaged in small-time operations that did little, if any, harm.

In comic contrast, Fields' antihero plays the most entertaining of contemporary victims, a browbeaten family man anchored to a going-nowhere position in small town America — though *It's a Gift*, a loose remake of Fields' silent picture *It's the Old Army Game* (1926), eventually offers an eleventh hour reprieve to a California paradise. (The turnaround is so extreme, even for comedy, that one might best "read" it as a satire of happy endings.) While Fields is inspired in either comedy mode, huckster or antihero, his henpecked husband occasionally lets a bit of larceny come through. For instance, when his screen wife in *Gift* forces him to share a sandwich with their brat of a son, the comedian bends the meat onto his side before dividing the bread.

Interestingly enough, the same year (1934) as the opening of the antiheroic *Gift*— Fields' greatest film — he also made what is arguably the comedian's best huckster picture, *The Old-Fashioned Way*. From its first moments, *Way* is a case study of any-con-for-the-production. The movie begins with a sheriff at the train depot about to serve Fields' showman, "The Great McGonigle," with a legal writ to keep him and his theater troupe in town because of unpaid bills. But McGonigle manages to come up behind the sheriff and wastes no time in setting fire to the document, which the officer had been holding behind his back. W.C. allows himself to be seen just as the blazing writ is beyond rescue. The mistakenly confident sheriff then tells him, "I have something for you!" As the surprised constable produces a flaming document from behind him, Fields (with the timing of the comic juggler he was) used this non-conventional blaze to light his cigar. McGonigle then tops the laugh by politely thanking the sheriff. As the reviewer for the *New York American* summarized, "McGonigle matches wits with local sheriffs all over the West ... [and] as the old saying has it, the sheriffs are practically disarmed."[4]

The manipulative McGonigle not only gets the best of adult establishment figures, he physically takes on oppressive youngsters like Baby LeRoy (Albert Wendelschaffer), managing to give him a kick in the backside. Comparing Fields' boot to the signature leg action of Charlie Chaplin's Tramp, the *New York World Telegram* critic went on to celebrate this kick as comic catharsis: releasing "the suppressed desires of countless adults, who have nearly been driven crazy by the abuses of some particularly noxious infant whose fond parents just beam on their offspring's antics and consider them cute."[5] Naturally, drop-kicking a kid is verboten to Fields' antiheroic character in *It's a Gift*, though an even more frustrating Baby LeRoy surfaces in this film, too. But as will be addressed shortly, Fields plays both exasperation and fifth columnist (soft-spoken comic asides) with equal verve.

While Fields' two alternate comedy personae were assisted greatly by the authors of two 1920s stage productions — Dorothy Donnelly's Broadway huckster play *Poppy* (1923, with W.C. starring as the title character con man) and J. P. McEvoy's antiheroic musical comedy revue *The Comic Supplement* (1925, in which Fields starred as part of the *Ziegfeld Follies*), the comedian's own writing roots were tied to the world of the antihero. Doing research for my first book on the comedian during the early 1980s, I happened upon his then seemingly forgotten copyrighted sketches at the Library of Congress.[6] Between 1918 and 1930, W.C. registered 23 separate comedy documents on 16 subjects (some sketches were copyrighted more than once when changes were made). This least known of his then-professional activities now looms as a fascinating look at the evolution of his antihero. Indeed, this documentation of Fields' victimized-male persona — his time usurped by dominating women, machines, and the urban setting in general — places the comedian's work in the vanguard of this character's development (see chapter 5, about the equally pioneering antiheroes Laurel and Hardy).

Without belaboring the significance of Fields' sketches, three copyrighted versions of his "The Family Ford" (October 16, 1919; September 3 and October 9, 1920) nicely demonstrate this antiheroic mindset. The sketch finds a family and friends attempting a motor outing. The occupants of the Ford are George and Mrs. Fliverton, Baby Rose Fliverton, Mrs. Fliverton's father, and friends Elsie May and Adel Smith. Predictably, the car serves as the comedy focus, from engine trouble to a flat tire. And appropriately for a skit which plays upon the victimization of twentieth-century man — frequently at the hands of machines — at one point the car's "engine starts of its own accord."[7] Fields further accents this mechanical bugaboo by frequently using the surname Fliverton — a thinly veiled reference to the most frustratingly funny of machines, the Model-T Ford, then frequently called a flivver. (Fields' original name for his *It's a Gift* character was Fliverton.) The flivver was so associated with comic problems that countless jokes circulated on the subject. For example, "The guy who owns a secondhand flivver may not have a quarrelsome disposition but he's always trying to start something."[8] Several comedy careers are also closely identified with the car, including that of Laurel and Hardy. Thus, to name a comedy family (actually several of them) Fliverton is strongly to suggest antiheroic tendencies, which a reading of the Fields sketches bears out.

"The Family Ford" is the foundation for the attempted Model-T exit and eventual road trip of the Harold Bissonette (Fields) family in *It's a Gift*. The routine's use of a blind character is also reminiscent of *Gift*'s celebrated inclusion of a sightless customer who nearly destroys the Bissonette grocery. There are small additional bits in "The Family Ford" which appear with only slight variation in later Fields films. For instance, Elsie May drops her hat while George (Fields) is pumping up an automobile inner tube. He pushes the hat away but it makes a complete circle and returns exactly where it started. This is repeated several times; in each case the hat is pushed in a different direction by George. Eventually, a frustrated Fields picks up the hat and throws it away. In the 1936 *Poppy* the comedian suffers from another returning hat, though he now is trying to play a small bass fiddle instead of change a tire.

Given that Fields was fond of showcasing his antiheroic screen comedy in a world of small-town, mealy-mouthed sanctimoniousness reflects his undoubted influence by what literature terms "the revolt from the village." This movement of the late 1910s and the 1920s focused on the dead end hypocrisy of small-town life — but "was in actuality an over-all attack on middle-class American civilization."[9] This new artistic wrinkle was precipitated by poet Edgar Lee Masters' *Spoon River Anthology* (1915), "though it required five years for the influence of that book to pass thoroughly over from poetry to prose."[10]

There were precedents in American literature, such as Mark Twain's inspired, biting short story "The Man That Corrupted Hadleyburg" (1900, Twain also being a Fields favorite).[11] But Masters' haunting collection of free-verse poems — each one spoken from the grave by a different individual whose life had often been wasted — found a more receptive environment. And while the contents of *Spoon River* might not sound like Fields, the general metaphor of Masters' examination of squandered *buried* lives is a cornerstone of any artist's work which (like Fields') attacks hypocrisy and its frequent companion, smugness. There are, however, darkly comic moments in Masters' work which sound quite Fieldsian. One such is prohibitionist Deacon Taylor admitting his death was not watermelon-related (as reported) but rather cirrhosis of the liver — the result of a thirty-year passion for a drug store bottle labeled "spiritus frumenti."[12] Not only does the Deacon Taylor poem key upon an often central thrust of Fields' shtick (alcohol), it also manages to put a piece of fruit to comic use. Playing a henpecked, overworked grocer in *It's a Gift*, Fields devotes a whole scene to another piece of fruit — the funny-sounding kumquat, a word uttered repeatedly during the segment.

Nineteenth century America's longtime love affair with the village, not to mention a nostalgic revival of interest in rural and/or small town populism during the

1930 Depression (see chapter 6), meant that "the revolt from the village" movement created a storm of controversy. But while other important works followed *Spoon River* (especially Sherwood Anderson's *Winesburg, Ohio*, 1919), it took Sinclair Lewis' *Main Street* (1920) "to bring to hundreds of thousands the protest against the village which these [earlier revolt] books brought to thousands.[13] And Lewis would soon follow *Main Street* with his equally iconic *Babbitt* (1922).

Lewis is of central importance to both the movement and a better understanding of Fields' ties with it. Both Lewis and the comedian attack "Main Street" hypocrisy, and while the title character of *Babbitt* is more a part of the establishment than Fields' screen antihero will ever be, both suffer under many of the same comic frustrations. In fact, Fields' celebrated "Sleeping Porch" routine (copyrighted in 1925 and recycled in *It's a Gift*) quite possibly owes more than a little to the 1922 publication of *Babbitt*. The novel, one of the greatest international publishing successes of all time, first introduces George F. Babbitt as a sleeping porch victim of noise:

> Rumble and bang of the milk-truck. Babbitt moaned, turned over.... The furnace-man slammed the basement door. A dog barked in the next yard ... the paper-carrier went by whistling, and the rolled-up *Advocate* thumped the front door. Babbitt roused, his stomach constricted with alarm. As he relaxed, he was pierced by the familiar and irritating rattle of someone cranking a Ford ... Not till the rising voices of the motor told him that the Ford was moving was he released from the panting tension.[14]

As will be addressed shortly, this Lewis comic set-up could be considered a partial primer for Fields' later "Sleeping Porch" sketch. But regardless of the links in this specific case, both men are pivotal satirical caricaturists who produced cartoon-like *portraits* of a frequently proud shallow-mindedness which anticipates by years painter Grant Wood's real portraits of the same subject (see especially Wood's *American Gothic*, 1930, and *Daughters of Revolution*, 1932).

Concerning the movie at hand, *It's a Gift*, one might best begin with Fields' second use of the pseudonym Charles Bogle (after *The Old-Fashioned Way*) for his original story credit. Like the comedian's favorite writer, Charles Dickens, the name Bogle demonstrates Fields' comic passion for funny-sounding names or words in general. Fittingly for *Gift*, the comedian gives his often frustrated screen character the most antiheroically amusing of names — Bissonette. Moreover, to milk this fact, the film frequently has characters give varied pronunciations of the name. Not saying Bissonette correctly also works on three additional levels. First, it further underlines the antiheroic nature of Fields' character. Second, his figure's perpetually patient attempts to demonstrate the correct pronunciation give his Bissonette a certain amusingly tattered dignity. Third, the ironic topper, and another example of the aforementioned "proud shallow-mindedness," is that Fields' character actually mispronounces his name! Appropriately for an antihero, when the movie ends with a wonderfully unlikely victory — Fields gets his ideal orange ranch — the following business sign still gets it wrong:

BISSONETTE'S
(PRONOUNCED BIS-ON-AY)*
BLUE BIRD ORANGES

*Correct pronunciation: Bis-on-ett

Gift also plays the amusing name game during the early morning "Sleeping Porch" sequence, when a traveling salesman interrupts Fields' attempt at rest by asking about the whereabouts of a Karl LaFong. The comedian then further exploits the kooky-sounding name by having both Bissonette and the salesman spell out Karl LaFong. Again, this is Fields managing to antiheroically milk the situation. That is, not only does the poor put-upon grocer have his down time interrupted by a thoughtless boob, the salesman comically belabors the situation by unnecessarily spelling out the name ... including the irritating detail of noting all capital letters. But unlike Bissonette's mistaken defense mechanism about correctly pronouncing his name, Fields' grocer scores some underdog payback points when he categorically nixes any knowledge of Karl LaFong by spelling said name back to the salesman.

Gift's other most entertaining showcase of funny-sounding names and/or words in general occurs at Bissonette's grocery. For one extended sequence Fields' harried businessman must simultaneously wait on two of the most demanding of customers — the chewing gum–seeking blind man Mr. Muckle (Charles Sellon), and the blustery James Fitchmueller (Morgan Wallace), who is demanding kumquats. Since Muckle is also deaf and tends to thoughtlessly break things by the constant swinging of his cane, Fields attempts to keep him seated. But this is easier said than done, and Bissonette is constantly forced to shout, "Sit down, Mr. Muckle!" Meanwhile, Mr. Fitchmueller is forever yelling, "How about my kumquats?" or simply, "Kumquats!" at an ever-increasing decibel level. Coupled with this verbal slapstick is the visual treat of a distracted Fields — over-wrapping a package of gum, comically grimacing as blind Muckle approaches a display of light bulbs, trying to again get the man seated, searching for kumquats, and racing (unsuccessfully) to protect his plate glass door from Muckle's overactive cane. (An entertaining topper to all this goofy grocery comedy occurs when Mr. Fitchmueller asks Bissonette just who is this blind Mr. Muckle. With the most deadpan delivery, the comedian replies, "He's the house detective at the Grand Hotel.")

In a 1935 *Movie Classic* interview, Fields confessed that while reading Dickens "was my start in collecting [funny] names," the comedian was pleased that "nearly all the names I have used on the screen are real people I have met in traveling around this crazy world."[15] For instance, Muckle was the name of a neighbor he had as a boy in Philadelphia. Going hand-in-hand with real names was Fields' strong believe in real slice-of-life situations for his comedy:

> I base my comedy on humanness, so I just watch people. We're all very funny only we don't know it. No one is original, and we all do about the same things, so I take the simplest, every day incidents, exaggerate them and turn them into an act and, people seeing themselves, laugh. You go into a grocery and buy some eggs. Coming out ... you drop them. Now, if that actually happened to you it wouldn't be funny, but when it happens to someone else, it [comically] visualizes the very fear you have so often had and it becomes highly amusing.[16]

(Consistent with this comedy theory, Fields' *Gift* originally had Muckle stepping in a basket of eggs. But the bit did not make the final cut.) Of course, Fields' attention to this theater-of-the-real comedy had been garnering critical and commercial success for some time. The 1934 *Gift* was largely stitched together from both 1920s copyrighted

More *It's a Gift* grocery problems for W.C. Fields (in trash can), with kumquats customer Morgan Wallace at left.

sketches by the comedian and like-minded antiheroic material from the previously mentioned J. P. McEvoy. Consequently, when *American Magazine* author Mary B. Mullett profiled the comedian in 1926, she began her article by praising the naturalness of his humor in the then *Ziegfeld Follies* sketches which would later anchor *Gift*: "We laughed most at the quiet little bits when we didn't feel that he was acting at all. He seemed to have wandered onto the stage out of real life. He was doing things which we too had done, or had seen other people do, dozens of times."[17]

In another article from later the same year (1926) Fields revealed that authoring his own sketches was making his transition to film easier. But even then he returned the subject to the importance of comic realism: "I'm egotistical enough to give them [filmmakers] a battle when they want to make a character do a thing I don't think he would do naturally."[18] Fields' concern for this topic went beyond some vague sense of artistic integrity. The topic was enough to make him confess an almost inability to function, if this sense of naturalism were breached:

> [I]f you do something you don't think you — as a certain character — should, you cannot chase it from your mind. Days and days later, your mind will still return to that action — and it becomes a perpetual mental irritant for the life of the picture. Even if the actor is wrong, it's almost worth while letting him have his way so that he'll keep his peace of mind.[19]

This rare revelation from a now obscure publication, *Motion Picture Classic*, goes a long way towards explaining how Fields eventually became all but impossible to direct. One had to simply let him play it his *natural* way.

As a final corollary to Fields' strong belief in realistic comedy, the comedian also enjoyed adding a touch of nasty to his naturalism. In a 1925 article entitled, "W.C. Fields Pleads for Rough Humor," he stated, "I don't like to have to be too nice. I'm not. No one is, or if they are, no one likes them. Things should be a little rough on the stage or in pictures just to be consistent."[20] Classic examples of this philosophy applied to Fields' own performances would include the aforementioned punting of Baby LeRoy by the "Great McGonigle" and Bissonette's bending the meat onto his side of the bread before *sharing* a sandwich with his son.

The comedian's application of "rough humor," however, goes much further than merely his own characters. A touch of nasty is what ultimately sells the darkly humorous blind Mr. Murkle scene, which was controversial comedy in 1934. The *Literary Digest* said, "Mr. Fields is the only comedian at large who could find fun in the adventures of a blind man in a grocery, and not cause the resulting efforts ... to seem revolting."[21] Fields defused the blind Mr. Murkle situation by, consistent with his rough-tinged theater-of-the-real philosophy, creating a character he described as "a son of a bitch."[22] Interestingly enough, there is a Charlie Chaplin connection here. In the aforementioned 1925 article on rough humor, Fields had observed, "Successful motion picture comedians have told me that their audiences would not stand for anything vulgar. Yet Chaplin, the greatest of all comedians, is vulgar."[23] Nine years later, several *Gift* reviewers made reference to Chaplin when praising the Mr. Murkle sequence. For instance, the *New York Times'* Andre Sennwald declared, "With the one exception of Charlie Chaplin, there is nobody but Mr. Fields who could manage the episode with the blind and deaf ... so as to make it seem genuinely and inescapably funny instead of just a trifle revolting."[24] (As suggested earlier, this was also a 1934 criticism repeat, since Chaplin had often been cited when discussing the equally controversial baby-booting scene in *The Old-Fashioned Way*.) Ultimately, one might summarize Fields' plea for natural comedy, regardless of its rough edges, by saying that while actors are often praised for shedding skin, it is more about revealing basic truths, funny or otherwise.

To paraphrase a song from the Beatles, *Gift* might be subtitled "A Day in the Life of a Comic Antihero." *Gift* begins with Bissonette trying to get ready for work. Thus, the picture's first great set-piece is the comedian's bathroom battle for control of the medicine-cabinet mirror. Though he arrives first to shave, his screen daughter (Jean Rouveral) quickly outflanks him, and he must work behind her. The girl's hair-combing and frequent opening and closing of the mirrored medicine-cabinet door nearly gives Fields whiplash. But then again, for this domestic victim, things can only get amusingly worse. When his daughter inadvertently combs some hair into his mouth he is reduced to a comic apoplexy — a poor man's imitation of the family cat trying to dislodge a fur ball. (This choking shtick was a patented bit of his comedy repertoire.) Recovered, the comedian turns a different direction and tries to shave from the reflection of a bathroom container. The next surprise attack occurs when the daughter begins gargling without warning. Nearly giving himself a fatal shaving wound, he warns, "You want me to cut my throat, keep it up." Without missing a beat comes

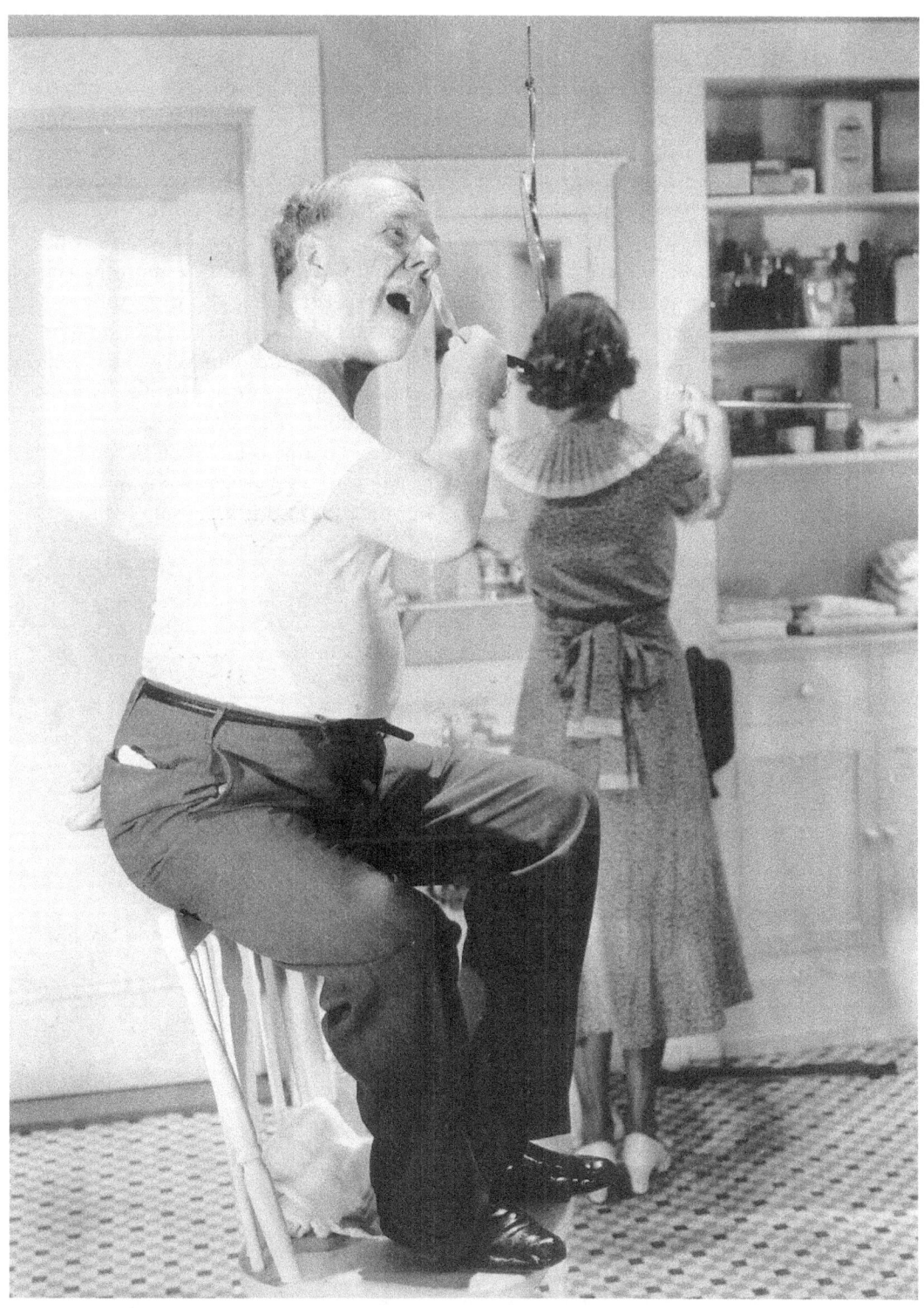

The comic dilemma of the *family* bathroom in *It's a Gift*, with a creative take on shaving by W.C. Fields, with a hand mirror tied to the light string.

another gargle and a frightened jump on Fields' part as he mumbles in an aside, "You evidently do."

Now W.C. ties a hand mirror to the overhead light string and tries to shave as the mirror revolves. Any ritual involving going round and round seems antiheroically appropriate, but he also risks another throat-slitting by waiting until the turning mirror is in front of him and then briefly shaving his neck with reckless abandon. Fields' next careless maneuver has him sitting precariously on the top of a chair ... from which he immediately falls. His last shaving tactic is to turn the still-revolving hand mirror face down while he lies on the chair underneath. Naturally, during all these morning contortions Fields does not notice the exit of his daughter. Paralleling this departure is the arrival of his screen wife (Kathleen Howard), who demands an explanation for his gymnastic approach to shaving. He innocently alludes to a daughter now very much gone. Once more he appears the fool to his domineering spouse. And Howard's definitive comic shrew castigates him, "Of all the driving idiots!" *Gift*'s string of acclaimed Fields sketches — connected by their shared antiheroic nature — are often topped by a final comic coup de grace from the henpecking Howard, even when she is not otherwise prominently featured in the routine (as was the case in this bathroom bit).

Baby LeRoy's *It's a Gift* opening of the molasses barrel spout closes W.C. Fields' (pictured) store.

This routine, which Fields had earlier filmed in the now seemingly lost silent movie *The Potters* (1927), makes for a provocative comparison with the memorable mirror scene in the Marx Brothers' *Duck Soup* (1933). In each case a comedian is driven to antiheroic distraction. But whereas W.C.'s plight is rooted in a frustrating domestic reality with which innumerable people can identify (and is consistent with his slice-of-life approach to comedy), Groucho's mirror dilemma is out-of-this-world surrealism ... at the hands of his sorcerer brother Harpo.

The second well-chosen Fields set piece for *Gift* is the previously examined comic goings-on at the grocery. The work is grounded, in part, in the sketch "The Drug Store" which the comedian had performed on stage as part of *The Comic Supplement* in the mid–1920s. Besides the previously noted antics of Mr. Muckle and Mr. Fitchmueller, this rendition of the material is also assisted by Baby LeRoy and one of Fields' favorite stooges — Tammany Young, who plays his assistant at the grocery. LeRoy and Young bring an effective comic close to the grocery segment with the child opening the spout of a molasses barrel, flooding the store with stickiness. When Fields questions his simpleminded sidekick on how this could have happened, Young vacuously says, "I told him I wouldn't do it if I was him." Fields' funny finis to the sketch has him placing a sign on his grocery door — "Closed on account of molasses."

The third pivotal playlet in *Gift* is inspired by the 1920s Fields stage sketch "The Naggers." It is early morning at the Bissonettes' and a wrong number gets Fields out of bed. Someone is trying to reach the local maternity hospital. After sharing this information with Kathleen Howard's Mrs. Bissonette, there is a brief icy silence before she states, "Funny thing they should call you up here at this hour of the night, from the maternity hospital." When Fields innocently reiterates that they merely wanted the maternity hospital, Howard snippetly responds, "Oh, now you change it!" As he starts to explain yet again, she cuts him off with "Don't make it any worse!" But the optimum word here is *worse*. Fully awake, Mrs. Bissonette now returns to her favorite daytime activity — nonstop complaining. The only good to come out of this comic tirade is that it eventually sends poor Bissonette out to the back porch and the movie's most inspired sketch — a variation of Fields' "Sleeping Porch" routine.

The comedian emphasized the significance of this playlet by actually entitling the *It's a Gift* story outline "Back Porch." Indeed, the picture's working title for much of the production was *Back Porch*. Regardless, as Bissonette looks for quiet away from his wife, Fields, blanket in tow (an over-age 1930s Linus), walks to the back porch on the second level of a three-story apartment complex and beds down on a rickety porch swing. But it is now later in the morning, and after the obligatory crash of the swing, when one of the support beams to which it is attached gives way, Fields must cope with an awakening neighborhood, from the milkman noisily delivering his bottles, to the pesky insurance salesman curious to discover the aforementioned Karl LaFong. The salesman's pitch could double as a summation of the antihero's ongoing plight: "If you buy a policy now you could retire when you're ninety on a comfortable income." Fields, the sometimes huckster, is now a potential victim of a huckster. (This insurance agent bugaboo lives on with later screen antiheroes, such as Woody Allen's observation in 1969's *Take the Money and Run*, that there are things worse than death, such as spending an evening with an insurance man.)

Another *Gift* back porch distraction involves a third-floor neighbor sending her daughter on an errand. Once on the ground floor the girl proceeds to engage the topside parent in a singsong conversation about just what to get and where to purchase it. Like the three-story building, the scene works on many levels. First, it is funny as another disruption of Fields' attempt to sleep, and it also precipitates a great example of his fifth columnism. When the daughter finally says to her mom, "You tell me where to go," the comedian's floor-between aside is, "I'd like to tell you both where to go." This immediately segues into the double-whammy penalty antiheroes sometimes have to suffer for the most modest of independent actions. That is, though Fields' aside made about as much noise as a mouse peeing on cotton, the loud neighbor above suddenly complains about the "shouting on the floor below." Moreover, W.C.'s wife then appears and insinuates that he is "getting pretty familiar" with their third-floor neighbor. Regardless of situation or setting, Mrs. Bissonette always seems to punctuate her husband's antiheroic misery.

The family's ensuing road trip to California, after Fields' grocer has used an inheritance to buy an orange grove ranch, borrows from still two more established stage sketches by the comedian. One involved the aforementioned "Family Ford" playlet and featured every type of Model-T merriment from engine problems to simply traveling with children. As his fellow antiheroic humorist Robert Benchley once wrote, "In America there are two classes of travel — first class, and with children."[25] The more celebrated, however, of the two sketches showcased in this road trip segment is the routine "The Picnic." The Bissonettes need a break from their motoring misadventures. Mistaking a private estate (filmed at Busch Gardens in Pasadena) for a public park, Fields drives right in and promptly knocks over a statue, with the comedian ad-libbing one of the movie's best lines, "She ran right in front of the car." Reducing a statue to pieces sets a precedent for what is to follow, rendering a formerly pristine pastoral setting into a Bissonette garbage dump. My personal favorite messy maneuver in this family of etiquette-impaired picnickers involves Fields' decision to open a can of tomatoes with a hatchet!

The comedian would later be bemused by a fan's continuity concern over this particular comedy bit, because shortly after giving his top multiple stains worthy of a Tide commercial, the shirt suddenly reverts to being spotlessly clean. Like both Charlie Chaplin and Will Rogers (see chapter 6), Fields was not one to be bothered by minor continuity derails missed by most viewers. But unlike Chaplin and Rogers comments along those lines, Fields, as was his habit, much preferred to play the storytelling huckster in real life. Consequently, since his tomato-stained *It's a Gift* shirt turns white again just as he is about to eat a sandwich during this derailed picnic, his tongue-in-cheek explanation was that somehow in mid-scene he had made a change: "My father ... told me always to be careful about tomatoes, and never to eat a sandwich unless my shirt was clean."[26]

Shortly after Bissonette and the family dog engage in a fight for a pillow that eventually results in a layer of feathers (pillow stuffings) being deposited over assorted picnic debris, the property owner and security arrive to run off this wayward family. But the family is now close to its final destination, and as the car drives by beautiful California orange groves, even bitchy Mrs. Bissonette begins to make noises like she might have been wrong. Naturally, this proves to be a short-lived development. When they reach their property the land looks as barren as a lunar landscape. And the "new" Bissonette house could have been the prototype for that dump in the later *Deliverance* (1972), where Georgia backwoods types have been in-breeding and cooking possum for years.

After a philosophical Fields explores the dwelling, a thoroughly disgusted Mrs. Bissonette (with children in tow) proceeds to leave the property on foot. Almost simultaneously, their overworked Model-T Ford, having covered 3000-plus rough pre-interstate miles from the family's New Jersey home, adds to Fields' antiheroic woes by suddenly imploding into a pile of junkyard metal. But a comedy miracle is brewing. When the transplanted grocer had first gotten near his new California home, he had stopped to ask directions of a Mr. Abernathy (Del Henderson). This good Samaritan and new neighbor would soon prove to be Bissonette's financial guardian angel. While the comedian's orange grove ranch was seemingly worthless, Mr. Abernathy would visit the now down-and-out former grocer and reveal that a wealthy local entrepreneur desperately needed Bissonette's land. Abernathy told him he could name his price.

Shortly thereafter, this comes to pass. There is some heated bargaining, during which time Fields utters those witty lines with which the chapter opens ("You're crazy. I'll be sober tomorrow and you'll be crazy for the rest of your life!"), and then Bissonette orchestrates both a large cash settlement *and* a paradise-like orange grove ranch. Fittingly, for a comedian driven by a theater-of-the-real foundation for his art, the *Gift* finale was shot at Fields' own "orange grove [Encino ranch, with W.C. amid his] tiled patios and lush lawns...."[27] This naturalism is further embellished by the last shot of the real-life alcoholic W.C. mixing himself the stiffest of drinks ... with just a touch of orange juice.

Paradoxical as it might now seem, one modest bit of *Gift* realism was mildly controversial. *Variety* was bothered by a line Fields has in the acclaimed bathroom sequence. When his screen daughter wishes to enter, Bissonette says it is okay—"I'm just shaving." *Variety*, the entertainment bible, felt lines like that were coarse-grained, making *Gift* "not for polite houses [theaters]."[28] But one must remember, the film was released the same year (1934) in which the censorship code went into effect (see the Mae West chapter for more on this subject). Period artists, whether in comedy or drama, had to work around restrictions unheard of today.

Gift is Fields' masterpiece, as well as the capstone picture of his breakout year (1934). The comedian appeared in no fewer than *five* films that year: *Six of a Kind*, *You're Telling Me*, *The Old-Fashioned Way*, *Mrs. Wiggs of the Cabbage Patch*, and *Gift*. While W.C. is superlative in all these outings, the pivotal pictures are the watershed huckster outing in *The Old-Fashioned Way*, and his defining antiheroic work—*It's a Gift*. In mid-1934, even before this definitive duo opened, Will Rogers would write, "[D]ear old 'Bill' W.C. Fields ... at last is coming into his own as one of the great comedians of our time. He is going like a house afire...."[29]

Consistent with this, the reviews for *Gift* were predictably stellar. What is provocative about these notices, however, is the missionary-like zeal with which the critics embraced Fields. For example, the *New York Herald Tribune*'s Richard Watts, Jr., opened his critique with this statement: "This department doesn't even talk to people who are not enthusiasts for the incomparable comic art of W.C. Fields."[30] The *New York World Telegram*'s William Boehnel began his review, "Come along to the ... superior screen item of the day and gaze — with unashamed delight, if you gaze as I did — upon the madcap antics of one William Claude Fields...."[31] And the *Literary Digest* observed, "[T]he modest author [Fields using his Charles Bogle pseudonym] has been wise enough to create a role permitting the great Fields to appear in virtually every scene, and to turn its plot into a veritable monolog for the funniest comedian of them all."[32]

Granted, this book is a testimonial to a number of beloved 1930s comedians, with notices from an army of period-praising pundits. But as someone who has sifted through countless critiques from this era, Fields' 1930s criticism "fans" seem more passionate about him than any other comedian, with the exception of Charlie Chaplin. Part of this is grounded in his earlier, much beloved stage work, especially from the 1920s — largely consisting of those famed sketches which he tweaked and creatively strung together for *It's a Gift*. This is at the heart of *Time* magazine's kudos for the comedy:

> Firmly established on that pinnacle of fame which great comedians have to reach before critics can discern in them the merits that have long been obvious to the public, W.C. Fields ... continues his policy of repeating for cinema audiences the routines that made him famed in the [*Ziegfeld*] *Follies*.[33]

And this high praise was from a magazine which, at that time, routinely gave short shrift to mere film comedies, if it reviewed them at all.

Maybe the most remarkable quality about *Gift* was its ability to elicit such passion over often understated frustrations of the common man. As the *London Times* said of his "quiet resignation" here, "[N]ot many screen comedians could keep this up throughout a film without becoming dull...."[34] But the everyman quality is also what gives the laughter its tragic overtones. A modern critic for *Film Comment* would state with wry insight that *Gift* demonstrates the small-town America is "still as dangerous as the frontier. W.C. Fields exemplifies most of what made this country endure. John Wayne is terrific but who can be John Wayne? Any of us can be, and have been, W.C. Fields."[35] But no one better captured this elegiac quality in Fields than yet another 1930s reviewer — the *New York Times*' Andrew Sennwald. Shortly after composing an already noted sterling critique of the movie, he was moved to write a heartfelt examination of Fields' antiheroic persona:

> Mr. Fields is a great comedian because he traffics in high and cosmic matters relating to man's eternal helplessness, frustration and defeat ... Not to be aware of the tragic overtones in the work of this middle-aged, whiskey-nosed, fumbling and wistfully incompetent gentleman is to be ignorant of the same tragic overtones in the comedy of Don Quixote....[36]

What makes Sennwald's sensitive insight into the quiet desperation component of Fields' art all the more poignant is that almost exactly a year later this gifted young critic (of James Agee–like promise) would be dead of an apparent suicide.[37]

Sennwald's special essay on the antiheroic Fields zeroes in briefly on characters comically "tormented by the problems involved in complex associations with other human beings."[38] This is a left-handed homage to Kathleen Howard's frightening Mrs. Bissonette, a figure loosely based upon the comedian's long-estranged relationship with his wife, Harriet (Hattie) Hughes Fields — more theater-of-the-real. But it is a characterization which still rings true. As a youngster I felt Mrs. Bissonette was simply a wonderfully imaginative but exaggerated Fieldsian "study" of relationships. Later, after being briefly involved with a younger version of Mrs. Bissonette, I was struck by the comedian's documentary-like skill in getting the characterization so disquietingly correct. Fields' Mrs. Bissonette could have inspired that modern joke explanation on why a certain marriage failed —"Well, we had religious differences. I was a Methodist, and she was the Antichrist." Regardless, Howard's bulldozing comic character is intertwined (or should one say *twisted*?) throughout the *Gift* sketches — forever contributing to the picture's antiheroic continuity.

Fields' standard film-ending reassertion of manhood is invariably subject to luck, such as *Gift*'s seemingly worthless orange grove, by chance representing a coveted location. This fits an antiheroic pattern charted by comedy theorist Steve Seidman, who suggested, "Fear of matriarchal power [*á la* Mrs. Bissonette] is such that it cannot be countered by the strength of the male. Rather it is dissolved by a near-magical occurrence."[39] (With Fields' talent for playing the realistically antiheroic husband, one might only wish he had played some of James Thurber's equally befuddled males, especially the title husband of the "Mr. and Mrs. Monroe" stories.[40])

Ironically, the realistic Fields would sometimes flirt with surrealism late in his screen career — such as diving out of an airplane without a parachute (for a bottle of booze!) in *Never Give a Sucker an Even Break* (1941). Yet, his creation of Mrs. Bissonette has such comic nightmare dimensions to it that she might qualify as her own special brand of surrealism. Regardless, it seems a miracle that so much laughter can be born of so much pain (whatever the catalyst). But that is often the tradition, the bittersweet beauty, the preciousness, of comedy.

CHAPTER 8

Joe E. Brown's *Alibi Ike* (1935)

> Only thing I ever *could* do was make people laugh ... And I can take only second billing for that talent. Nature met me more than halfway when it threw a handful of features together and called it a face.
> — Joe E. Brown (1944)[1]

While this clown with the comic slit eyes, vacuous puss, signature big mouth, and glass-cracking yell came into the world as Joe Evan Brown (July 28, 1892), the funnyman would later answer to many affectionately comic nicknames during a career covering nearly seven decades: "cavernous-mouthed comedian," "Grand Canyon," "crater-mouthed comic," "funny face," and "monster-mouthed." Raconteur Brown liked to claim that he once had a Major League offer based entirely upon the size of his mouth. That is, if he could not put a glove on a batted ball, Joe could open his mouth and catch it between his teeth! However, it is only fair to say that there is a certain tin type beauty, a hardy stalwartness, about Brown's face. The *New York Times*' review of the comedian's *Earthworm Tractors* (1936) said, in part, "It is true that it [Brown's mug] looks like something done with mirrors, a Coney Island illusion ... and living proof that nature ... is still greater than [makeup guru] Max Factor. But, for all its irregularities, it is also a face which has about it a certain rugged beauty, like the Maine coastline."[2]

With all due respect to Brown's ability to raise funny to the level of fable, ably assisted by that comedy fortune in a face, his initial entrance into the world of entertainment had nothing to do with laughter. Moreover, like Brown's 1930s comic contemporaries W.C. Fields (who began as a juggler) and Will Rogers (who started as a trick rope cowboy), Funny Face's show business commencement did not even involve speech — Joe was first a circus acrobat.

Brown would go on to be a pioneering sound comedian, but the plasticity of his mug brings to mind the silent cinema clowns, with the exception of Buster Keaton's "Great Stoneface." Along similar lines, Brown's screen characters often embraced a small town innocence more typical of silent comedy, such as personified by the all-American funnyman Harold Lloyd. Joe's youthful heartland heroes contrasted with the older, more cynical Depression era clown norm of W.C. Fields, Groucho Marx, Mae West, and Jimmy Durante. That being said, however, Brown did fluctuate between two small town types — a milquetoast antihero, and a breezy egotistical smart aleck. And Joe's fast-talking latter figure, who often doubled as an athlete, had a confident nonchalance consistent with his more worldly 1930s comedy contemporaries. For example, when Brown's baseball title character in *Elmer the Great* (1933) overhears Sterling Holloway's wish that he could bat like him, Joe responds, "Yes, so does Babe Ruth."

To this Holloway replies, "Oh, if you were only as good as you think you are."

"Say, I'm better than I think I am," answers Brown.

Joe's baseball take on his smart aleck is an athletically talented, entertainingly unlettered sort, whose ego has tall tale tendencies. For instance, when his Elmer is not casually claiming Babe Ruth envies him, he amusingly alibis over why his (Elmer's) last swing did not produce a home run: "Shucks, that one hit the fence. I'll put the next one over. I'm always afraid of breaking windows." This bravado is not inconsistent with the huckster swagger of a W.C. Fields or Mae West. But there is a difference; Brown's character is a delightful fool, while the con artists Fields and West are in definite diverting control.

Still, there is a reason why Brown's most winsome work occurs in a baseball uniform, his diamond trilogy: *Fireman, Save My Child* (1932), *Elmer the Great* (1933), and *Alibi Ike* (1935). The comedian both acknowledged this in his autobiography, and offered an explanation, "I think my best motion pictures were baseball stories. But pictures are only fantasies. My real-life [diamond] interests were stronger than that. I even mixed baseball with business [from having a Warner Brothers team, his parent studio, to being a part-owner of the Kansas City Blues]."[3] Yet, one can flesh this out further by simply stating that baseball was an integral part of Brown's life from childhood on. As he once shared with *Time* magazine, while "he did not get into show business until he was nine ... he was a confirmed baseball fan at four."[4] A pivotal hero of Brown's youth was an early baseball superstar — Ty Cobb. But Joe's admiration went beyond a diamond skill level. Cobb's drive reflected the moxie Brown had to embrace to survive a hard luck childhood of the 1890s depression. That is, Joe related to the fact that Cobb always "insisted that he was not superbly endowed as an athlete, only that he had greater desire."[5] Despite Brown's obvious talent as a multi-faceted performer, he, too, forever felt his success was directly linked to a blue-collar baseball mentality.

In an immigrant-rich melting pot era in this country, youngsters (like Brown) playing baseball was a fun way to embrace being an American. As period populist poet Walt Whitman observed, "America's game [baseball] ... belongs to our institutions, fits into them [as] significantly as our constitutions [sic], [and] laws: Is just as important in the sum total of our historic life."[6] Or, more succinctly, French historian Jacques Barzun stated, "To know the heart and mind of America, one must learn baseball."[7] Plus, patriotic Brown both enjoyed and excelled at the entertainment/spectacle aspect of the game. Along related lines, major league baseball as we know it today, with American and National League champions meeting in an annual World Series, was born during Brown's youth, and it is easy to see why the sport was a central defining component for him. One might call it the background music of his life.

Baseball surfaces throughout Brown's life and career in ten meaningful ways. First, there was simply the joyous factor of playing, which lasted long after his youth. As late as the 1930s, Brown's Warners contract would necessitate they fund his studio team.

Perennial baseball player Joe E. Brown is pictured here in his studio team uniform (circa mid–1930s).

(Joe's friend, fellow comedian, and baseball aficionado Buster Keaton often provided the rival diamond nine.) Second, the new national game was so popular in the early 1900s that semi-professional teams popped up everywhere. Consequently, one of young Brown's perennial part-time jobs was playing for various baseball clubs. Third, Joe so excelled as a ballplayer that the New York Yankees flirted with the idea of adding him to their minor league farm system. (*Time* magazine would later describe a Brown major league exhibition game double for the Boston Red Sox as "what may have been the happiest moment of his life."[8])

Fourth, as a touring vaudevillian Brown frequently found himself in the company of on-the-road baseball players. Like his friend and fellow legendary comedian Will Rogers, Brown often worked out with different major league teams at various baseball parks. Fifth, as previously noted, Brown's greatest films, in a headliner capacity, were his diamond pictures. And period critics often coupled their praise for Joe's comedy with the acknowledgment that his proven talent in the sport made the subject a natural for the comedian's movies. To illustrate, *The Hollywood Reporter* made just this declaration about *Fireman, Save My Child*, and spiced it up with comparisons to two radically different period personalities — "putting Joe E. Brown in a baseball picture was as sound a piece of casting as showing [Jascha] Heifetz as a violinist. It's his [Brown's] meat and he shows that he's as much at home on a baseball diamond as [Al] Capone with a bodyguard."[9] Along related lines, the *New York Times*' rave review of *Elmer the Great* noted, "Mr. Brown is no greenhorn when it comes to baseball, for he was a professional player in his younger days, and this fact helps to make *Elmer* ... all the more interesting."[10] And the *New York Daily Mirror* said of *Alibi Ike*, "Joe E. Brown, whose immoderate passion for baseball is quite as well-known as his spectacular mouth, plays the title role with vast enthusiasm."[11]

Of course, Brown drew upon both his own diamond skills *and* memories of other notable players. He would later write of *Elmer the Great*, "the best thing about the part was that during the days when I played ball on small town teams in Ohio, Indiana, and Michigan I had come to know and admire many Elmers."[12] But besides the fortuitous development that sports roles, especially baseball, allowed Brown to showcase his athletic gifts and experience, film comedies revolving around sports "provided a natural excuse for physical comedy."[13]

The sixth meaningful way in which baseball surfaced in Brown's life occurred during World War II. The comedian was so identified with the sport that when he entertained troops throughout the first half of the 1940s, popular demand required that part of his stand-up shtick be diamond-oriented. Surprisingly, or maybe not so surprisingly, when one such wartime performance later involved meeting some Japanese prisoners, those "who could speak English said they had seen his *Elmer the Great* movies. [And] they wanted to talk baseball."[14] (Even prior to the war, one of Brown's signature responses to spontaneous public attention from his fans was to go into an exaggerated corkscrew wind-up — a comic bit he first devised for his Elmer characterization.)

Interestingly enough, baseball went beyond just a source of entertainment material for Brown's World War II military tours. He spent a great deal of time with soldiers and sailors in small group sessions, from visiting hospitals to eating with the men in mess hall settings. Though small talk was never a problem with a born raconteur like Brown, he found his typical baseball fan knowledge of the game was a natural ice breaker and a source of conversation with men in uniform. After all, this was a time when the sport was truly the *national* pastime, and Japanese soldiers would even attempt to bait American forces by yelling, "To hell with Babe Ruth."[15] Brown also modestly saw himself as merely a visiting symbol of home — a poignant reminder of a native land that also defined itself, in part, by baseball:

> I'd know it wasn't just me talking ... It was home itself; it was the days when he was a high school kid and the neighborhood theater was showing one of my pictures. It was the old lost times when everything was right, and Mom was baking an apple pie ... and the kids on his block were getting up a baseball team ...[16]

Along related lines, one of Brown's war charities also athletically assisted men in uniform. Fittingly for the sports-obsessed comedian, Joe had founded the All-Pacific Recreation Fund, which supplied athletic equipment to American military men serving in the Pacific theater. By 1944, over $50,000 worth of sports supplies had found their way to the troops.[17] Consistent with this athletic perspective, Brown also continued to raise military relief funds stateside throughout the war by sponsoring charity baseball games and other sports events.

Seventh, not only was baseball something Brown never tired of, it was also a way of periodically recharging his batteries. For example, in 1940 he returned to the stage in a production of *Elmer*. And in 1947 Brown recorded a double album entitled *How to Play Baseball*, with the comedian explaining the national pastime to a youngster named Elmer. Eighth, the man with the famous mouth long maintained professional ties with the sport, from being a 1953 New York Yankees television announcer to doubling that same year as the president of the national Pony Leagues (for 13- and 14-year-old youngsters).[18] Ninth, the ongoing significance of the sport was such that throughout the comedian's long life his conversations were peppered with baseball references. For instance, while facing surgery at seventy-two, he metaphorically kidded with reporters about handling anxiety: "Get on second base and run. This is the fellow [himself] that couldn't hit a curve ball."[19] Tenth, the comic passed his passion for the game onto his beloved surviving son, Joe L. Brown, who spent his adult life in professional baseball. The 1955 capstone to that career was Joe L. becoming general manager of the Pittsburgh Pirates![20]

One might even note a final "Baseball Brown" addendum — whether the comedian was pioneering in the collection of diamond memorabilia, or guesting on 1930s radio as a play-by-play announcer for the Chicago Cubs (two of his three movies had him playing a Cubbie), baseball was always central to his existence. In fact, Brown's philosophy of life used an aggressive Ty Cobb–like diamond metaphor: "I always played baseball the same as I do anything else. Just because there are two men out and we are ten runs behind in the ninth doesn't make the game finished ... no game is over until there are three men out in the ninth inning."[21]

Given all these baseball connections, it was only a matter of time before Brown made a diamond picture. National game or not, however, there was then a knock against baseball pictures — the belief that the sport could not score at the all-important box office.[22] Quality baseball-related material in film had often been limited to featured moments in movies largely devoted to other subjects, such as Buster Keaton's inspired visit to Yankee Stadium in *The Cameraman* (1928), where he gives a masterful solo demonstration of batting and base running. That same year, 1928, Harold Lloyd made his underrated *Speedy*, a sometime tribute to the sport that also featured Yankee great Babe Ruth. But in late 1930 Brown had made a baseball believer out of Warners producer Darryl Zanuck when the comedian's limited-run holiday stage appearance in a Los Angeles production of Ring Lardner and George M. Cohan's *Elmer the Great* was a smash success.[23] (Impressively, Brown's version was a greater hit with audiences than the Broadway original, which starred celebrated actor Walter Huston in the title role.)

Lardner (1885–1933) is no longer a household name. But in 1914 he had both elevated baseball stories to comic literature and affectionately derailed the notion of the noble bloodless diamond hero. The initial catalyst was a series of Lardner *Saturday Evening Post* short stories later collected in book form as *You Know Me Al: A Busher's Letters*.[24] The pieces, a fictional correspondence from a rookie Chicago White Sox pitcher (Jack Keefe) to a hometown (bush league, or small time) friend, chronicled the comic misadventures of an entertainingly self-centered rube in the Major Leagues. Keefe is barely literate, and part of the humor comes from the misspellings and hyperbole, a comic form of writing especially popular with a late nineteenth century collection of American writers known as the "Literary Comedians."[25] But Lardner peppered his prose with a wonderful ear for dialogue and American slang, especially as it applied to baseball. Besides an immediate popularity with the public, such acclaimed period literary heavyweights as H. L. Mencken and Virginia Woolf would eventually praise his gift for the language. At his best, Lardner did not so much take the air out of the national pastime as just remind us it was part of the human comedy, too. Lardner's later diamond tales, such as the short story "Alibi Ike" (1915) and the play *Elmer the Great* (1928), continued in the tradition of those original Jack Keefe comic letters.

Brown's aforementioned baseball trilogy of the 1930s, *Fireman, Save My Child, Elmer The Great*, and *Alibi Ike*, might also be subtitled a "Ring Lardner Salute." While the opening picture was technically not from a Lardner source, the original story was so similar (including a hick pitcher and a Lardner-like title — "The Bush Leaguer"), that many film reviewers noted the obvious connection.[26] Ironically, there are even some basic Lardner-Keefe components showcased in *Fireman* which do not surface in the two later Brown adaptations of Lardner's work. The most obvious example involves the easy vulnerability to baseball groupies of the standard Lardner player. Indeed, a goodly portion of *You Know Me Al* documents Keefe being taken for the proverbial ride by two different women.

Brown's *Fireman* character, Smokey Joe Grant, is an inventor-fireman from the small Kansas town of Rosedale. He is also a gifted pitcher, with the most entertaining corkscrew wind-up, where Joe's arms briefly twist around his head before unloading the ball. Brown the inventor is obsessed with marketing his fire extinguisher bomb. Fittingly, the device is designed in the shape of a baseball — all the better to "pitch" into a fire. Since the invention takes precedence over everything else, baseball often gets short shrift. Of course, for the boy/man Smokey Joe, everything is a distraction, especially fire engines and loud sirens. But if truth be told, all three of Brown's screen baseball players have more than a little in common with pioneering Major League zany Rube Waddell (1876–1914), a pitcher whose fascination with fire engines even delayed games, as he pondered their path from the mound. Baseball historian Lowell Reidenbaugh's description of Waddell, as someone "who pitched like a superman but whose child-like nature required infinite managerial patience and tact," could double as a description of

This scene from *Fireman, Save My Child*, with Joe E. Brown and Evalyn Knapp, effectively captures the sense of yesteryear which permeates the comedian's baseball films.

all Brown's ballplayers, with an accent on "Rube." (During the 1940s Brown was even in negotiations to star in a biography film of Waddell, but unfortunately nothing came of the project.[27]) As if to accent a connection between Waddell and the Joe of *Fireman*, the movie's early Rosedale scenes seem to mirror the turn-of-the-century heyday of the original Rube. That is, the Rosedale fire engine is pulled by horses, and the bucolic main street looks like Tom Sawyer and Huck Finn might appear at any time. Only later, when Joe is pitching for the St. Louis Cardinals, does one realize this is *not* a period piece. But this sense of yesteryear permeates much of the Brown oeuvre, especially when he is on a diamond.

Fireman proved to be a smash success, with the entertainment industry bible *Variety* calling it "Surefire comedy material providing Joe E. Brown with the best part he's had since [getting] in pictures."[28] Under the title "*Fireman* Corking Comedy," *The Hollywood Reporter* pushed the positive meter further by amusingly stating, "[T]he Burbank boys [Warner Brothers] have a piece that will easily take rank as one of the best comedies of this season ... with more good hearty laughs than a case of Scotch."[29] For certain, it was rare to dislike Brown in 1932, the release date of *Fireman*. The picture's popularity help put him, for the first time, on filmland's most coveted list — the annual top ten box office stars.[30] (Of this text's focus nine comics and/or teams, only Will Rogers, Mae West, and Eddie Cantor would ever appear on this top ten pantheon. Brown resurfaced on the list in both 1935 and 1936.)

After the early 1932 critical and commercial success of *Fireman*, Brown and Warner Brothers were anxious to make another baseball picture. By September of that year, negotiations had acquired the rights of the Lardner-Cohan play *Elmer the Great* from Paramount, which had adapted the stage vehicle to the screen as *Fast Company* (1929, with Jack Oakie). But as previously noted, West Coast fans of Brown and/or baseball already identified the character with the comedian after his popular late 1930 Los Angeles stage production of *Elmer*. The cinematically prolific Brown appeared in two other 1932 pictures, *The Tenderfoot* and *You Said a Mouthful*, before making the 1933 *Elmer*. Though *Elmer* is largely a faithful adaptation, the film makes the title character a great home run hitter instead of a masterful pitcher (*à la* Lardner's Jack Keefe). Brown's movie Elmer remains, however, the same talented, amusingly unlettered, small town egotist of the play. Indeed, these are traits which apply to all three of Lardner's signature baseball characters — Keefe, Alibi Ike, and Elmer. And since their baseball skills are only rivaled by a propensity to brag, all three figures have a tendency to comically alibi, too, when their tall tale–like hype does not produce.

Given that all of Lardner's prose players are similar smart aleck rubes, one could contend that Warners was perfectly in keeping with the humorist by making Elmer a power hitter, since Ike had been a slugger, too. Brown's screen version of *Elmer* opens in the small Indiana town of Gentryville. Periodically during the picture, an instrumental rendition of the song "Back Home Again in Indiana" is used as sort of a movie mantra for simpler small town life. As with the beginning of *Fireman*, the visible means of transportation suggests an earlier time period — a Chicago Cubs representative, in a horse-drawn sleigh, has come to sign Elmer. Also, as in *Fireman*, our comic antihero is less than excited about this opportunity. But whereas he was distracted by the inventing bug in that picture, this time around he cannot bear the thought of leaving small town sweetheart, Nellie (Patricia Ellis).

Only Ellis' character has the power to make Elmer exit tiny Gentryville. Nellie does the sacrificial thing; she both breaks it off with Elmer, and also fires him from his store delivery position, where she had been the boss. With this, he signs the Cubs contract and is next seen at spring training, where he puts on an impressive display of hitting. (Baseball, for the time being, seems to have distracted him from a broken heart.) Brown's demeanor in and around the batter's box is especially entertaining, too. Before setting himself up to hit, he flips his bat in the air one-half revolution, catching the fat end of the stick. He then quickly reverses the process, and grabs the slender portion of the bat — all with one rapid hand movement. In the batter's box he displays a pronounced lean towards the pitcher, topped off with a conspicuous leer, like his eyes are assuming a special batter's focus. The characterization is inspiringly unique, something new for the modern fan. As a footnote to the fan, one should credit Brown with a novel scheme. A more typical approach to this situation, as demonstrated by a comedy genius like Buster Keaton or Red Skelton, is to nail in wonderful detail every *typical* batting nuance, from stooping for some dirt with which to dry the hands, to that hitter's wiggle as he digs in at the plate.

Not surprisingly, Brown's Elmer gets the Cubs to the World Series, just as his Smokey Joe took the St. Louis Cardinals to the "Fall Classic" in *Fireman*. And in both cases, this would ultimately mean a victory against the New York Yankees' famous "Murderers' Row" of hitters, including newsreel footage of Brown's friend and legendary slugger Lou Gehrig. (Friendship is a good thing, because through the movie magic of editing Brown's *Fireman* pitcher proceeds to strike out Gehrig on three pitches!) But the World Series scenes in 1933 *Elmer* were, in part, the product of Brown and a Warner film crew going east the previous autumn to shoot "Fall Classic" filler footage. Gehrig was again the Yankee most prominently showcased in the finished picture.

"Murderers' Row" was not Elmer's only challenge. In light of today's ongoing controversy about Pete Rose's gambling past, the film adds a modern twist when Brown's rube became innocently involved with a betting ring. His best friend on the Cubs, High Hips Healy (Frank McHugh), takes Elmer to a gambling house where the food and drinks are free, courtesy of all the suckers management fleeces. Healy figures his slugger friend, with that comically gargantuan appetite, will enjoy all the gratis items. Innocent Elmer, whose idea of a "drink" order is a "raspberry soda pop *à la mode*," initially limits himself to matters of the stomach. But eventually, like a curious child, he wants to play some of the gambling games. Unfortunately, Healy (McHugh was often teamed with friend Brown at Warners) is not much brighter than Elmer and neglects to inform his friend that he is running up a large gambling debt. But in the simpler Hollywood world of 1930s clown comedies, Elmer manages to survive the scandal by later proving he bet on his Cardinals to win!

Elmer proved to be a huge critical and commercial success. While the *New York Herald Tribune* described the picture as "bordering on entertainment perfection," *The Hollywood Reporter*'s opening praise was in baseball terms, which then segued into affectionate humor: "Chalk up a home run for Director Mervyn LeRoy and Joe E.

Brown ... *Elmer the Great* is excellent from Brown's first yawn, which is nearly a blackout, to his last slide to a muddy home base, another near black-out."[31]

The admiring *New York Times* critique even documented how an enthusiastic Radio City Music Hall crowd was caught in "rapt attention during a closing stage [at bat] of the proceedings, most of the spectators were fearful lest Elmer might strike out, like [actor] DeWolf Hopper's [famous rendition of] Mighty Casey."[32]

Despite all the urban kudos for Brown's small town Elmer, the *New York Sun* reviewer suggested the film would register even stronger "in the rural districts."[33] The best 1930s gauge of the small town-rural market can be found in "What the Picture Did For Me" section of a period publication called the *Motion Picture Herald*. This portion of the *Herald* reprinted paragraph-length blurbs about then current pictures from hinterland theater owners across the country. A sampling of the glowing *Elmer* notices found in this *Herald* section would more than suggest the *Sun* critic was correct. From Shenandoah, Pennsylvania, came passionate praise that ultimately turned poetic:

> A sparkling and hilariously funny baseball yarn with that sensitive, wide open mouth of Joe E. Brown amidst the battery delivering home run entertainment and handling out laughs that literally knocked the audience in the aisles with his funny antics. Some observers laughed so hard that most of the gags were blotted out ... Play it and see Joe E. Brown's mouth swallow the grinning face of old man depression from view....[34]

A small theater owner in Malta, Montana, mixed high compliments with low comedy of his own, "A knockout for laughs ... that will earn you more good will than free storage for homeless mother-in-laws."[35] In tracking more than a dozen of these *Elmer* small market mini-reviews over several months (today's simultaneous saturation theater booking was decades away), I found all the critiques to be equally celebratory.

This is the popular platform upon which Brown would launch his third and greatest diamond picture—*Alibi Ike*. But being a sports-orientated, prolific filmmaker, the comedian would sandwich four other pictures in between *Elmer* and *Alibi Ike*—*Son of a Sailor* (1933), *Very Honorable Guy*, *The Circus Clown*, and *6-Day Bike Rider* (all 1934). Suffice it to say that the three best movies in the grouping had Brown doubling as an athlete: a boxing sailor, a gymnastic clown, and a champion cyclist. But his most entertaining sports-related picture, baseball or otherwise, is *Alibi Ike*.

This film wins the brass ring for three reasons, besides another inspired performance from Brown. First, unlike his previous two cinematic baseball stars, who were both initially reluctant players (distracted by fires and love), Ike is totally focused on the game. In fact, his first appearance in the picture (smashing through the center field fence in an out-of-control automobile) is a perfect metaphor for the explosive enthusiasm he brings to the sport. Second, Brown has an impressive supporting cast, starting with a future two-time Academy Award winner as his leading lady, Olivia de Havilland. The previous year (1934), famed German stage producer-director Max Reinhardt had chosen her to appear as Hermia in both a Hollywood Bowl production of *A Midsummer Night's Dream*, and Warners' 1935 screen adaptation (which would include Brown and an all-star cast). This Reinhardt attention had gotten de Havilland a Warners contract, with her first screen appearance being *Alibi Ike*, though the *Midsummer* screen adaptation was actually shot prior to Brown's baseball film. *Alibi Ike*'s cast also featured the gruff but lovable William Frawley as the Cubs' manager. Best remembered today as Fred Mertz in the classic TV sitcom *I Love Lucy* (1951–57), Williams also had many memorable movie roles in support of comedy kingpins—*Professor Beware* (1938, Harold Lloyd), *Monsieur Verdoux* (1947, Charlie Chaplin), and *The Lemon Drop Kid* (1951, Bob Hope). Besides Frawley, *Alibi Ike* had two other high-profile character actors—Roscoe Karns and Ruth Donnelly, both of whom specialized in playing fast-talking insiders.

A third justification for calling *Alibi Ike* Brown's best sports picture is tied to the strong writing. For example, when Frawley's character asks Ike how many games he won in the minors the previous year, Brown's pitcher unloads the movie's best comic alibi, "Only twenty-eight, had malaria most of the season." But the humor does not stop there. Frawley's manager gets a comic comeback, "Where can I send the rest of our pitchers to get it [malaria]?" Or, when Frawley wants to see his rookie at the plate, Brown alibis, "Of course, I don't bat my best on Wednesday." The manager's snappy reply even tops the busher, "Don't you worry about that, I'll cancel all the Wednesday games." Writing credit must go to both Lardner (with a variation of the malaria line in the original short story, too[36]), and screenwriter William Wister Haines.

Besides the comedy of Joe E. Brown, *Alibi Ike* featured the gifted support of character actor William Frawley (left).

Paradoxically, while Hollywood changed Lardner's Elmer from a pitcher to a hitter, they reversed the process with Ike — the slugger became a great hurler. The catalyst for this transformation was probably twofold. First, the previous year St. Louis pitching star Dizzy Dean had emerged as the living embodiment of a Ring Lardner egotistical, alibi-spouting country boy. Moreover, when Brown interacted with Dean, both during and after the celebrated 1934 World Series, the public undoubtedly further connected these two entertainers as similar free spirits. For example, one news account documented a comical mutual admiration society between the two before stating, "Mr. Brown's sport trophy room in his Beverly Hills home will be considerably enriched through its owner's attendance at the recent world series ... Dizzy Dean presented him with the Cardinal uniform he wore while he was blanking the Tigers in the final and deciding contest...."[37] Plus, the zany antics of Dizzy were soon not limited to the sports page. On April 15, 1935, he made the cover of *Time* magazine, with the accompanying article noting:

> It was clear that with Shirley Temple, Father Coughlin, the Dionne Quintuplets and Mrs. Roosevelt, Jerome Herman Dean was definitely one of that small company of super-celebrities whose names, faces and occupations are familiar to every U. S. citizen and whose antics, gracious or absurd, become the legend of the time.[38]

Thus, it was only natural that Warners' *Alibi Ike* would attempt to trade upon the Lardner-Dean-Brown connections, such as this bit of dialogue from William Frawley's manager after Brown's egotistical Ike vainly states that he must not realize who he is. Frawley retorts, "Sure I do. You're Dizzy Dean. But you've had your face lifted to fool the batters." Therefore, the Lardner-Dean-Brown link is often addressed in period reviews, from the *New York American*'s opening, "A Dizzy, Daffy (Dean) comedy of the baseball diamond, starring Joe Brown in a character as only Ring Lardner could conceive...," to the *Hollywood Reporter* observation, "Joe E. is cast as [a] screwball, more than slightly resembling the great Dizzy Dean."[39] The *New York Herald Tribune* even gave their review opening a soothsayer's slant: "Back in the days when Ring Lardner, with an artist's foresight was predicting the career of Dizzy Dean, he created an epic character called Alibi Ike."[40]

A second possible reason to turn Ike into a pitcher is to capitalize on all his comic parallels with Lardner's hurler Jack Keefe, created just a year before Ike (1914). For instance, when one reads the Keefe stories collected as *You Know Me Al: A Busher's Letters*, one immediately thinks he should have been called Alibi, too. For instance, here is Keefe's take on how the great Ty Cobb got on base: "I pitched a spitter and Cobb bunts it right at me. I would of threw him out a block but I stubbed my toe in a rough place and fell down. This is the roughest ground I ever seen Al."[41] Or, listen to why Keefe's single could have been a double — "I took my healthy [cut] at the next one [pitch] and slapped it over first base. I guess I could of made two bases on it but I didn't want to tire myself out."[42]

There are enough parallels between all three of Brown's small town simple-minded braggart ballplayers that sometimes even the comedian got confused. To illustrate,

Brown's portrayal of Elmer, going back to a 1930s stage production, was embellished by the comedian's interest in pioneering Philadelphia Phillies pitcher Harry Frank "The Giant Killer" Coveleski, who was especially effective against the New York Giants. During Brown's vaudeville days he closely followed Coveleski's career and was fascinated by the player's goofy lumbering walk, a sort of lazy swagger, with prominent arm-swinging. The comedian adopted the gait and deliberate mannerisms for his take on Elmer. In the comedian's autobiography he reveals that there is even a comic Coveleski incident recycled in his *Elmer* movie, where the title character's full wind-up with a man on first allowed the base runner to steal second.[43] When the manager complained, the pitcher, with his brain in neutral, alibied that he had somehow been unaware of the runner, which provoked an inspired touch of managerial sarcasm that went over the player's head. *However*, in Brown's screen version of *Elmer* his title character is *not* a pitcher. The comedian is remembering a scene from *Alibi Ike*. The sequence unwinds just as described, with William Frawley's manager then calling the team together, and with tongue firmly in cheek, observing:

> From now on there ain't going to be no more secrets. I mean not telling each other what's going on. Here's a guy [Ike] that wound up with a runner on first just because nobody told him the man was there. Now, after this when a man gets to first base, I don't want anyone to keep it secret from the pitcher!

Like Coveleski, Ike thinks the manager is criticizing the team, and compliments their leader, "That a boy, Cap [Frawley]...." To add to the confusion (or is that just character consistency), Lardner describes a scene reminiscent of the Coveleski-Ike example in one of his Jack Keefe stories from *You Know Me Al: A Busher's Letters*: "Cobb was on first base. First thing I knowed he had stole second while I held the ball. [Manager] Callahan yells Wake up out there and I says Why don't your catcher tell me when they are going to steal."[44]

Regardless, Brown's *Alibi Ike* chronicles the success of Lardner's title character during his rookie season with the Chicago Cubs. As in the author's original short story, this is a figure who alibis about everything, including the game of pool. After making a difficult shot against a teammate (impressively staged with an overhead camera placement), Alibi echoes his name by observing, "I ain't so good at this game, we don't play much pool back home." Ike's perennial excuses also lead to a pivotal scene in both Lardner's story and the adaptation — the temporary derailing of the character's romance. After Brown's Ike is kidded about being engaged, he says, "Sometimes a fella don't know exactly what he's getting into. Take a good-lookin' girl and a fella does just about what she wants him to do. When a fella gets to feeling sorry for a girl, it's all off [he's hooked]."

Unfortunately, this banter with his buddies is overheard by Dolly (Olivia de Havilland) and she calls off the engagement. (Ironically, though the statement might be inflammatory for a lover, there is more comic common sense here than in the usual dialogue from a Lardner ballplayer.) Not surprisingly, the loss of Dolly impacts Elmer's pitching and the Cubs' chances for a pennant.

At this point the screen adaptation interjects a new wrinkle — gamblers put pressure upon Ike to lose his last two starts for the Cubs. With the Chicago team heavily favored when Alibi pitches, this would be a huge windfall for the betting racket. And after Brown's character drops the first game through grief at losing Dolly, the gamblers mistakenly feel Ike is playing along. When they realize otherwise, the pitcher is kidnapped. (The 1932 abduction of Charles Lindbergh's baby helped fuel both the fear of kidnapping in real life, and its depiction in the popular arts of this era.)

The abduction of Ike allows the picture to replicate a finale factor of Brown's two previous baseball films — the comedian's ballplayer only reaches the pivotal game at the eleventh hour. This time Ike escapes his kidnappers by way of using the very ambulance in which he had been abducted. When he ultimately crashes said vehicle through the outfield wall at the pennant-deciding game, the picture has come full circle from his similar stadium wall–shattering introduction.

The plate umpire will not delay this night game for Brown's Ike to get in uniform. But a forgiving Dolly is at the park and she manages to briefly shut down the stadium power and the resulting blackout enables Ike to change. But the uniform we suddenly see him in is many sizes too big. Brown's subsequent comic shtick is amplified by what is literally a clown costume. (This anticipates the oversized uniform synonymous with Max Patkin's later "Clown Prince" of baseball character, which was highlighted in *Bull Durham*, 1988.) Brown's outfit soon proves to be an amusing liability, too, when Ike loses an in-play ball within this maze of clothing and the Giants tie the score. But when the Cubs come to bat in the bottom of the ninth, Ike hits a game-winning, inside-the-park home run. His amusingly speedy circling of the bases, encased in the oversized outfit, is then inspiringly topped by his eluding of the catcher's tag with a gymnastic somersault *over* said player and a safe slide home. The Cubs win the pennant and in a brief epilogue, Ike marries Dolly.

This extremely entertaining baseball saga is further assisted by several additional ties to the national game, both from the sport's past history, and mid-1930s developments. First, besides using footage of real Major Leaguers, there are pertinent references to legendary ballplayers. Besides the aforementioned Frawley reference to Dizzy Dean, this manager also draws a parallel between Ike and Rube Waddell, the fire engine–obsessed pitcher who was an unofficial model for Brown's character in *Fireman, Save My Child*. Frawley himself plays a figure named Cap, which goes back to Lardner's original story. This is an obvious reference to pioneering ballplayer Cap Anson, the Hall of Famer sometimes considered the game's first superstar. More to the point for the Chicago Cubs-focused *Alibi Ike*, Anson was also the very successful manager of Chicago's First National League team.

Brown's title character antics in *Alibi Ike* also play upon famous incidents associated with celebrated baseball stars. At one point Ike attempts to show off his pitching by calling his teammates to the mound and throwing with no defensive support behind him. This tall tale–like example of ego has been attributed to a plethora of pitchers, from Waddell and Dean, to Satchel Paige. (What is more, Brown would replicate this stunt in a 1935 season-ending exhibition appearance for Hollywood's then minor league team. Calling in his outfielders, the comedian would strike out famed song and screen writer Harry Ruby — who was also a huge baseball fan.) When Brown's Alibi Ike drives his car onto the field, one is reminded of legendary pitcher Christy Mathewson. While "Matty" did not crash his automobile through walls, he did use the presence of an expensive car as an intimidation factor. Mathewson could also be a free spirit, such as his weakness for coasting with a big lead. In one such situation he loaded the bases and immediately had a manager reading him the riot act. His response, "Take it easy, it's more fun this way."[45] He then struck out the side.

Late in the film, a newsboy asks Brown's character a variation of the famous line allegedly requested by a boy of Shoeless Joe Jackson when he was first accused of helping "fix" the 1919 World Series—"Say it ain't so, Joe." The connection with Ike is that he, too, is thought to be in on a gambling fix, though that is not the case. In fact, *Alibi Ike* reverses the process by ultimately having the newsboy be an informant for the betting ring. Brown's picture even has a Major League footnote that involves the comedian himself. During the previous year's (1934) World Series, Detroit pitcher Schoolboy Rowe claimed that a strong handshake from Brown had injured his hand, a ludicrous claim which produced comic comments across the country. Brown's favorite hometown paper, the *Toledo Times*, made the comedian out to be a second Paul Bunyan: "Joe, an enthusiastic baseball fan, is reported to have shaken Schoolboy Rowe's hand so lustily before today's game that he fractured several small bones in the hurler's right hand [!]"[46] But humorist Will Rogers' syndicated daily newspaper telegram avoided hyperbole and went straight to comic indignation, "My old friend, Joe E. Brown, didn't [sic] wound anybody by a handshake. If he did he must have hit 'em."[47] Flash forward to 1935's *Alibi Ike*: Brown's character declines to shake hands with his manager before pitching in the finale, feeling it would be safer to wait until after the game! (Earlier in the picture Ike had blamed a homer he gave up on having received too many congratulatory handshakes after one of his wins.) As the *Los Angeles Times*' review observed, "A sports reporter really should cover *Alibi Ike* at Warner's downtown theater. It's that technical so far as its baseball is concerned."[48]

Brown's picture was also up on the latest developments in Major League baseball. *Alibi Ike*'s crucial concluding contest is a night game. Though this phenomenon can be first traced to two obscure late nineteenth century games, the Major League's groundbreaking regularly scheduled night games began with seven Cincinnati Reds contests during the 1935 season.[49] The initial game (May 24) occurred just two months before the East Coast opening of *Alibi Ike*.

For all the attention to baseball detail showered upon *Alibi Ike*, the picture does pose one error. While Brown's Cubs are said to be playing the New York Giants, the uniforms of their rivals showcase the logo of the St. Louis Cardinals. The editing sequences usually mask this discrepancy but occasionally it is glaringly apparent. There is no obvious explanation but two theories come to mind. First, since Brown's characterization was influenced by Harry Frank "The Giant Killer" Coveleski, whose long ago pitching exploits once derailed a pennant drive by the New York Giants, maybe Warners and/or Brown decided to honor this connection. Second, *Alibi Ike* generated a lot of ties being drawn between Lardner's character and St. Louis' Dizzy Dean. Maybe the powers that be felt having Brown's movie team then play the Cardinals would be overkill.

This small potatoes discrepancy notwithstanding, *Alibi Ike* was yet another critical and commercial hit for Brown. As the reviewer for *The Hollywood Reporter* said, "With Joe E. Brown in a baseball story its happiness ahead for everybody, producer, audience and critics."[50] The *New York Post* called it "a one hundred and ten per cent

American comedy-drama ... and if it fails to move you either to mirth or excitement then you better go back to Union Square or wait until the next Russian film comes to the Cameo [theater]."[51] The *New York Times*' high praise started by calling Brown a studio icon—"Joe E. Brown, who is to Warners what Garbo is to Metro [MGM] and Shirley Temple is to Fox, returns to Times Square (via the Cameo) in a genuinely amusing little comedy patterned after one of Ring Lardner's most famous baseball stories...."[52] The title of *New York Evening Journal* critic Rose Pelswick's review might have best summed up all these kudos—"Joe E. Brown Amusingly Plays Goofy Pitcher in Baseball Classic."[53]

As was the norm by this time, Brown's direct links with the national game were grist for reviews. This recognition could be purely informational, such as the *New York Sun* critic Eileen Creelman stating his "knowledge of baseball includes some professional playing as well as a current part ownership in a team ..."[54] But reviewers could also wax poetic on the subject, as *New York Daily News* critic Wanda Hale did in her *Alibi Ike* critique:

> It is said of [Brown] that had he never learned his funny face was his fortune he should have followed the game of hit and run for a livelihood. Thus when Joseph dons a monkey suit and performs a feat of magic with what our sports writers call "the old apple," he does so with more than cinematic proficiency.[55]

Mixing Brown's lifelong love of baseball with critical hosannas such as these, and having 1935 find him back on the box office top ten list, it's no wonder that he would consider his best films baseball stories. (In the 1940s he called *Elmer* his favorite diamond picture but late in his life Brown gave that personal title to *Alibi Ike*.[56]) For such a quintessential American comedian, what would make more sense than defining himself through the national game? Moreover, here was a man (Brown) who simply derived a great deal of pleasure (like any baseball fan) by merely interacting with his sports heroes, from the aforementioned Dizzy Dean, to Babe Ruth. And what was most telling of his talent, these great athletes also enjoyed being with Brown. This is amusingly documented as early as a 1930 World Series photo opportunity for a lucky news photographer. Brown and Ruth were talking during a game (the Yankees did *not* make the Series that year!) and the journalist asked the comedian, "Make a funny face, Joe." Brown kiddingly refused, claiming, "That's work for me." But this gave Ruth a chance to affectionately zing his friend, "It [a funny face] comes natural with him."[57]

Brown would have appreciated contemporary sports columnist Sandy Gray's later observation, "No matter how tough life may be ... [baseball] gives a fan a separate universe of heroics and drama ... [I]t's like being engrossed in a season-long movie ... with the World Series as the last chapter; it may be fiction, but you gotta believe it matters."[58] And with Brown's baseball comedy, the national game only gets better.

As Robert Frost once said, "Some baseball is the fate of us all."[59]

CHAPTER 9

The Marx Brothers' *A Night at the Opera* (1935)

> When I invite a woman to dinner, I expect her to look at my face. That's the price she has to pay.
> — Groucho to Margaret Dumont in *A Night at the Opera*

While *Duck Soup* (1933, see chapter 4) is the Marx Brothers' greatest film, it was not a commercial success.[1] Indeed, the movie performed so poorly at the box office, after the huge financial success of their earlier Paramount pictures, that *Duck Soup* ended the team's association with that studio. *A Night at the Opera*, the first of five Marx Brothers films for MGM (they had also done five for Paramount), was the team's comeback picture. But the term "comeback" is too modest a word. Thanks, in part, to the brilliant comedy writing of George S. Kaufman and Morrie Ryskind (who shared a Pulitzer Prize with Ira Gershwin for *Of Thee I Sing*, 1931–32), *Opera* would become one of the Marxes' signature movies, as well as their best MGM outing. Beyond becoming an instant comedy classic, it also had an important impact upon a then new film genre — screwball comedy — which will be addressed later in the text.

The road to *A Night at the Opera* had involved some interesting turns. At loose ends after their split with Paramount, the comedian brothers went in several separate directions, from Harpo's trip as a cultural ambassador to the Soviet Union in late 1933 (this closely followed President Franklin D. Roosevelt's diplomatic recognition of the Communist country), to Groucho and Chico's short-lived 1934 pun-entitled *Marx of Time* radio program. Moreover, the team became a threesome when Zeppo quit to join a theatrical agency. His presence in the Marx movies had been relatively minor, never being allowed to develop an identifiable character. But one fewer brother was still a loss. (Conversely, during contract negotiations with MGM, Groucho kiddingly claimed, "Without Zeppo, we're worth twice as much."[2])

Though there was talk of other studios picking up the team, no strong offers were forthcoming. Eventually, as had happened in the past, Chico's card playing habits got things going again. The acclaimed Irving Thalberg, MGM head of production, was a bridge-playing friend of Chico's. Thalberg "decided" he wanted to hire the Marx Brothers, although "Mr. Persuasion" (Chico) probably had something to do with it.

9. The Marx Brothers' *A Night at the Opera* (1935)

Regardless, support from the "Boy Genius" of Hollywood — later the model for the title character of F. Scott Fitzgerald's unfinished final novel *The Last Tycoon* — was no little accomplishment. *But* there would be a price. Thalberg had specific thoughts on reshaping both the team and its relationship to the story, however thin the story might be. In fact, a stronger, more plausible story was something Thalberg wanted, as well as better pacing of comic lines — to eliminate responsive audiences drowning out other comic lines. Thalberg said *Duck Soup* "was a very funny picture but you don't need that many laughs in a movie."[3] He went on to suggest he could do twice the gross with half the jokes, if he could incorporate a more believable story. Thalberg also wanted to add a romance to interest women. (The antisocial cynicism and sometimes womanizing, sometimes misogynous nature of Depression clowns like the Marx Brothers and W.C. Fields hardly endeared them to many women.) To broaden their audiences still further, Thalberg wanted the Marxes' characters made more sympathetic, something that was most specifically directed at the antisocial personae of Harpo and Groucho. Plus, eccentric comic behavior should be more directly tied to the plot, as in the assistance of the film's romantic couple.

Even a partial homogenizing of Groucho and Harpo comes as a shock after the organized chaos of the Paramount pictures. As the *New Statesman and Nation* reviewer of the earlier *Horse Feathers* (1932) wrote, they are "the only film artists in Europe or America that do not make some appeal to sentimentality."[4] Thus, *A Night at the Opera*

On the set of *A Night at the Opera*, with the remaining Marx Brothers and director Sam Wood.

is disappointing when it attempts to give Harpo and Groucho pathos, be it the beating of Harpo by the singing star villain Lassparri (Walter Woolf King) or Groucho being booted down three flights of stairs by a minor character. Thankfully, *Opera* keeps such moments to a minimum, and allows some payback, such as Harpo eventually knocking out Lassparri and immediately reviving him — so the mad mute can knock him out again! Still, the Marxes today are largely defined through their earlier unadulterated aggressive comic personae. And while *Opera* remains rightfully celebrated in the Marx Brothers canon, it ranks below the comically uncompromising *Duck Soup*. Consequently, when the American Film Institute selected their 100 funniest movies in 2000, *Duck Soup* ranked fifth and *Opera* was twelfth. (*Some Like It Hot*, 1959, finished first.) More pointedly, when the AFI had earlier (1998) picked the 100 greatest movies (inclusive of all genres), *Duck Soup* was the only Marx movie on the list. (*Citizen Kane*, 1941, took the top spot.)

Ironically, there was even a popular minor showcase of Marx aggression (keying on Harpo) which opened shortly after *Opera*: Disney's cartoon *Mickey's Polo Team* (1936). This short subject has Mickey, Donald, Goofy, and the Big Bad Wolf competing against Harpo, Chaplin, and Laurel and Hardy. Harpo is easily the roughest comedy player, no small accomplishment when your competition includes the Big Bad Wolf. The cartoon Harpo's ensemble of tricks, perfectly in keeping with the live-action Paramount Harpo, including everything from a boxing glove that springs from his hat, to the coat-hidden appearance of a blowtorch (produced just as magically by the real Harpo in *Duck Soup*). The fact that the cartoon Harpo steals the show and that Disney is not exactly a poor surveyor of popular culture tastes suggest that a comically unsympathetic Harpo had not yet overstayed his welcome.

Of course, just as chapter 4 (on *Duck Soup*) documented a 1930s general belief that any feature-length entertainment should not have comedy straight through, some period critics praised making the Marxes more sympathetic. For example, a 1937 *Stage* magazine essay observed, the team "learned that audiences may laugh at but resent such [pure aggressive] action.... If you'll recall, in *A Night at the Opera* you were on the Marxes' side. They were sympathetic. Everyone they mistreated had it coming to him"[5] Certainly *Opera*'s box office clout would be more evidence in favor of Thalberg's makeover. But to play devil's advocate, an argument could be made that *Opera*'s success with mid-1930s audiences was not so much because of Thalberg-engineered changes but rather due to the producer's financial generosity. Most importantly, this meant a willingness to pay the $100,000 it would take to get George Kaufman involved in the production. For the Marxes and much of the country, Kaufman was at or near the top of America's wealth of comedy writers. His string of Broadway successes (including the Marx Brothers' *The Cocoanuts* and *Animal Crackers*) had made him a sort of pre–World War II Neil Simon.

The Thalberg-proposed transformation had initially received a mixed reaction from the Marxes. For instance, Groucho's son Arthur later wrote that his father had reservations about Thalberg's goal that *Opera* "have something in it for everybody — even female picturegoers": "Father had always felt that it was pointless to try to make a broad comedy that would appeal to women, too. From past experience, he had found out that it was mostly men who enjoyed the Marx Brothers."[6]

Still, when the great Thalberg was interested in reviving your screen career.... Moreover, one of the suggestions which came out of the Marxes' talks with the producer met with everyone's approval — road test the material for the team's first MGM picture. After all, the Marxes' first two movies (Paramount's *The Cocoanuts*, 1929, and *Animal Crackers*, 1930), had been based on fine-tuned stage hits, both of which had started with shakedown tours. This had not been the case with the team's three subsequent Paramount films. While the written-for-the screen *Monkey Business* (1931) and *Horse Feathers* (1932) had been critical and commercial hits, the box office numbers had not been there for an equally original *Duck Soup*. *Duck Soup* director Leo McCarey's normal working habits, a product of his silent film comedy past, had involved bringing in ideas on scraps of paper and shooting material in an improvisational or nearly improvisational manner daily.

Though there were other writers on *Duck Soup*, McCarey still clearly left his signature on the film.[7] Therefore, when *Duck Soup* then did not do expected big business, it would seem to represent more evidence for using road-tested material. Though the Marxes had handpicked McCarey, any production doubts they might have had would not be unique to them. In 1937, because of McCarey's unorthodox working style, the leading man (Cary Grant) of the director's classic screwball comedy *The Awful Truth* attempted (unsuccessfully) to buy out of his contract during production.[8] But unlike *Duck Soup*, the greatness of *The Awful Truth* was recognized immediately, and ultimately won McCarey his first Best Director Academy Award.

Going on the road with new sketch material was yet another example of Thalberg's financial generosity towards the Marxes. This successful practice would be repeated for their next MGM picture, *A Day at the Races* (1937, an even bigger box office hit than *Opera*). Yet, with Thalberg's premature 1937 death, MGM largely pulled the plug on costly team tours.

The Marx Brothers' *Opera* test tour, entitled *Scenes from a Night at the Opera*, hit the road in spring of 1935. The fifty-minute vaudeville-like act played four times daily for almost a month, and focused on cities in the western United States. Tour stops included Santa Monica, Seattle, Portland, Salt Lake City, and San Francisco. The road show was a huge success, both with the audiences and the comedy-tweaking Marxes, though Groucho had some second thoughts after the final performance in San Francisco. Thalberg had been in front row attendance and never laughed! But unbeknownst to the Marxes, the producer had seen several of their road shows and simply knew and *loved* the polished performances.

The tour was significant for several reasons. First, and most obviously, it was the groundwork for a great comedy, the semi-dehorning of Groucho and Harpo notwithstanding. Period literature suggests the greatest tour beneficiary was the stateroom scene.[9] This is the sequence in which Groucho discovers his ocean liner quarters are the smallest on record. Delivery of his large steamer trunk, from which stowaways Chico, Harpo, and romantic lead Allan Jones emerge, fills the place up. But this is only the comedy beginning. Somehow this tiny stateroom will soon also include a steward, two maids, a ship's engineer, a manicurist, a huge assistant to the engineer, a young girl looking for her Aunt Minnie, a charwoman, and four waiters with food. The comedy topper arrives when Groucho's perennial high society target,

Margaret Dumont, opens the stateroom door and everyone comes tumbling into the hall.

The beauty of the stateroom scene is that it combines the most amusing ongoing visual incongruity with very witty patter. For example, when the young girl arrives and asks if her Aunt Minnie is there, Groucho's character observes, "Well, you can come in and prowl around if you want to. If she isn't in here, you can probably find somebody just as good." Or, when the manicurist asks the mustached one if he wants his nails long or short, Groucho says, "You'd better make 'em short. It's getting kind of crowded in here. I don't know, this isn't the way I pictured an ocean voyage."

So how did the tour help create the now acclaimed stateroom scene? As originally conceived, the midget room and giant steamer trunk were merely an excuse to get a laugh from Groucho being forced to go into the hall to undress. But a suddenly modest Groucho had reservations about appearing on stage in his garters — killing the reason for the undersized stateroom. Thus, what evolved was the decision to hold a regular comedy convention in this doll house–sized compartment. This was well-received by vaudeville audiences. But the troupe found that every time they added more bodies the laughs increased. Plus, Harpo wrote in his autobiography that the sketch still opened a bit flat until he and Groucho improvised the following shtick:

> So this night we did it our way. Groucho, ordering a meal from the steward while being jostled into the corner of the jammed-up stateroom, said, "And a hard-boiled egg...." I honked my horn. "Make it two hard-boiled eggs," said Groucho. The audience broke up....[10]

The "two hard-boiled eggs" and Harpo's honking became a repeated refrain during the sketch, eventually segueing into an even zanier Groucho meal order:

> And two-hard boiled eggs. (A honk is heard.) Make that three hard-boiled eggs. (Another honk is heard.) And one duck egg. Uh, have you got any stewed prunes? (Yes says the steward.) Well, give them some black coffee. That'll sober them up.

A second reason the *Opera* road tour was important, beyond both polishing and developing comedy material, was simply allowing the team to be a creative partner on the new material. While they always had a tendency to tweak original sketch ideas, no matter how important the author, a road audience gave them an effective comedy gauge with which to make it their own. Ironically, on both the *Opera* tour and the subsequent road show for *A Day at the Races*, Groucho would sometimes be criticized for underselling material. But the comedian's defense was always the same; he could easily generate a laugh from anything, with those elevator eyebrows and painted mustache. Groucho simply wanted to first see how the material would stand with a minimalist presentation. Actress Lillian Roth, the young heroine of the Marxes' *Animal Crackers*, addressed this subject when she once explained why she had ruined take after take of a scene she shared with Groucho:

9. The Marx Brothers' *A Night at the Opera* (1935) 131

***A Night at the Opera*'s** famed stateroom scene, with Groucho on the left, Chico in the center, and Harpo sleeping on top.

> I burst into giggles every time he said [his line]. The line itself wasn't so hilarious but I knew Groucho was going to say it with the big cigar jutting from his clenched teeth, his eyebrows palpitating, and that he would be off afterwards in that runaway crouch of his; and the thought of what was coming was too much for me.[11]

The New Republic's pioneeringly significant early film critic Otis Ferguson made a similar but more succinct assessment in his *Opera* review: Groucho "would be funny in still photographs...."[12] Of course, as a footnote to funny, all great screen clowns can milk laughter from less than memorable lines. For instance, in W.C. Fields' acclaimed *It's a Gift* (1934, see chapter 7), *The Hollywood Reporter*'s glowing review still claimed, "without a Fields to mouth it, the dialogue would be so-so."[13]

A third explanation for the significance of the *Opera* tour was how it generated interest in the eventual movie. Indeed, the spring road tour was still the primary focus of attention in many of the picture's end-of-the-year reviews. The *Brooklyn Eagle*'s critique was even entitled, "Testing a Film — for Laughs," and claimed that, "For the first time in motion picture history a film was to be 'previewed,' 'cut,' and gauged for laughs before the picture was actually placed in production."[14] Sometimes period reviews for

Opera combined an ongoing fascination about the Marxes' testing tour with jokes stating the team was improved by the loss of Zeppo. For example, *Newsweek*'s critique comically claimed that the Marxes got to do their shakedown tour after Zeppo "threatened to rejoin the team if Thalberg didn't give in."[15]

Even without the kidding of poor Zeppo (a major mid-1930s target), the *Opera* tour continued to generate a great deal of comic-tinged public interest well after the picture's opening. Alva Johnston's amusing autumn 1936 article, "The Scientific Side of Lunacy," would posit, "The only possible advance in efficiency [beyond a pre-film tour] would be to load the public on belt conveyers and make it laugh with mechanical ticklers."[16] And despite Groucho's aforementioned doubts about generating female fans for the Marxes, Johnston's tongue-in-cheek essay appeared in *Woman's Home Companion*!

For those fans who had been living under the proverbial rock at the time of *Opera*'s original test run, MGM even hinted at the tour in their print ads, too: "At a cost of $1,000,000, MGM has plotted the BIG COMEDY SHOW that you'll vote the funniest ever made! A year to make!"[17] (Another unusual ad campaign twist for the time was including plugs for the picture from other MGM stars, such as the following obviously ghost-written copy from Academy Award–winning actor Wallace Beery: "Three times as funny as anything I've ever seen ... but after all there's three times as many comedians in the picture."[18]) For all the tour's overexposure, its tweaking of the inventive source material resulted in some of the Marxes' most notable sketches.

After the aforementioned unforgettable stateroom scene, arguably *Opera*'s most inspired routine is the contract scene, where Groucho and Chico derail the world of legalese. The mustached one thinks he is signing a star, but as usually happens when he interacts with a brother, Chico gets the better of him—though his client (romantic lead Allan Jones) will eventually rise from the chorus. Regardless, the mix of Groucho's absurdity and Chico's ice cream Italian is a delight. Here is a sample:

> CHICO: Well, I dunno 'bout that.
>
> GROUCHO: *Now* what's the matter?
>
> CHICO: I don't like-a the second party [part] either.
>
> GROUCHO: Well, you shoulda come to the first party. We didn't get home 'til around four in the morning. I was blind for three days.

The brothers visually punctuate this verbal slapstick by periodically tearing offending clauses from their matching documents—certainly an attractive comic development for anyone who has ever waded through a contract. (Groucho and Chico also begin their contract routine again as the movie comes to a close.)

While Groucho is the verbal absurdity star of the contract sketch, Chico assumes that mantle in another memorable *Opera* routine—the aviators at New York's City Hall. As the movie's comic action moves from Italy to the staging of "a night at the opera" in New York, the ocean liner stowaways (Chico, Harpo, and Jones) need a cover to exit the ship. With three bearded flyers onboard, scissors-happy Harpo hatches a plan for himself and his sidekicks to double as this trio (after snipping their beards) when disembarking. This was familiar territory for the team, since *Monkey Business* features the notable ocean liner sketch, where all four Marxes individually attempt to go through customs by imitating entertainer Maurice Chevalier, whose passport the team has somehow managed to acquire. The only flaw in Harpo's *Opera* aviator scam is that the real flyers turn out to be famous, so a disguised Chico has to give a speech at City Hall. Here is an excerpt:

> So now I tell you how we fly to America. The first time-a we start-a, we getta halfway across when we run out of gasoline and we gotta go back. Then I take-a twice as mucha gasoline. This time we were just about to land, maybe three feet, when what do you think? We run out of gasoline again. Then we go back again and getta more gas. This time I take-a plenty gas. Well-a, we getta halfway over ... when what do you thinka happen? We forgetta the airplane....

Interestingly enough, this sketch was also assisted by road show tweaking. Originally, Chico's speech about aviation woes was loosely attributed to flying legend Charles Lindbergh. "At no performance did anyone laugh. When, however, Chico related the experience about himself, the entire audience was in the aisles."[19]

The topper to such verbal gems as the contract scene and the aviation speech is *Opera*'s finale, when the Marxes create assorted mayhem to disrupt the New York opera debut of the film's nasty tenor (Walter Woolf King). Their temporary derailing of the proceedings includes: Harpo in a quasi-sword dual with the conductor, switching the orchestra music to "Take Me Out to the Ball Game"; Chico and Harpo playing catch; Groucho selling peanuts in the aisle; Harpo swinging like Tarzan above the stage — which also causes various canvas backdrops to come down; Harpo defying gravity by literally running up the curtain, and the ultimate kidnapping of King. This crazy comedy conclusion remains a special crowd-pleaser, with some of the funniest bits being brief cutaways. For instance, my favorite laugh in the whole picture is a Groucho throwaway line during this runaway close. One first sees and hears a creepy Halloween-like gypsy woman in the cast singing mournfully — with the movie then comically cutting to Groucho in a balcony saying, "Boogie-boogie" — complimented by that funny face and his manic hand gestures.

Stage magazine critic Clifton Fadiman was so taken with the film's finale that he imaginatively described it as "resembling Bedlam rearranged by Mr. Thurber."[20] This amusing analogy, reminiscent to me of the James Thurber drawing accompanying his essay "The Day the Dam Broke" in *My Life and Hard Times* (1933), where a tidal wave of people pours through the author's hometown of Columbus, Ohio, might even be better linked to the flood of people pouring out of *Opera*'s stateroom scene.[21] Moreover, Fadiman's reference to the humorist was probably the catalyst for a goofy 1937 Thurber tribute to the Marxes in *Stage*, claiming the team ...

> ... are not to be confused with — or even by, as far as that goes — the author of *Das Kapital*, who wore a beard and looked a little like Sanity Clause (Karl Marx 1818–1883). The Marx Brothers (1776–2937) are not, as a matter of fact, to be confused by anybody.[22]

Another period critic especially taken with *Opera*'s close was Joseph Alsop, Jr. But instead of making a literary link with American humor (*à la* Thurber), Alsop defined the close as a prime example of surrealism — the movement that originated in 1920s France and attempted to express in art the workings of the unconscious. Though not the first author even then to draw the Marx-surrealism parallel (see, for example, Antonin Artaud's 1932 essay "Les Frères Marx au Cinéma du Panthéon"[23]), Alsop's *New York Herald Tribune* article was ambitious for mid–1930s mainstream American newspapers. I draw attention to the work because it showcased an international high-art link being given to Groucho and company and yet still redefined surrealism with an American comedy — Marx Brothers — slant. Alsop's approach to surrealism remains, like that of the Marxes, decidedly fluid, as if to suggest that all the weirdness anyone could want is available in everyday life.

This piece is also entertaining for the fun it has celebrating this home-grown crazy comedy while kidding (in Marx Brothers tradition) the lofty European surrealism stereotypes. To illustrate, Alsop comically contrasts *Opera* with two scenes in Luis Buñuel and Salvador Dalí's *Andalusian Dog* (1928), which is generally considered the beginning of surrealist cinema: "You will not find in it a single slit eyeball, or even one ant crawling out of a hole in a ... hand but then, there are the Marxes, and they are quite sufficient."[24] Alsop might have added a further surrealistic connection between Dalí and the punning tendencies of Groucho and Chico. That is, art historian E.H. Gombrich later observed:

> Dali's way of letting each form represent several things at the same time may focus our attention on the many possible meanings of each colour and form — much in the way in which a successful pun may make us aware of the function of words and their meaning.[25]

One is tempted, of course, to credit the Marxes with pushing their often-dark humor beyond surrealism.[26] The main difference between black comedy and surrealism, as defined by humor historian Max F. Schulz, is that surrealism keys on "internal disorder" of the subconscious mind, while black comedy generally suggests that disorder is now the external, real state of things.[27] Certainly a pivotal element in the rediscovery of the Marxes during the chaotic 1960s was based on the fact that surrealism was more and more becoming the day-to-day norm. Along these lines, dark humorist Chandler Brossard had the following late 1960s thoughts on the antiwar movement: "The true absurdists of our time are not the avant-garde at all; they are institutional [military complex] realists."[28]

Regardless of how one defines the loopy antics of the mad Marxes, one cannot leave the subject of surrealism without noting Dalí's embrace of Harpo. In the artist's 1937 *Harper's Bazaar* article, "Surrealism in Hollywood," he called the mute Marx "the most fascinating and the most surrealistic character in Hollywood ... because for Harpo there exists no essential difference between a butterfly and a minute steak...."[29] Just as this Dalí essay also includes a Harpo-inspired drawing by the artist, Marie Seton's 1939 *Theatre Arts* article, "S. Dalí + 3 Marxes =," features five Dalí paintings for which Harpo and his brothers are the catalyst.[30] These works represented part of a Dalí series that was done as an abstract storyboard of sorts for an equally abstract and unrealized team-inspired Dalí script. The point of Seton's article, which also touched upon both Lewis

Carroll and the American literary humor movement known as "lunatic comedy" (which included Robert Benchley and Donald Ogden Stewart), was that the Marxes were live-action surrealist performers. But if truth be told, Dalí was a surrealist performer, too. For instance, in 1936, the year after *Opera,* the artist gave a lecture at the International Surrealist Exhibition (London) while "wearing lead boots and a deep-sea diving suit (to symbolize his dive into the unconscious) and nearly suffocated to death. The public and press took notice."[31] Indeed, this sounds decidedly like something Harpo would do.

Sometimes, however, the surrealistic tendencies of the Marxes were simply used by reviewers as a source for their own team-related comedy. To illustrate, the *New York Sun*'s film critic stated, "If these [*Opera* review] sentences don't make much sense, which they don't, neither do the Marxes. You'll be goofy, too, after seeing them."[32] And as the pivotal pop culture author Gilbert Seldes wrote in 1937, the Marxes' surrealistic tendencies are also what separated the team from their comedy contemporaries:

> The Marx Brothers are not human ... they are completely fantastic and they seem completely mad. You never recognize yourself in any one of them as you do in Fields, nor ever see them express the essence of emotion as Chaplin does. Again and again the Marx Brothers act as we act in dreams [surrealism], or as we would act if we dared, if the whole world were created for our pleasure.[33]

The close to Seldes' surrealism statement also segues this study to another quintessential component of Marx magic—what the French refer to as the "Spirit of the Stairway" (Esprit d'Escalier). This refers to those random, fleeting public moments when one needs a comic comeback but fails. Only after leaving the event (on the proverbial staircase) does the perfect witticism come to mind. But the "Spirit of the Stairway" *never* happens to the verbal Marxes—Groucho and Chico. In fact, one could argue that beyond all the celebrated Marx sketches, the greatest single crowd-pleasing component to their comedy is Groucho's propensity to pepper his performance with countless classic put-downs.

Some notable *Opera* comeback examples would include a suspicious detective questioning Groucho about allegedly being a hermit, yet having a table set for four. The mustached one would respond, "That's nothing. My alarm is set for eight." On another occasion the team's frequent co-star, Margaret Dumont, berates Groucho for sitting on her bed, and asks him, "What would people say?" He quickly replies, "They'd probably say you're a very lucky woman." Since Dumont's *Opera* character is wealthy, which is the norm in all her Marx Brothers appearances, Groucho often mixes his insults with quasi-romantic patter. After one such advance she tells him they need to keep things on a business basis, to which he observes, "How do you like that? Every time I get romantic with you, you want to talk business. I don't know, there's something about me that brings out the business in every woman." As *New York Post* reviewer Thornton Delehanty stated, to Groucho "falls the prize bits of dialogue, and the stream of inanities is so unremitting that one simply has not time to pick oneself up between laughs."[34]

Not surprisingly, the *Post*'s praise was typical of the period reviews, with several

Groucho with his favorite society matron target, Margaret Dumont, in *A Night at the Opera*.

publications, including the *New York World Telegram* and the *New York Daily News*, calling *Opera* the team's funniest film.[35] Rose Pelswick's *New York Evening Journal* critique sounded Thalberg-like when it linked kudos to a "more closely-knit story than they've [the Marxes] had in their former film efforts...."[36] But the *New York Herald Tribune*'s equally positive review comically minimized the significance of a tighter narrative: "There possibly is a trifle more plot ... than was to be found, usually with a microscope, in the earlier Marx wonderworks, but such a thing really does no great harm...."[37]

The most ambitiously balanced period critique was Clifton Fadiman's aforementioned *Stage* review, entertainingly entitled "A New High in Low Comedy." He also felt this was the team's funniest film. But Fadiman questioned whether the "sanitation" of the Marxes represented "progress": "[T]he provinces did not take kindly to Harpo's satyriasis, to Groucho's innuendos ... [such] as his all-inclusive invitation to Mrs. Rittenhouse [Margaret Dumont]: 'Won't you come in and lie down?' in *Animal Crackers*."[38] This section of the review wisely hints at a factor seldom linked to Thalberg's makeover of the Marxes — the censorship code came to Hollywood in 1934, the year between the commercial failure of 1933's *Duck Soup* and 1935's *Opera* comeback. (For more on the code see chapter 3 — Mae West.)

In Fadiman's far-reaching review he addressed everything from W.C. Fields' tendencies towards understatement (versus the Marxes' "prodigal overstatement"), to the suggestion that the team's surreal tendencies would be well served by hiring fantasy-oriented director René Clair.[39] But maybe the critique's most provocative component is its close, in which Fadiman claims, through an unnamed source, that the Marxes' next picture would involve one of three subjects: the circus, the World's Fair, or a department store. Though this did not come to pass, two of the Marxes' four pictures which followed *A Day at the Races* (1937) did use these settings for a backdrop: *At the Circus* (1939) and *The Big Store* (1941).

Given Fadiman's special contacts, or "gifts," it might have been interesting to have had him uncover more about Harpo's 1934 desire to speak in *Opera*. The *Los Angeles Times* reported:

> Harpo wants to talk! Chico and Groucho don't want him to. They blame it all on his recent triumphant invasion of Russia. It has gone to his head. He not only wants to talk but he wants to get arty in their next picture [*Opera*] — the Russian influence.[40]

Two weeks later the *Los Angeles Times* ran a story on what was undoubtedly the projected "arty" segment for *Opera*— Harpo comically interacting with two Russian actresses who impersonate Groucho and Chico. This had been a big hit on Harpo's Soviet tour, after a Russian "government contest was conducted" to choose these two performers.[41] MGM was supposedly considering bringing both actresses (Helen Ketatk and Iona Brotsky) to Hollywood. Nothing came of either this or Harpo's verbal aspirations. But a fascinating Groucho and Chico compromise on Harpo speaking merits noting. The talking Marxes "suggested to Harpo that if he wanted to speak he should merely say what he is thinking, just as [characters did] in *Strange Interlude* [1932]. Harpo turned thumbs down on this idea. If he talks he is going to say plenty."[42] The Marxes had already parodied the earlier stage production of *Strange Interlude* in their *Animal Crackers*, with Groucho comically speaking his inner thoughts. Of course, another variation on this spoofing of internal monologues would be to borrow a page from Joe E. Brown's *You Said a Mouthful* (1932). In this picture when Brown goes comically deep-dish with his own "strange interlude," the comedian's amusingly mournful inner thoughts are simply heard in voice-over. This latter approach might have proven less jarring for Harpo's fans, had he gone through with it. Paradoxically, while the comedian flirted with speaking in *Opera*, he would later turn down a $55,000 offer to speak in *A Night in Casablanca* (1946). Ultimately, the mute Marx stayed that way for character consistency, though Chico and Groucho had kiddingly threatened to go silent if Harpo started talking!

Possibly *Opera*'s most neglected legacy is its impact upon the then new film genre of screwball comedy. This variation on American farce is usually first dated from *It Happened One Night* and *Twentieth Century* (both 1934, the year before *Opera*). But what is forgotten today is the period significance of the screwball classic *My Man Godfrey* (1936).[43] More than any of its predecessors, *Godfrey* offered a whole house full of screwballs. Thus, for many period critics, this picture represented a more obvious starting point for the genre. For example, Kate Cameron's *New York Daily News* review of *Bringing Up Baby* (1938) placed it in the tradition of "the whole crazy variety of screen comedies that began with *My Man Godfrey*."[44] Moreover, the now acclaimed 1930s critic Otis Ferguson credited the movie with being the first to rate the screwball label — "With *My Man Godfrey* in the middle of 1936, the discovery of the word screwball ... helped build the thesis of an absolutely new style in comedy."[45] One "new" twist for screwball comedy was having the genre's romantic couples acting with the surprising incongruity of personality comedians (*à la* the Marx Brothers), doing comic business formerly assigned to supporting players. And even before *Godfrey*, the screen clowns most often footnoted in early period reviews of groundbreaking screwball comedies were the Marxes. For instance, the *Los Angeles Times'* review of *Twentieth Century* praised this "element of surprise as it has not been maintained since the last Marx Brothers' nonsense."[46]

Regardless, part of *Godfrey's* special status would seem to have a connection to the huge critical and commercial success of the Marxes' 1935 *Opera*, which opened less than a year before *Godfrey*. Despite being repackaged and somewhat homogenized, there was still enough inspired surreal silliness in *Opera* for the Marxes to be quickly recanonized as the kings of crazy. Premiering in late 1935, *Opera's* popularity, and that era's pre-saturation booking tendencies, had the picture playing in many markets well into 1936. Thanks to *Opera*, manic movies seemed to be the wave of the future. Consequently, the late summer launching of the screwy *Godfrey* undoubtedly benefited from this surreal lead-in.

Still, the *Opera-Godfrey* connection went beyond convenient timing. Both movies were co-scripted by the same man, the sometime playwright Morrie Ryskind. He scripted the team's *The Cocoanuts* and *Animal Crackers*, adapting them from the stage plays he had co-authored with Kaufman. And after *Godfrey*, he would return to the team yet again with the screen adaptation of *Room Service* (1938). While one might debate at length just how much influence Ryskind had on the iconoclastic Marxes, there can be little doubt that his insider status with them was an excellent starting point for the penning of a watershed screwball comedy. Plus, *Godfrey* is the most Marx Brothers–like screwball comedy of the 1930s. As the *Variety* reviewer observed, the film's focus family has definite "psychopathic ward tendencies"— a description which would double quite nicely for that Marx family, too![47]

A closing summation for the mad Marxes brings to mind a provocative analogy that writer Jim Knipfel makes in his darkly comic memoir *Quitting the Nairobi Trio*. The title is a reference to comedian Ernie Kovacs' surreal Nairobi Trio sketch, where three characters (in ape masks, trench coats, bowler hats, and gloves) mime a performance of the strange song "Solfeggio." Moving mechanically, one ape conducts, the second plays the piano, and the third uses the conductor's noodle like a drum. Metaphorically, Knipfel sees life as an ongoing series of self-destructive slapstick sketches. The secret for survival is to recognize this fact, and then "Figure out who — or what — was holding the drumsticks over my head early enough so I could dodge them, before they caved in the back of my skull."[48] The beauty of the Marx's *Opera* is that it provides a comic primer for many of life's drumstick moments (from interacting with pompous people, to navigating the slippery slopes of contract legalese), *and* ultimately provides the viewer with an ongoing comedy catharsis. That is, while most of us, warning or no warning, will suffer countless drumstick moments in life (victims of the "Spirit of the Stairway"), we can always savor victory vicariously through the Marxes. They quite literally, to borrow an apt phrase from Alan Alda, gift us with a "poetry of the funny bone."[49]

CHAPTER 10

Charlie Chaplin's *Modern Times* (1936)

> I wondered what would happen to the progress of the mechanical age if one person decided to act like a bull in a china shop ... I decided it would make a good story to take a little man and make him thumb his nose at all recognized rules and conventions.
> — Charlie Chaplin in 1936[1]

This Charlie Chaplin (1889–1977) epiphany for what became *Modern Times* occurred when the comedian drove past "a mass of people coming out of factory ... and was overwhelmed with the knowledge that the theme ... of modern times is mass production."[2] But just as the picture was variously known during the shoot as *The Masses*, *The Factory*, and *Production No. 5* (being Chaplin's fifth feature), there was undoubtedly a series of catalysts in the birth of the story. For example, as a boy the comedian had briefly worked as a printer's assistant and he was terrified of this large machine—"I thought it was going to devour me."[3] Over thirty years later the most metaphorically memorable scene of *Modern Times* has Charlie being swallowed by an enormous machine. Moreover, while the 1936 Chaplin quote which opens the chapter was seminal to the comedian at the time of the picture's release, nearly forty years later he remembered a pivotal 1930s conversation with a *New York World* reporter: "Hearing that I was visiting Detroit, he had told me of the factory-belt system there—a harrowing story of big industry luring healthy young men off the farms who, after four or five years at the belt system, became nervous wrecks."[4]

Ironically, given all these creative sparks for what became *Modern Times*, there were a number of false starts on other projects preceding the production. Following the release of Chaplin's previous film (*City Lights*, 1931), the comedian pondered doing a Napoleon picture as he went on a lengthy triumphant world tour.[5] Though this glorified vacation stretched until mid–1932, with the writing of a book about the tour occupying the rest of the year (*A Comedian Sees the World*, 1933[6]), a Napoleon movie continued to fascinate the comedian. (Chaplin would eventually collaborate with John Strachey on the unproduced 1936 script *Napoleon's Return from St. Helena*.) Like the later

10. Charlie Chaplin's *Modern Times* (1936)   141

Chaplin's Charlie gets swallowed by the *Modern Times* machine.

celebrated director Stanley Kubrick, who also obsessed about doing a Napoleon film, Chaplin would not realize this goal.

Even as Chaplin flirted with a picture about the French emperor, a front page August 1932 *Hollywood Reporter* article stated the comedian would write and direct a serious screen drama — but would not star. The newspaper added that just as Chaplin had written and directed the innovative film drama *A Woman of Paris* (1923, with only a cameo by the comic), he was "anxious to make the 'perfect talking picture' — one which will carry his own ideas of new technique and methods for handling sound with dramatic action."[7] But a year later (August 1933) the comedian's business manager Alf Reeves stated Chaplin soon would begin production on what sounds like the eventual *Modern Times*. Paulette Goddard was to play "a tomboy character in the picture, which will be laid in the lower part of any big city with factories."[8]

Yet in January 1934, another front page *Hollywood Reporter* news item revealed that the comedian had discarded a third potential picture project and presumably returned to *Modern Times*:

> Latest from the Charlie Chaplin front is that the comedian has decided to make his new picture entirely silent, with synchronized music and effects. Chaplin has abandoned the idea of making a talkie in which he would himself play the role of a deaf mute.[9]

Even on the eve of starting the *Modern Times* shoot, which would essentially be a silent film, the comedian had sound movie aspirations:

> Charlie Chaplin has decided to talk and, moreover, he is writing his own dialogue for the production he chooses to call ... "Production No. 5." Charlie has been yelling into microphones ... trying to get his voice to sound like something. He has been under the training of some of the best voice teachers in Hollywood, and now it seems to jell (his voice) and he has decided to talk.[10]

Chaplin's stop-start creative antics between *City Lights* and *Modern Times* were later reflected in the opening of Robert Forsythe's positive *New Masses* review of *Modern Times*: "If you have had fears, prepare to shed them; Charlie Chaplin is on the side of the angels. After years of rumors, charges and counter-charges, reports of censorship and hints of disaster, his new film ... had its [successful] world premiere...."[11] (Forsythe was the pseudonym used by the scholar and sometimes journal editor Kyle Crichton when critiquing for Communist publications like the *New Masses*.) Forsythe/Crichton would go on to credit *Modern Times* as being the "first time an American film was daring to challenge the superiority of an industrial civilization based upon the creed of men who sit at flat-topped desks and press buttons demanding more speed from tortured employees."[12] Though this leftist political praise was not uniformly shared in 1936 (a subject to which the text will return), a better reason to designate *Modern Times* a watershed point in Chaplin's career rests upon two points. This is both the comedian's last silent film and the final appearance of his timeless Tramp, though a semblance of him remains in the Jewish barber of *The Great Dictator* (1940). But when *Modern Times* was released, not even Chaplin, who was letting more and more time pass between production, had decided on the future fate of Charlie. Yet a close, often metaphorical, reading of the movie suggests that there were few or no other options available. This view rests upon three key factors to which Chaplin subjected (however subliminally) the character of Charlie.

First, while peppering his pictures with political topics was not new to Chaplin, the concept of "modern times" had never before intruded so strongly into the Tramp's world; for the first time his ongoing existence seemed threatened by change.[13] As Robert Warshow has suggested, prior to *Modern Times* Charlie and society often were at odds but there seemed to be no real threat to the continued independence of a professional free spirit like the Tramp. But after the early 1930s, changes in society had created a condition that represented an ongoing threat to the individual.[14] Not surprisingly, the machine society of *Modern Times*, as well as the fascist one of *The Great Dictator*, quite literally threaten the life of Chaplin's underdog alter ego.

Modern Times is structured upon the institutionalism of this change in society. As if comically anticipating the later documentary filmmaker Frederick Wiseman's obsession with institutional life, Chaplin's film divides its time among a factory, a large department store, a prison, and a restaurant. In fact, a tongue-in-cheek Otis Ferguson, reviewing the picture for *The New Republic*, suggested it was a feature simply composed of the following short subjects: "*The Shop, The Jailbird, The Watchman,* and *The Singing Waiter.*"¹⁵ Each of the settings, and particularly that of the factory, has a markedly debilitating effect on Charlie.

In the factory, Charlie's job is to tighten nuts on an assembly line — a line whose speed is constantly being increased, as if in reference to the ever-changing clock face over which the opening title (*Modern Times*) is superimposed. Eventually Charlie's enslavement to the assembly line (he misses tightening a nut, and proceeds to go after it) causes his aforementioned cataclysmic swallow by the machine — an industrial age Jonah. As the pivotal early Chaplin biographer Theodore Huff has amusingly put it, "the endless nut tightening finally drives Charlie nuts."¹⁶ Yet this comic breakdown (equipped with two wrenches, he tries to tighten everything in sight, including some provocatively placed buttons on a woman's blouse) represents a defeat over Charlie to which no other living antagonist has ever come close.

Charlie's road to the sanitarium is also assisted by other modern elements in the factory. With large monitors placed in strategic places, Charlie cannot even steal a quick smoke in the washroom without being reprimanded by a big screen boss. This

Modern Times' "endless nut tightening finally drives Charlie nuts."

totalitarian touch from Chaplin was the later inspiration for George Orwell's "Big Brother is watching you" telescreens in the renowned novel *1984*.[17] (As a footnote to Orwell, he was an even bigger fan of Chaplin's *The Great Dictator*, and "he called for the [British] government to subsidize showings of it so it could be seen by poor people who could not afford seats...."[18]) And the Kevin Brownlow documentary *The Tramp and the Dictator* (2004) suggests that it was no accident that the *Modern Times* big screen factory boss (Allan Garcia) resembles Henry Ford — this was a satirical dig at the industrialist who invented the debilitating mass market assembly line.

The Tramp's mental and physical health is further endangered by the boss' desire to increase productivity by slipping workers into an automatic feeding device that will streamline the lunch process. Charlie gets to be the guinea pig for this culinary torture device, which begins to malfunction early in the demonstration, attacking the defenseless Charlie with everything from a renegade ear of corn to a blotter-like mechanical napkin that keeps smacking him in the mouth. Fittingly, for a machine, it even attempts to force-feed him some steel nuts mistakenly placed on his dessert dish. For most period critics, this automatic feeding device going awry was the picture's most popular sketch. For instance, the *New York Evening Journal* reviewer Rose Pelswick observed, "The best of the gags is one in which Chaplin ... is fed by a mechanical food server that goes out of commission with riotous results."[19] But the *London Daily Telegraph*'s Campbell Dixon elevated the routine to cinema pantheon status: "I laughed at this sequence till I cried. If only 200 feet [of movie stock] in all film history could be preserved, this is what I should choose."[20] Moreover, variations of this sketch would later surface in numerous comedies, including Bob Hope and Bing Crosby's *Road to Hong Kong* (1962) and Woody Allen's *Bananas* (1971).

Of course, one cannot leave *Modern Times*' factory setting without noting another influence. The assembly line which drives Charlie nuts was the catalyst for what is arguably Lucille Ball's greatest television sketch. First broadcast in a 1952 episode of *I Love Lucy* (1951–57), the routine in question finds Lucy and small screen close friend Ethel Mertz (Vivian Vance) working on a candy shop conveyor belt wrapping chocolates. Like Charlie's *Modern Times* factory job, where he finally cannot keep up, Lucy and Ethel soon suffer the same comic fate. While they do not succumb to a nervous breakdown (*à la* Charlie), their frantic attempts to handle the surplus candy (from eating the chocolate, to putting it inside their clothing) is consistent with Charlie's quiet comic desperation.

Chaplin's own *Modern Times* assembly line routine is sometimes linked to the conveyor belt comedy of director René Clair's *A Nous la Liberté* (1931). Clair's production company brought a plagiarism suit against Chaplin, though it never came to court. A screening of the brilliant *Liberté* shows little similarity between its satirical examination of factory mechanization and Chaplin's *Modern Times* take on the subject. Clair took no part in the suit. The French artist claimed he had borrowed liberally from Chaplin through the years, and was simply flattered if the creator of Charlie had been inspired by *Liberté*. Chaplin claimed to have never seen Clair's film. Amusingly, Chaplin said that the only assembly line routine that might have impacted him was a brief conveyor belt bit in Walt Disney's short subject Silly Symphony cartoon *Santa's Workshop* (1932).

Following *Modern Times'* brief Charlie sojourn in a sanitarium, and various misadventures around the city, the Tramp finds himself in prison, mistakenly jailed as a violent Communist leader. Once again, Charlie's lifestyle is completely institutionalized, from the matching cells to the mass dinner scene where, row after row, the prisoners sit down at long gray tables. Though nothing occurs here that is quite so metaphorically dramatic as being swallowed by a machine, Chaplin does create a comically inspired cocaine sequence, where a fellow inmate has hidden some "nose powder" in a salt shaker. Naturally, Charlie manages to get under the influence, and his formerly antiheroic inmate is suddenly more than a match for the prison bully. This instant strength and/or drug-induced bravery is reminiscent of Charlie accidentally sitting on a drug needle in *Easy Street* (1917) and abruptly being able to take on a whole street gang. Though his hopped-up *Modern Times* sequence plays as innocuously comic today, it remains a puzzle on how this got by 1930s censors, given that anything to do with drugs was strictly verboten.

More disturbing for students of Charlie, the *Modern Times* Tramp reveals the extent of his institutionalization merely by not wanting to leave the prison, even after he is pardoned. Times must really have changed when a "Tramp" cannot get along in the outside world, especially one who has formerly been so fiercely independent. Yet as the earlier congested city montage of this "modern times" selection suggests, Charlie is no longer up to this type of stress after his factory-induced nervous breakdown. As if to underline this, not long after his release from his security blanket haven in prison, Charlie dines on a huge restaurant feast for which he has no money — in order to return to prison.*

For Chaplin's signature figure to avoid life is not in the spirit of the Charlie of old but rather an old Charlie. The hallmark of his earlier work was the innovative manner in which he *avoided* the law, such as his ability in *The Rink* (1916) to literally "roll" circles around the police. On those occasions when the authorities did catch him, director Chaplin rarely allowed the viewer the sight of Charlie in the lock-up. If anything, prison in a Chaplin film had formerly represented an occasion for a brilliant escape, such as the lively chase of *The Adventurer* (1917), or the lovely irony of clerical disguise in *The Pilgrim* (1923). Significantly, both of these films start *not* with an incarcerated victim but rather with an already escaping Charlie.

One could argue that time had caught up with Charlie, by way of prison, in *City Lights*. Despite not using a lock-up as an escape here, with his release the Tramp had never looked quite so beaten and disheveled — which heightened the pathos of his interaction with the former blind girl at the close (see chapter 1). Regardless, it is a shock to find the *Modern Times* Tramp so enamored of the safety of the penal cell, even one sporting the added bourgeois touch of a Lincoln portrait. True, Charlie does have near free rein here, but that is only because he has single-handedly *stopped* an earlier escape attempt by others — another paradox for Charlie, normally the ally of anything having to do with freedom. But unhappily for the prison-domesticated Charlie, he is pardoned. When he later escapes arrest after the "free" lunch he originally took to return

---

*Red Skelton would later base his annual Freddie the Freeloader Christmas television show on this premise. Freddie, the most popular of The Red Skelton Show *(1951–71) characters, was also inspired by Chaplin's Tramp.*

to prison, it is only because of the childlike intensity of the lovely, coaxing street gamin (Paulette Goddard) he has befriended. But when had Charlie ever needed coaxing to escape before?

The apparent age of the comedy character is another factor at this point. As early as *City Lights*, the Tramp is starting to show signs of age. In *Modern Times*, much of this is minimized by the general lack of close-ups — something film theorist Béla Balázs has claimed was necessary in order that Chaplin avoid any apparent mechanical problems the absence of sound would have implied in dramatic close-up.[21] Still, *Modern Times* presents the viewer with a noticeably older Tramp, and age does not set well with his comedy character.

The ability of any comedy character to age relates directly to the premise on which the character is based. For example, with clowns of childlike innocence, such as Chaplin contemporaries Stan Laurel and Harry Langdon, the aging process is devastating — they literally lose their premise for comedy. Conversely, with figures like Groucho Marx or W.C. Fields, where humor is based upon cynical worldly experience (and more than a touch of the dirty old man), age actually enhances their appeal. They literally grow into this type.

The comedy persona of the Tramp, though hardly based in innocence, still does not age well. Because of Charlie's ability to master almost any task and his ease at taking on other shapes and forms (from posing as a floor lamp in *The Adventurer*, to a mechanical figure in *The Circus*, 1928), Chaplin authors have often seen the magic of Charlie in godlike terms — particularly as Pan, the free-spirited god of the forests in Greek mythology. Robert Payne actually entitled his book on the comedian *The Great God Pan: A Biography of the Tramp Played by Charles Chaplin*.[22] Such comparisons were being made so early in Chaplin's career that they probably caused the rather self-conscious, though charming, dream sequence of *Sunnyside* (1919), where Charlie dances with four lovely wood nymphs in a meadow.

Needless to say, gods do not age. And though nothing in *Modern Times* is quite so shocking as the Lillian Ross photograph of an elderly Chaplin assuming the pose of Pan — the comedian "curls his forefingers alongside the ends of his eyebrows [like horns] and raises a prancing leg, like Pan" (from her brief book, *Moments With Chaplin*[23]), Charlie shows enough age in *Modern Times* to suggest that the saga of the Tramp had best close. Ironically, the later critic-historian Walter Kerr would draw a *Modern Times*–Pan analogy which creates pathos in the most paradoxical of ways — losing one's hold on sanity. After Charlie has been swallowed by the machine, Kerr calls him a "deranged Pan that is the only Pan the twentieth-century can know ... a nervous collapse has set him loose among imagined Elysian Fields...."[24]

Yet another institutional setting in *Modern Times* is that of a multi-storied department store, where Charlie finds work as a night watchman. The store's many showrooms seem to represent a microcosm of "modern times," and as if to accent the ever-accelerating pace of life, Charlie finds it necessary to don roller skates to maintain the speed required for his rounds. This allows Chaplin to both replicate the ballet-like grace he earlier demonstrated on skates in *The Rink* (1916), as well as mix in some Harold Lloyd–like "thrill comedy," where Charlie's blindfolded skating skills brings him close to railing-less precipices.

But just as the Marx Brothers would find that there is nothing simple about even a microcosm (in their own *The Big Store*, 1941), so Charlie would also encounter a problem. His heart would go out to fellow victims of "modern times"—unemployed workers who were robbing the store, workers who were also friends from the factory assembly line days. When authorities discover the robbery at the store's opening the next morning, a "closing" of sorts takes place for Charlie—he is returned to prison. His "meeting" with former factory mates and the resulting trip back to the hoosegow bring his multi-faceted encounter with institutionalism full circle.

The second key factor that serves as a *Modern Times* harbinger of the Tramp's swan song focuses on his relationship with the lovely gamin Goddard (Chaplin's real-life companion and later third wife). Goddard, as Theodore Huff has noted, is "different from both the old, passive Chaplin heroine, and the tempestuous Georgia" of *The Gold Rush* (1925).[25] But whereas Huff drops his Goddard focus after noting her vitality and spontaneity, it is necessary to take this perception of her distinctiveness one step further.

This vitality and spontaneity very much reflect that this is the first and only time we have a Chaplin heroine created in the image of Charlie. The situation is reminiscent of the duel focus narrative found in *The Kid* (1921), where Chaplin's delightfully diminutive co-star and title character (child star Jackie Coogan) is simply a miniature version of Charlie. Inspired by his close relationship with Goddard (with whom he remained friendly even after their divorce—a Chaplin rarity), the comedian also saw the gamin as the catalyst of the whole film. (Goddard was his most gifted leading lady—and the first to sustain an acting career outside the Chaplin milieu.)

Traditionally, Charlie acted as a father figure for his heroines, from his masterly scrubbing of Edna Purviance's face in *The Vagabond* (1916) to his care for the blind girl in *City Lights*. But in *Modern Times* this parental role is most definitely shared, almost as if director Chaplin is acknowledging the new role of women in "modern times." There is no doubting this gamin is often the one who takes care of Charlie—a unique reversal. She does everything from finding them a rickety but serviceable home to getting him a job as a singing waiter. But most importantly, just as Goddard represents an inspiration for Chaplin as director, the gamin works the same magic on the character of the Tramp. For instance, Charlie's love for her is what generates an unheard of development for the "Tramp"—to voluntarily want to settle down! From the point at which they team up, the spirit of the Charlie of old has returned, a true "Artful Dodger," in the semantic sense (to borrow from Charles Dickens, a Chaplin favorite). He again has no need of prisons and regains his former elusiveness during run-ins with the law.

The gamin makes this possible because she is a younger, "streetwise" version of Charlie. Whereas earlier heroines were often several notches above him in social class (especially with Edna Purviance), this gamin has been orphaned into the streets. In addition, Goddard's character takes to this Tramp-like situation with all the physical intensity of a young Charlie (previous heroines were rather restrained in their actions). She shows tenacity in caring for her young siblings, bringing to mind the Tramp's care of Jackie Coogan in *The Kid*, and she brings a grace to her improvisational street dancing that is much like Charlie's quasi-ballet salute to Pan in *Sunnyside*.

Chaplin continues to allow the Tramp some parental action, such as getting the gamin food in the department store cafeteria and tucking her in for the night in the bedding supply section. But she still comes across as more of an equal than any other Chaplin heroine. The comedian seems to accent this by the film's close — the gamin accompanies Charlie down one final road, the first and only time the exit shuffle, his classic film signature, has been shared. Memorably, and another thing which says "finis" here, is that this last joint exit is on a paved road — "modern times" indeed.

The third and final element that seems to signal that *Modern Times* will be the close of Charlie's journey comes in the often derivative nature of the comedy material itself. That is, many of the routines, though brilliantly funny, are close variations of things Chaplin had done before, from the aforementioned homage to *The Rink*, to his assorted problems as a waiter, a comedy situation he had essayed on several earlier occasions, starting with *Caught in a Cabaret* (1914). Of course, one could argue that Chaplin was more prone to the use and/or reuse of established material. The comedian once told his son, Charles Chaplin, Jr., the secret of his cinematic success:

> [T]he gag that is sure to go over is the one where the audience has been tipped off in advance. That's why I like to use old gags. Like the [*Modern Times*] diving scene [where Charlie dives into what appears to be deep water but it is really very shallow] — it's been done so many times everyone is already familiar with what is going to happen. All you have to worry about is your interpretation.[26]

In humor theory this is known as comedy of anticipation.

A certain degree of derivative material, moreover, is to be expected when dealing with what theorist Balázs calls "true personalities of the screen," among whom he lists Chaplin — those stars who do not so much act as play the "same personality" in each film, where the heavy viewer identification is a product of the fact that this "old acquaintance" turns up in each new film.[27] But the often derivative nature of *Modern Times*, despite the time update, seems to go beyond the needs of viewer identification. Balázs' hypothesis asks not for recycled routines but rather recycled spirit — a consistency of attitude in the character as he responds to *new* situations.

There is nothing usual about the problem of derivative material, if, in fact, it *is* a problem. For example, as numerous writers have suggested, the Marx Brothers' movies essentially repeated a variation on the same theme. Yet, it does not detract from the greatness of their specific comedy pattern, though as Woody Allen has noted, it does suggest a failure to grow.[28] Of course, in defense of the Marxes, most pantheon screen comedians (including Allen) repeat variations on a similar theme.

When *Modern Times* came out, however, the derivative nature of the film often met with celebration rather than criticism, because of both the great popularity of Charlie and the rarity with which his films were appearing. It was as if to say an old Charlie was better than no Charlie. For instance, *New York Times* critic Frank S. Nugent closed his glowing review, after chronicling several derivative strands, with: "This morning, there is good news: Chaplin is back again."[29] *The Nation*'s Mark Van Doren observed:

> [T]he audience showed by all the ancient signs that it knew what was coming ... [but] Charlie Chaplin was not disappointing. He was exactly as good as he had ever been before ... which is a way of saying that *Modern Times* is one of the most interesting spectacles to be seen in America today.[30]

Stating it was "the old Chaplin at his best," *Variety* said that Charlie "in anything is b.o. [box office], and in *Modern Times* ... it's box office with a capital B. The picture is grand fun...."[31]

Consistent with such praise, many *Modern Times* reviews reflected the unadulterated hosannas not heard since the release of Chaplin's *City Lights*, five years earlier. Indeed, critiques often footnoted that fact. Thus, the *London Daily Telegraph* said, "Last night ... an audience that included half the film and stage stars of England laughed as I have not heard an audience laugh since ... *The Gold Rush* and *City Lights*."[32] And the *New York World Telegram*'s William Boehnel noted, in a review entitled, "Chaplin Still Supreme in His *Modern Times*": "[L]ast night I saw the funniest motion picture since this same Chaplin produced *City Lights* nearly half a decade ago."[33] As Nugent later wrote in the *New York Times*, after this wave of critical kudos, "The polls are closed, the returns are in and Charlie Chaplin has been re-elected king of the clowns."[34]

Unlike the uniformly rave reviews for *City Lights*, however, *Modern Times* did have a few naysayers—most often addressing the political satire that the aforementioned Robert Forsythe so praised in his *New Masses* critique. Consequently, the *Brooklyn Eagle*'s Winston Burdett felt that Chaplin's "sentimental weakness for the little fellow he has been impersonating all these years got the better of his intentions as a satirist."[35] The *New York Daily Mirror* felt *Modern Times*' "chief weakness seems to lie in Mr. Chaplin's determination to be 'significant' [only to then key upon old-time slapstick] and his having begun the film several years ago at a time when his message was more pertinent."[36] Some critics, like the *New Republic*'s Otis Ferguson, were simply bothered by an old-fashioned comedy being called *Modern Times*.[37] As a Chaplin biographer, John McCabe, observed, "*Modern Times* is simply misnamed. If it had been given the title [critic] Alexander Woollcott used to describe his beloved Tramp, *Charlie As Ever Was*, critical reproaches might have been muted."[38] One should hasten to add that none of this critical quibbling resulted in any *Modern Times* pans.

The closest thing to a pan came not from critics but rather from totalitarian countries, with *Modern Times* being banned in Nazi Germany and Fascist Italy. The official problem, as reported in the German press, was that the picture was "tainted with Soviet propaganda."[39] But there was then a mistaken belief that Chaplin was Jewish, and the persecution of Jews was rapidly escalating in Germany. That this was at the heart of at least the German ban is given greater credence by the fact that an earlier 1930s revival of *The Gold Rush*—in no way a leftist film—was also banned there. And though World War II in Europe was still three years away (1939), German neighbors were sensitive to these actions. For example, Vienna film censors cut the *Modern Times* scene where Charlie picks up a red warning flag that has fallen off a truck and innocently finds himself suddenly leading a parade of Communist radicals.[40]

Still, whereas Chaplin's loyalty to silence in *City Lights* had seemed quite justified because of the early crudeness of Hollywood's transition to sound, which he satirized at the start of the film, many saw the continued silence of *Modern Times* as an anachronism, despite the ongoing praise for its slapstick. Chaplin himself later noted in his autobiography that he approached the next project, what would become *The Great Dictator* (1940), with the "feeling that the art of pantomime was gradually becoming obsolete ... a discouraging thought."[41]

All things considered, therefore, *Modern Times* begins to take on the quality today's recording industry might label "Chaplin's Greatest Hits" (historian Huff calls it a "Chaplin anthology"[42]), a phenomenon that does not traditionally appear until the close of an artist's career. Chaplin seems to accent this finale quality by the one *new* element he brought to the film — allowing Charlie to speak briefly for the first and only time. The speech is actually a delightful gibberish song, "a sort of Katzenjammer French," whose nonsense lyrics he improvises after losing the originals.[43] Thus, director Chaplin creates a lovely device with which to preserve the formerly silent universality of Charlie's character: The Tramp is given his own language. Chaplin had, however, put himself into a corner.

What kind of sound encore could he do? Gibberish would hardly work on an expanded scale, yet limiting himself to merely one language would immediately destroy the air of universality. There was also the problem that the Tramp would be speaking with an English accent, hardly the stuff of an everyman universality. Consequently, to preserve the uniqueness of Charlie, retirement was the only real option. Chaplin did flirt with a *Modern Times* close that copied the pathos-driven unrequited love conclusion of *City Lights*: After being separated late in the former film, Charlie returns to find that the gamin has become a nun. But more happily for a *Modern Times* tale that wraps

The lovely gamin (Paulette Goddard) writes the song lyrics on Charlie's cuff in *Modern Times*.

up the saga of the Tramp, Chaplin decided to let Charlie make his final exit with a lovely companion.

The preceding observations *now* seem to "document" *Modern Times* as a logical close to the celebrated career of cinema's most iconic figure. Chaplin would go on to create a number of other film characters, often with Tramp-like qualities (including the Bluebeard Monsieur Verdoux), but Charlie now belonged to the ages.

CHAPTER 11

Laurel and Hardy's *Way Out West* (1937)

> SHARON LYNNE: "Is it true he's dead?"
> LAUREL: "Well, we hope he is — they buried him!"
> — From *Way Out West*

As early as 1931, Depression America's unofficial spokesman for the common man, Will Rogers, would call Laurel and Hardy Hollywood's "best team of comedians" and the "favorites with all us movie folks, as well as the audiences...."[1] Rogers' remarks anticipate a later axiom about the duo, "Nobody likes Laurel and Hardy ... except the people." As film historian Leonard Maltin once wrote, "Chaplin commanded more attention, Keaton inspired a sense of awe and wonderment, but it's doubtful that anyone ever generated more laughter, or more love, than Laurel & Hardy."[2] While this book's examination of *Way Out West* and *Sons of the Desert* (1933, see chapter 5) suggests that period reviewers should be given more credit for acknowledging the artistry of the team, Laurel and Hardy's propensity for a magnified slice-of-life comedy undoubtedly minimized critical attention. For instance, the British documentary filmmaker and sometimes critic Basil Wright stated in a 1937 article on the team: "Whether or not they are to be listed with the great clowns depends on your affections. Maybe they are too near your personal heart. Their troubles are your troubles— magnified to the stars."[3] But later in Wright's essay he would become more defensive about Laurel and Hardy as comedians of the common man:

> Maybe you don't find them funny? Then you are my enemy, and I hope you will many times be forced to sit through a Laurel and Hardy feature film, tortured by the unceasing laughter of an audience of ordinary people who realize, if only subconsciously, that they are looking at a film which sums up more simply than any philosophical treatise the need for laughter....[4]

Two years prior to Wright's article, another prominent British documentary filmmaker and occasional critic, John Grierson, had written of this Laurel and Hardy everyman quality in a more succinct but no less eloquent manner: "They are perhaps the Civil Servants of comedy."[5] How fitting that a duo whose work so often begins with a people-orientated theater-of-the-real catalyst had two such articulate *documentary* champions.

Ironically, however, some of the period kudos for *Way Out West* (which rivaled the notices for their greatest film, *Sons of the Desert*) were driven by atypical developments, such as a Western parody framework which eschews many of their signature situations. Why would this generate greater critical hosannas? For the same reason that spoofing their tough guy images won Academy Awards for Humphrey Bogart, John Wayne, and Lee Marvin. It shows a self-referential sense of humor. Now, while *Way Out West* does not get too radical, such as Laurel roughing up Hardy, or the duo joining the Indians, a greater movie awareness is at work here. For example, early in the film Hardy loses several articles of clothing and repairs to another room to get dressed. Through the magic of movies he is back much too soon. Laurel immediately asks, "How'd you get dressed so quick?" Hardy's knowing parody reply: "None of your business!"

Regardless, *Way Out West* is a very funny movie. And since America's most archetypal genre is the Western, most major comedians eventually do a cowboy spoof, from Buster Keaton's *Go West* (1925), to Owen Wilson and Jackie Chan's *Shanghai Noon* (2000). In-between examples, besides Laurel and Hardy's spoof, would include W.C. Fields and Mae West's *My Little Chickadee* (1940), the Marx Brothers' *Go West* (1940), Abbott and Costello's *The Wistful Widow of Wagon Gap* (1947), Martin and Lewis' *Pardners* (1956), and the Steve Martin, Chevy Chase, Martin Short collaboration *1Three Amigos!* (1986). Plus, Bob Hope practically turned Western parody into his own special domain with *The Paleface* (1948), *Fancy Pants* (1950), *Son of Paleface* (1952), and *Alias Jesse James* (1959).

The first rule of parody is to be amusing even without viewer expertise on the subject (in this case, Westerns) under affectionate comic attack.[6] Thus, *Way Out West* opens with its most fundamentally funny contrast — placing comic antiheroes Laurel and Hardy in macho sagebrush land. Moreover, the team avoids the standard spoofing shtick of dressing as cowboys and assuming colorful Western names, such as Mae West's Flower Belle Lee in *My Little Chickadee*. Instead, there is a refreshingly goofy charm to the duo still answering to Stanley and Ollie and appearing in garb similar to what they might wear in a non-period picture, including the all-important derbies. *Variety*'s review made special note of this: "They wear their usual costumes, despite the cowboy-western surroundings."[7] They further accent this visual oddity, "Laurel and Hardy out West," by essentially acting like Stanley and Ollie, notwithstanding the occasional elements of movie awareness. Consequently, it is as if they have just exited a comedy time machine and are doing parody fieldwork.

In otherwise keeping to a broadly Western terrain familiar to most viewers, *Way Out West* is more of an integrated feature than is often the Laurel and Hardy norm.[8] The comedy duo find themselves heading to Brushwood Gulch to deliver a gold mine title to the now-orphaned Mary Roberts (Rosina Lawrence), so virtuously portrayed as to be a send-up of the genre's traditionally overly sweet heroine. Like Mark Twain's own Western spoof, *Roughing It* (1872), Stanley and Ollie find plenty of painfully comic diversions along the way, from hitching a stagecoach ride to confronting the traditional crooked saloon owner bearing a fitting name — Mickey Finn (played by longtime team nemesis James Finlayson). Naturally, good triumphs in the end, though true to comic antihero form, Laurel and Hardy's lives never become any easier.

In Laurel and Hardy's *Way Out West* misadventure, they give the gold mine deed to the wrong person (Sharon Lynne), a con orchestrated by James Finlayson (at right).

The film begins with Ollie being victimized by a sinkhole in a shallow stream, while Stanley safely and obliviously walks across. As regular as old-fashioned reel changes, Hardy takes another "bath" in the stream at the movie's mid-point, as well as its conclusion. This sinkhole symmetry makes the repetition work. For those interested in comic genealogy, Laurel and Hardy style, the sinkhole is no doubt the forefather of all those wonderful bottomless mud puddles that often turn up in the team's modern-setting films.

Another basic parody component is the compounding phenomenon. Although a spoof usually has a focus genre to derail, it often includes eclectic references to other structures or texts. An inspired *Way Out West* example of compounding occurs when Laurel needs to stop a stagecoach. Playing upon the phenomenal success and viewer recognition of director Frank Capra's acclaimed *It Happened One Night* (1934), Laurel borrows from the conclusion of that film's classic hitchhiking scene. In *Night*, Clark Gable has exhausted his supply of hitchhiking hand gestures and the lovely Claudette Colbert offers to give him a "hand," or more precisely, a leg. She pulls up her skirt to expose one of the beautiful limbs for which she was famous on Broadway. Naturally, a car immediately screeches to a halt, with an editing cut to a braking tire for added comedy effect. In *Way Out West*, Stanley and Ollie also find themselves hitchhiking, and when it looks like the stagecoach is going to pass them by, Laurel, in the spirit of Colbert, pulls up a pants leg and — amazingly — stops the coach. Ever conscious of details, there is also a cut to the braking stagecoach wheel.

Though without the comedy buildup of *Night* (Gable initially both fails at numerous hitchhiking techniques and pooh-poohs novice Colbert's offer of assistance), Stanley's exposure of a less-than-lovely limb works for five funny reasons. First, it is a parody of the earlier film and the comedy contrast of a Colbert limb and Stan's. Second, it is parody of sexuality in general; this is not something a man would normally do. (Thus, one does not have to be in on the specific parody reference to find it amusing.) Third, it is also, in part, a takeoff on Laurel's screen character, since any sexual awareness (regardless of gender) invariably seems alien to him — this would normally be the action of a more worldly character. Fourth, Stanley's feminine action (exposing his leg) is, however, comically consistent with the couple-like nature so often associated with the team, where the bossy Ollie is sometimes seen as the "man" and the often submissive Stanley (including his signature crying shtick) is the stereotypical "woman." Fifth, Laurel's success at stopping the coach is a comic affront to Ollie not unlike the one Colbert administered to Gable. An ongoing Laurel and Hardy premise has always been that despite the general comic incompetence of both their screen characters, the seemingly more-dense Stanley frequently betters his partner. (As with Ollie's movie awareness in the aforementioned quick change scene, Stanley's ability to activate this *Night*-like sequence suggests a character cognizance on his part in keeping with parody's self-conscious nature.)

Being true to their antiheroic norm, Laurel and Hardy are initially tricked into giving the gold mine deed to the wrong person — the sexy saloon wife of James Finlayson, Lola Marcel (Sharon Lynne). The team's subsequent attempt to get said document back triggers the movie's funniest and most creatively sustained comic scene — a mix of both broad physical comedy and a parody of the traditional seduction scene.

Confronting the crooked couple in their living quarters above the saloon, Laurel and Hardy are soon involved in what film historian John McCabe has entertainingly described as "a four-part roundelay of grabbing, snatching, losing, regaining, again losing, and once more regaining ... battle with the Finns for the deed."[9] Like a neighborhood football match, the document is hiked, passed, and fumbled into several four-way pile-ups on the floor, with the deed causing nonstop comedy chaos. When every amusing maneuver has been exhausted here, including windy Ollie's ability to blow the deed away from the outstretched hands of the prostrate Finns, phase two of this comic battle royal kicks in.

With the document-possessing Stanley retreating to a bedroom, sexy Lola follows him in and locks the door. Like a frightened little boy, he hides the deed inside his shirt and prepares for the worst. Lola sheds her fur wrap and slowly comes toward Stanley, her provocatively tight-fitting gown suggesting a comic reversal of the traditional male-instigated sex scene. Given the utter innocence of Laurel's persona, it is the perfect situation for a parody seduction, especially with Lola having a story-related reason to get inside his clothing. While mock rapes of Stanley date from as early as the Leo McCarey–supervised *Putting Pants on Philip* (1927), this particular rendition is the most effective for three reasons. First, Laurel had never before been teamed with such an

The football-like pile-up to get the *Way Out West* deed, with (top to bottom) James Finlayson, Sharon Lynne, Stan Laurel, and Oliver Hardy.

attractive antagonist. Second, consistent with the parody status of *Way Out West*, this particular seduction spoof is played more broadly than earlier examples, with the duo rolling around on the bed, under the bed, and all about the room. Third, the sequence is further bolstered by adding another wonderful bit of Laurel shtick — uncontrollable laughter.

Lola's attempts to get the deed have quite literally tickled Stanley. Once she realizes how susceptible to tickling he is, she makes this her primary mode of attack. The scene's segue to laughter is a perfect transition, since the sexual innuendo can only go so far, and being tickled by roving fingers is actually quite believable. But Laurel manages to further stamp the sequence with brilliance ... by drawing out the laughter. As often happens on these rare, wonderful laughter jags — everything strikes one as funny, no matter how inappropriate. Consequently, when Lola finally gets the document from him, he laughs harder. When Hardy soon steals it back and leads the Finns on a merry chase around the adjacent room, it is even funnier to Stanley. And he is so intoxicated by laughter that when Ollie does a deed hand-off, Stanley purposely puts it back down his front — he wants *more* tickling. As Lola goes back to work on him, he ultimately provides the perfect scene topper — voluntarily giving up the document because the laughter has pushed him to the comic — "I can't stand it!" — breaking point. The beauty of the sequence, despite the parody and the exaggeration, is that the tickling-laughter component goes back to that one-foot-in-reality premise that their mentor McCarey had mapped out for the team in the beginning (see chapter 5).

11. Laurel and Hardy's *Way Out West* (1937)

With the phenomenal mid–1930s popularity of Gene Autry, "B" Westerns were soon full of singing cowboys, from Autry's own Republic Studio also developing Roy Rogers, to Warner Brothers showcasing the underrated Dick Foran. This unusual sagebrush development undoubtedly fueled the two musical parody numbers in *Way Out West*. The first one finds Laurel and Hardy in front of Mickey Finn's Palace (saloon). Some seated cowboys (Chill Wills and the Avalon Boys) are singing the old Western song "At the Ball, That's All." This is the catalyst for Stanley and Ollie to suddenly go into their own eccentric dance routine. While there is nothing remotely Western about it (and therein lies part of the parody), it is a charming display of their joint physical grace, and a polite appreciation of the entertainment values of this new — for them — setting. (The scene is marred only by having an obviously false rear projection backdrop of a Western street.)

The team's second musical number occurs later in the saloon. A single cowboy is singing "The Trail of the Lonesome Pine," and Laurel and Hardy pleasantly join in, harmonizing most effectively. But just as one thinks no parody will surface, Stanley's voice comically switches to a deep bass (Chill Wills). The team's smooth harmonizing broken, a disgruntled Ollie stops singing and pantomimes to the bartender that he wants the keg-tapping mallet. Once supplied, he smacks Stanley on the noodle. However, instead of stifling his suddenly bass companion, Laurel's singing voice now switches

In order to recover the *Way Out West* deed, sexy Sharon Lynne resorts to tickling Stan Laurel.

An informal moment on the *Way Out West* set, with Laurel and Hardy and their mule Dinah.

to a woman's falsetto (Rosina Lawrence). A bemused Hardy does not know what to make of this — but he ultimately gets satisfaction when Stanley passes out at the end of the number! The routine is a good example of what realist film theorist Siegfried Kracauer referred to as creating comedy by way of "speech undermined from within," which encourages the viewer to focus upon the more important visual nature of the medium.[10] Laurel and Hardy's sideswiping of one's verbal expectation in this scene from *Way Out West* might be likened to Charlie Chaplin's use of distorted sound for the public speakers at the beginning of *City Lights* (1931), a sequence much admired by Kracauer. A final footnote to Laurel and Hardy's rendition of "The Trail of the Lonesome Pine" is that it became a hit record ... in 1975. Released as a novelty number in Great Britain, Stanley and Ollie's single went to number two on the pop charts!

Way Out West's lengthy parody wrap-up finds Laurel and Hardy bungling their way to a deed-possessing happy ending by breaking into the saloon during the middle of the night. Trying to rob a safe might be a typical Western plot point, but there is never anything typical about Stanley and Ollie. The funniest single gag in this lengthy misadventure involves a block and tackle system the boys have worked out to hoist Hardy, with the help of their trusty mule Dinah (the smartest member of the trio), to the saloon's second floor. With a hardworking Laurel methodically pulling Hardy up, they are on the verge of success when Stanley suddenly states, "Wait until I spit on my hands." Ollie's expression morphs from acknowledgment to realization of just what that means — Laurel letting go of the rope. And the comic force of Hardy's fall is effectively milked visually by having his body make an indentation in the ground. Based upon my numerous class screenings of the film, this fall often generates the single biggest laugh from audiences.

Other comic developments will range from a second block and tackle miscue (resulting in a suddenly airborne Dinah the donkey), to Laurel and Hardy hiding in a piano and Finlayson *playing* them into submission. There is even a touch of what appears to be borrowed McCarey material. In the director's earlier Marx Brothers movie *Duck Soup* (1933, see chapter 4), Chico and Harpo have also broken into a residence with designs on the safe. Chico begins to ascend a staircase, just after reminding his mad mute brother about the need for quiet. Harpo then proceeds to reset a clock (triggering chimes), accidentally activates a music box–like figurine, and innocently begins playing some piano wire — harp-style. Chico is, with good reason, beside himself. Along similar lines in the later *Way Out West*, the quiet-conscious Hardy is halfway up the saloon staircase when Laurel randomly decides to play a slot machine ... and naturally wins — resulting in the loud cascading sound of coins. Nominal leader Hardy is less than pleased.

This prolonged breaking-and-entering sequence also includes a brief throwaway scene that is seldom noted in commentaries about the picture but which brilliantly showcases both Laurel's visual comedy and his economy in storytelling. Stanley and Ollie's noisy antics have awakened Mary Roberts, for whom the gold mine is intended. (Like a comedy Cinderella, she has become a working ward of the Finns.) Naturally, she demands an explanation as to what Laurel and Hardy are doing in the saloon at that hour. To keep the sound down, Stanley takes her into the saloon's meat locker to explain. Thanks to the standard window in the cooler door, the viewer has the pleasure of watching Laurel pantomime the team's whole comedy of errors concerning the deed. This is an entertainingly inventive way to fulfill a plot necessity (briefing Mary), without boring the viewer with a simple verbal rehash. Plus, Stanley's abbreviated mime almost comically reinvents the material, while still allowing one to savor the high points, such as the tickling escapade with sexy Lola.

Though *Way Out West* does not recycle any specific Laurel and Hardy routines, as with all personality comedians, certain comedy patterns do reoccur. One such example involves Stanley eating Ollie's hat. Laurel's goat-like dining habits frequently surface in the team's films, such as his propensity to eat wax fruit in *Sons of the Desert* (see chapter 5). But whereas Charlie Chaplin eats a boot out of necessity in *The Gold Rush* (1925), and Harpo Marx's surreal other-worldliness has him downing buttons and nibbling on a telephone in *The Cocoanuts* (1929), Laurel normally eats the odd item because of inspired stupidity. However, in *Way Out West*, the hat is forced on Laurel as a self-prescribed punishment. Stanley had earlier stated that if they did not retrieve the deed, he would eat Ollie's derby. Since that had not yet happened, the always parental Hardy was teaching him a lesson.

While this begins as a penalty, with Laurel's first derby bite being hard to force down, the blockhead factor quickly kicks in, and Stanley is soon happily munching away. Moreover, he even pulls out a handkerchief to use as a napkin for his neck, and fishes a salt shaker from another pocket to season this seemingly delectable derby. During these goofy developments, Hardy gives the viewer one of his patented direct address looks, as if to say, "Can you believe this guy?" But eventually Ollie is curious and he decides to try a bite himself, with comically obvious results — he has to spit it out. Like Chaplin's boot-eating companion from *The Gold Rush* (Mack Swain), Hardy finds articles of clothing less than appetizing. (Interestingly, in the Marx Brothers milieu, Groucho and Chico are never tempted to try the other-worldly eating habits of their surreal sibling, Harpo. This further accents the unique difference of Harpo.)

Unfortunately, there is one reoccurring *Way Out West* gag which plays as inconsistent for Laurel's character — by snapping his finger, he can turn his thumb into a lighter. Since McCarey teamed and molded Laurel and Hardy in the late 1920s, the foundation of their comedy has always been one foot in reality. McCarey would later write about this as "The Could-Be Quality."[11] In a 1937 joint interview, shortly after *Way Out West* was released, the team was still in agreement about that connection to reality. The duo discussed their efforts to find a reasonable story explanation on why the Brushwood Gulch sheriff had it in for them (the duo innocently flirted with his wife on the stagecoach into town). Hardy even makes a blanket statement about comic reality which is a bit ironic, given the aforementioned hat-eating scene: "Nothing is funny unless people can believe it could have happened. That's why impossible things like a comedian coming along and eating doorknobs isn't funny. Nobody eats doorknobs."[12]

Regardless, while Stanley's flaming thumb is undoubtedly funny for some, it is inconsistent with the delightfully dumb persona of Laurel. If he really had such magical skills, there is no reason for his comic suffering through all the team's problems; Stanley could solve everything with just a little hocus-pocus. Such power both undercuts Laurel's normally wonderful incompetency and breaks the duo's "could-be" foundation. In contrast, such a fantasy characteristic would be perfectly in keeping with the mischievous Pan-like persona of Stanley's contemporary Harpo, whose surrealistic antics, not to mention his surrealistic pockets, frequently seem other-worldly.

One might better demonstrate the more typical difference between Harpo and Laurel's screen characters by contrasting the manner in which they respond to the same comedy set-up. In *Horse Feathers* (1932) Groucho admonishes Harpo: "Young man, you'll find as you grow older you can't burn the candle at both ends." But Harpo triumphs by then producing a candle doing just that — one of the most amusing examples of the pocket wizardry that is the mad mute's ongoing wardrobe. In *Them Thar Hills* (1934) the gifted Laurel and Hardy regular Billy Gilbert tells Stanley: "You can't burn a candle at both ends." Laurel replies, "We don't. We burn electric lights." In each case the response is consistent with the viewer's comedy expectations for the character — the other-worldly sorcery of Harpo, and the inspired stupidity of Stanley.

Denying Laurel this bit of magic might be comedic blasphemy to some. One could conceivably link it to his screen persona by arguing, "Stan is so dumb he doesn't even know one can't do that." Coupled to this is the added explanation: Ollie fails and/or quickly withdraws from such magic because he knows it should not work. That is, after repeated *Way Out West* attempts, Hardy finally lights up his *own* thumb with a snap of his fingers ... and promptly scares himself into "magic" retirement. (In the Marx Brothers world, Groucho and Chico seldom emulate Harpo, just as they avoid his odd "food" choices.) But having both Laurel and Hardy sport flaming thumbs just adds to the consistency problems, since it chafes at the perimeters of their personae, and violates the realism premise they forever embrace when comedy theory is the subject. (The team's most thorough period take on "could happen" comedy was a Laurel interview he gave to Britain's *Film Weekly* in 1935.[13])

I am also reminded of a comment made by director and film comedy guru Frank Capra on the "integrity of characterization." In the filmmaker's autobiography he writes about his frustration over collaborating with comedian Harry Langdon and director Harry Edwards on the orchestration of Langdon's screen persona: "It was amazing to me that neither Langdon nor Edwards really understood, or took seriously, this integrity of characterization — which made Langdon what he was. A funny gag was a funny gag to them, whether in character or not."[14]

Of course, Langdon's later deviation from that path led to his downfall as a major film comedian, while Capra became one of cinema's most celebrated auteurs, with classic pictures in several comedy genres: *It Happened One Night* (1934, screwball comedy), *Arsenic and Old Lace* (1944, dark comedy), and assorted populist pictures — *Mr. Deeds Goes to Town* (1936), *Mr. Smith Goes to Washington* (1939), *Meet John Doe* (1941), and *It's a Wonderful Life* (1946). Paradoxically, Langdon's original Capra-constructed character would anticipate much about the McCarey-molded Laurel. Along related lines, Langdon would later take co-writing credits on several Laurel and Hardy films, as well as play a supporting player in a Hardy solo outing, *Zenobia* (1939).

Flaming thumb or no flaming thumb, *Way Out West* was a hit with critics and the public. Several reviewers even felt compelled to document audience responses of comedy catharsis proportions. *New York Daily News* critic Dorothy Masters observed, "If the floorboards hold out under standing-room-only weight and the rafters survive the Vesuvius-rivaling bellows of audience lung power, you'll be privileged to share in hilarity at the Rialto [theatre]...."[15] Her review was even entitled, "Laurel-Hardy Comedy Jeopardizes Theatre." *New York Post* critic Archer Winsten's praise of the picture was grounded in a single audience member case study:

> Near where I was sitting a child got completely out of control when Stan Laurel stole some meat that had been rejected by a bar customer as "tougher than shoe leather" and mended the hole in his shoe with it.... I noticed that the [comically] hysterical abandon was hereditary. Papa had it, too.[16]

Again, the review's telling title said it all: "Laurel and Hardy Panic Rialto With Their Act." Ironically, Winsten was not really a Laurel and Hardy fan. But he had the honesty to chronicle their comedians-of-the-people status, and the insight to recognize its significance: "You can't pass off that sort of thing [a spontaneous audience response] lightly even if you fail to share the merriment."[17]

Most period critics, however, expressed no such personal reservations. Indeed, several of them used *Way Out West* as a happy excuse to reaffirm the importance of old-fashioned physical comedy. No one wrote more eloquently along these lines than the *New York Times* reviewer Frank S. Nugent, who would later script several of director John Ford's most honored Westerns, such as *The Searchers* (1956). Nugent opened his *Way Out West* critique with this poetic play upon words: "Too many books are being written on the anatomy of humor and none on the humor of anatomy."[18] Playing upon Laurel and Hardy's Western setting, *New York World Telegram* critic William Boehnel called the duo "the last frontier" of low comedy, which "may not be as slick and smart as its more refined counterpart but it is usually eminently more enjoyable and certainly more eternal."[19] But the *London Times* waxed the most poetic, likening their brief feature (65 minutes) to a short story, and movingly describing the loss to cinema if even the team's less memorable padded-for-length features should stop:

> They are always amusing in a film equivalent to the short story.... But even if [their] directors persist in a mistaken policy of turning good short stories into disappointing long ones it will be a sad moment if ever the hardy laurels should wither.[20]

The idea for the team's parody Western is often attributed to Laurel's wife Ruth, though the couple would separate before production began on the picture. Whether the story idea is hers or not, parody is something Laurel had frequently done in his pre–Hardy days, such as his short subject spoof of Rudolph Valentino's *Blood and Sand* (1922) called *Mud and Sand* (1922), with the comedian playing Rudolph Vaselino! Given this background, the success of *Way Out West*, and the fact that Laurel had taken a rare producer credit on the film, might have led one to expect more parodies from the team. They could have even revisited the West, since the duo had only skimmed the sagebrush surface. (For instance, their original *Way Out West* script had an Indian finale which was entirely dropped.[21]) Moreover, Hardy's propensity for direct address (looking at the camera when Laurel exasperated him) was a spoof-like action, since it drew attention to the filmmaking process, as did parody. But a new Laurel contract arrangement with Roach took the team in a different direction. One could long speculate on the course Laurel and Hardy's career might have taken, if they had had the autonomy of Charlie Chaplin.

At its most basic level, Laurel and Hardy's heritage is linked to the physical and/or psychological differences which define all great teams. As *New Yorker* critic John Lahr, son of famed comedian Bert Lahr, poetically observed, "Light needs shadow to intensify its brilliance, and so it is with comics, which is why ... the [rotund] blowhard Oliver Hardy was partnered by the [thin] milquetoast Stan Laurel."[22] But Laurel and Hardy's legacy is also tied to the groundbreaking evolution of the comic antihero, which was examined at length in chapter 5, with Hardy hardly being so domineering to the rest of the world. Though the team's antiheroic nature is probably most effectively showcased in a modern setting like *Sons of the Desert*, the duo are 100 percent antiheroic, whatever the time or place. But part of the team's special link to the common person, beyond the all-important believability factor, is something noted by *Village Voice* critic William Paul: "Few other comedians can so effectively convey the joy of immediate experience, and this is ultimately what L & H comedy is about."[23] In *Way Out West*, this "immediate experience" joy might best be linked to their spontaneous soft-shoe number in front of the saloon, or Laurel's loving-it tickle scene. But whatever sequence one chooses, the ultimate gift of Laurel and Hardy is transferring that "immediate experience" joy to the viewer.

CHAPTER 12

Bob Hope's
The Cat and the Canary (1939)

> When another *Cat and the Canary* character asks Bob Hope if big, empty houses scare him, the comedian replies, "Not me, I used to be in vaudeville." But later he confesses, "I'm so scared even my goose pimples have goose pimples."

Fittingly, for a comedian whose focus film in this study, *The Cat and the Canary* (1939), came out at the end of the decade, Bob Hope's (1903–2003) career belonged to the future more than anyone else featured in this text. Moreover, with the exception of Charlie Chaplin, Hope is also the only one highlighted herein that would undoubtedly have listed a decade other than the 1930s as his screen heyday. But that should in no way detract from the uniqueness of *Canary*, which as Hope himself later wrote, "was the turning point for my movie career."[1] Prior to this, he had been largely relegated to "B" films. In his first comic memoir, *They Got Me Covered* (1941), the comedian stated, "I [had] made so many 'B' pictures I began to get fan mail from hornets ... and for me that was an improvement."[2]

By the late 1930s Hope had created a comedy character which could fluctuate between the most cowardly incompetent of comic antiheroes and the cool, egotistical, womanizing wise guy. This was a breakthrough development in the world of personality comedians, with numerous screen clowns (such as Red Skelton and Danny Kaye) soon emulating him. But Hope was the unquestionable master, whether in his later "Road" pictures with Bing Crosby, or spoofing film noir detectives in the classic *My Favorite Brunette* (1947). Sometimes Hope's comic verbal duality was simply in the mix of a cocky breezy delivery ... derailed at the close. For example, *Brunette* includes the following Hope parody of noir tough guy voice-over narration: "You see, I wanted to be a detective, too. It only took brains, courage, and a gun. And I had the gun."

If all this sounds very familiar, Woody Allen, the greatest film comedy auteur of the modern era (post–1960), has affectionately highjacked the Hope dual personality. This is something Allen freely admits, especially in his moving cinematic tribute to Hope, *My Favorite Comedian*, which was part of the 1979 New York Film Festival. Allen has confessed:

There are certain moments in his older movies when I think he's the best thing I have ever seen. It's everything I can do at times not to imitate him. It's hard to tell when I do, because I'm so unlike him physically and in tone of voice but once you know I do it, it's absolutely unmistakable.[3]

Allen's Hope-like duality is probably best showcased in *Love and Death* (1975), especially when he attempts to put on a brave front shortly before his execution. Woody starts out tough but quickly reverts to a cowardly antihero: "Yea, though I walk through the Valley of the Shadow of Death — or on second thought, even better, though I run through the Valley of the Shadow of Death — that way I'll get out quicker."

Allen's films are also rich with Hope-like cracks which smack of the older comedian's breezy casualness, such as an often noted Woody comment from his science fiction parody *Sleeper* (1973). An evil leader had been killed, but the government is prepared to clone him back into existence by way of surviving nose. Allen's assignment is to get said nose and destroy it. As the comedian bluffs his way into the medical facility, his banter includes a typical Hope-ism — "We're here to see the nose. We hear it's running." Allen's modern age aping of Hope also allows an audience to appreciate how the often woman-obsessed ski-nose might have sounded in a less-censored era. For instance, when Woody's *Love and Death* character is told sex without love is an empty experience, he responds, "Yes, but as empty experiences go, it's one of the best."

Hope's persona had been honed, in part, on his popular *Pepsodent* radio show, which had gone on the air in the fall of 1938. By the following season the comedian's ratings had even passed those of his friend and soon to be co-star Bing Crosby. (Hope only trailed radio giants Charlie McCarthy & Edgar Bergen, Jack Benny, and Fibber McGee & Molly.[4]) But Hope's strong numbers in his inaugural season were the catalyst for the comic's parent studio (Paramount) to bump him up to the "A" picture bracket with *Canary*. And just as Allen had hero-worshipped Hope, the making of *Canary* enabled Hope to meet the comedian he most admired — Charlie Chaplin, the husband of his co-star, Paulette Goddard. After telling Chaplin how much he revered *Modern Times* (1936, see chapter 10) and enjoyed working with Paulette, Hope received the *Canary* "review" he would always most cherish: "Young man," Chaplin said, "I've been watching the rushes of *The Cat and the Canary* every night. I want you to know that you are one of the best timers of comedy I have ever seen."[5] For a young man (Hope) who started his show business career by doing impersonations of Chaplin's Tramp, it does not get any better than that.

While Hope's later film career would be peppered with numerous broad parodies, from the aforementioned *My Favorite Brunette*, to Western spoofs like *The Paleface* (1948) and *Son of Paleface* (1952), *Canary* is a reaffirmation parody.[6] As noted with Mae West's *She Done Him Wrong* (1933, see chapter 3), this approach to spoofing maintains enough of the traditional genre values under comic attack as to often not even be perceived as parody. That is, *Canary* represents a standard haunted house tale, complete with murder victim, sliding panels, secret passages, a creepy housekeeper, and a will being read at midnight. In fact, earlier adaptations of the play, both on stage and in the movies, were presented as straight murder mysteries — what might be called a prototype for all "old dark house" thrillers. When Paramount bought the property from the studio most synonymous with the horror genre (Universal), they decided to comically open it up with a wisecracking Hope. But he is a funny fellow in what is still a scary movie, at least for period audiences. This reaffirmation approach makes for an entertaining tension between genre expectations (in this case, a thriller — to be frightened) and a spoof that is funny without defusing the scary scenario.

Variety hinted at this more ambitious parody duality when it said Hope "carries a straight dramatic characterization, with comedy quips and situations dropping into the plot naturally to accentuate the laugh...."[7] Moreover, while no one missed the inspired addition of the comically coward Hope, many critics still focused on the story's scare factor. For instance, the opening comments of the *New York Daily Worker*'s Howard Rushmore promised "as many goose pimples as its predecessors."[8] *New York Daily Mirror* reviewer Robert Coleman began his critique by crediting director Elliott Nugent for including "all of the thrills that marked the play and added a few for good measure. The result is as exciting as reading ghost stories by candlelight near midnight on Halloween."[9] And the *New York Journal American*'s Rose Pelswick called *Canary* "a mystery thriller done with a sense of humor."[10]

Besides gifting audiences with a more entertainingly complex comedy, *Canary*'s reaffirmation parody approach works on several additional levels. First, Paramount scored points for being innovative. *New York Daily News* critic Kate Cameron praised *Canary*'s something-old-is-new-again duality, after an opening to her review that sounds amazingly contemporary: "Hollywood has gone in for remakes on a large scale during

Bob Hope and Paulette Goddard in front of *The Cat and the Canary*'s "old dark house."

the last year, and has taken a verbal trouncing from most of the critics and patrons for trying to disguise old stuff under new and false labels."[11]

Second, by keeping the *Canary* focus on thrills and chills, there is less pressure on Hope to carry the picture, as would have been the case if this had been a broad "we're not taking the plot seriously" parody. Third, the scary framework also gives viewers another reason to identify with Hope (beyond being a good-looking funnyman). Frightened ourselves, we relate to his easy admissions of fear, just as we admire that equally easy wit. Thus, when the spooky, medium-like housekeeper (Gale Sounstrgaard) tells Hope there are spirits all around him, he replies, "Well, could you put some in a glass with a little ice? I need it badly."

Fourth, the duality inherent to *Canary*'s reaffirmation parody also complements the two-part nature of Hope's new groundbreaking comedy character. To illustrate, the comedian's quick character fluctuations (from coward to smart aleck wise guy and back again) needs an anchor genre with a legitimate fear factor (like the thriller) to maximize the humor from being less than heroic. Previous Hope pictures, including his feature film debut in support of W.C. Fields in *The Big Broadcast of 1938* (1938, which also gave the ski-nosed comic his "Thanks for the Memory" theme song), never provided the scare springboard of *Canary*. A fifth and final bonus to this reaffirmation parody approach is that even when Hope's quips misfire, the scary situation give them a certain "whistling in the dark" poignancy. The *New York Post* even praised Hope lines delivered "rather apologetically, which makes it all right ... [though] it isn't"—putting on a brave face.[12]

As a footnote to this final factor, some of those flat lines are purposely scripted in order to provide a foundation for a follow-up joke. For example, when Hope is being delivered by small boat to this spooky old house in the bayous of Louisiana (not Florida, a mistake in some period reviews), the already nervous comedian tells a joke which elicits no response from his frightening Creole ferryman. When the comic acts incredulous, the stoic guide tells him he heard the joke last year on Jack Benny's radio show! The fact that radio personality Hope is actually playing a radio star in the story, and that the Creole character looks like the last person in the world to even have a radio (let alone be a Benny fan), merely adds to the humor. At a later junction in the film, after another failed joke in a time of stress, Hope gets rid of a pistol with the excuse, "I don't need a gun with jokes like that." (The scripted flat line set-up is an old comic device which Hope had, even then, incorporated into his *Pepsodent* radio program.)

Like Hope's later wannabe private eye in *My Favorite Brunette*, there are also elements of the comedian's *Canary* character which drive the story along parody detective lines. Though Hope's given *Canary* occupation is radio actor, most of his assignments appear to have been murder mysteries. Thus, his character, Wally Campbell, is forever second-guessing every *Canary* plot twist, based upon these past radio assignments. Not surprisingly, this often makes him sound like a private eye on a case. This provides some added ballast to his cocksure façade ... over a not-so-sure character. Otherwise, Hope's persona would simply be reduced to playing the cowardly fool. Moreover, his moments of temporary insight and fleeting bravado further complement *Canary*'s reaffirmation duality—playing this spoof for both thrills *and* laughs.

Hope's detective-like *Canary* character also helps reinforce another parody component — an educational slant often defined as "creative criticism." That is, to create effective parody, one must be thoroughly versed in the subject being spoofed. But parody is the most palatable of critical approaches, offering insights through laughter. Hope's humor is driven by audiences recognizing *Canary*'s stereotypical haunted house story. However, as a private eye–like figure periodically spouting standard murder

Bob Hope and Paulette Goddard cower before *The Cat and the Canary*'s sinister medium-like housekeeper Gale Sondergaard.

mystery plot points, Hope helps keep that "creative criticism" element entertainingly front and center.

Interestingly, when MGM used this Bob Hope–like reaffirmation parody approach to launch Red Skelton to star status with *Whistling in the Dark* (1941), they further pushed the detective slant. Skelton's character in *Dark* is a radio star whose specialty is cooking up seemingly perfect murder plots, only to provide last-minute loopholes for the police to do their thing. The narrative catalyst occurs when Skelton's radio character is kidnapped by a cultist mob anxious to have him concoct a perfect real-life murder. As with Hope in *Canary*, the fun is then derived from the antihero/wise guy dichotomy which follows. Consequently, while Skelton's detective-like radio personality is professorially cool in demystifying his pretend murder scenarios (as is Hope when relating similar radio mystery plots in *Canary*), both comedians are often nervous Nellies around real murderers. Or, to comically paraphrase, they can talk the talk, but they almost always trip on the walk.

This Hope-Skelton connection was no mere coincidence. *Canary* had been a huge critical and commercial success, followed by an equally popular Hope-Goddard thriller follow-up, *The Ghost Breakers* (1940). This was a film formula ripe for the borrowing, especially in Hollywood where, as the twisted axiom goes, "all things are created sequel." And even before the nation's critics sang the Hope-like praises of Skelton in *Dark*, MGM believed its young comedian could tap into the mass popularity of the ski-nosed star. References to the studio's optimism sometimes even found their way into the picture's reviews. Indeed, the *New York Morning Telegraph*'s *Dark* critique opened with: "The talk is that the MGM studios fondly believe they've discovered another Bob Hope in the personality of a lad named Red Skelton ... it would appear that this belief is not altogether unjustified."[13]

Certainly Skelton's *Dark* patter had that Hope-like quick fluctuation from smart aleck to coward. For instance, one of the *Dark* mobsters growls at Red, "Quit stalling ... You get in my hair!"

Skelton's reply is equally tough, "Yeah, well, I'll tell you something!"

The gangster's comeback is an even harsher, "What?"

A suddenly intimidated Red meekly answers, "You could use a shampoo."

Like Hope's *Canary*, Skelton's *Dark* was a breakout film for him, spawning two sequels (*Whistling in Dixie*, 1942, and *Whistling in Brooklyn*, 1944) and other memorable MGM movies. But back in 1941, NBC radio, like MGM, was also anxious to encourage the Bob Hope-Red Skelton comparisons which so many movie critics had noted in that year's late summer *Dark* reviews. And why not? Besides Hope's already highly rated NBC radio program (with Bob soon to be named broadcast comedian of the year by *Radio Daily*[14]), a poll of the nation's film exhibitors (for the twelve-month period ending August 31, 1941) had the comedian included for the first time among the top five male box office draws.[15] Thus, when Skelton's radio program had its October 7, 1941, debut, NBC placed it in a time slot right after Hope. This was, and is, classic programming at its most basic — give a new show a strong and similar lead-in. Whether looking into the modern era with Woody Allen, or surveying Hope's comedy contemporaries, it was hard to avoid the Hope influence.

Hope's career-making *Canary* character is most significant for its wise guy/antihero duality. But it also showcases other comedy components perfect for parody, the genre to which Hope most often would gravitate in the future. One could argue that the first principle of Hope is draw comedy out of cowardice. All his best spoof films do just that. The comedian's scaredy-cat philosophy is best crystallized in his telling remark about family fears in the Western parody *The Paleface*: "Brave men run in my family." But for all Hope's inspired spoof films, it is hard to top the fright atmosphere of *Canary* and *The Ghost Breakers*. Thanks to this ambience, even the simplest Hope crack can generate laughter, such as his *Canary* observation, "There isn't anything living that I'm afraid of ... hardly."

Just as Hope entertained well into his 90s, a second basic "make 'em laugh" principle for the comic is an indefatigable high voltage spirit. While he does not deliver lines in quite the machine gun patter of a Groucho Marx, Hope's quips still come at a blistering pace, earning him the nickname "Rapid Robert." And in a parody predicated upon goose pimples, sometimes a steady stream of wisecracks, successful or otherwise, produces a certain entertainment comfort zone for all concerned. The *New York Post* reviewer for the *Canary* sequel, *The Ghost Breakers*, implied just this point with the comic observation, "And if [Hope] can't laugh them [scary phenomena] off, he quips them into helplessness."[16] Plus, Hope's need for the random comedy chatter can also provide added background which reinforces his everyman quality. For example, the first time the lights begin to flicker in *Canary*'s creepy old house in the bayou, Hope comments, "They do that when you don't pay your bill." Besides the fundamental comedy thrust involved here—incongruity (not the standard explanation for power problems in a haunted house), Hope's observation suggests he knows about not having enough money to cover one's expenses. Bingo. Most viewers have either been in that position, or at least had an occasion to briefly worry about it. Consequently, Hope scores more common man points, like the universality of being easily frightened by things which go bump in the night.

Hope's everyman quality, in fact, qualifies as a third element of his comedy character. Along those lines, the comedian's son, Tony, would observe:

> Part of the American spirit has always been to poke fun at the pompous. That seems to me to be the cornerstone of his humor, to align himself with the view of the common man and pull the pompous down to the level by saying what the common man would've said if he'd had another 15 seconds to phrase it.[17]

Thus, Hope describes the dishonest wealthy eccentric whose will has brought the *Canary* cast to the bayous of Louisiana as "so crooked that when he died they had to screw him into the ground." But hand-in-hand with that everyman quality are Hope's good looks, the ski-nose notwithstanding. Sure, he traded upon being "a coward with phony bravado" (the comedian's own description), but the viewer also identified with his being a handsome wit.[18] Compare him with Don Knotts, another cowardly comic, who even remade Hope's *The Paleface* as *The Shakiest Gun in the West* (1968). Knotts, though forever synonymous with his Barney Fife character on television's *Andy Griffith Show* (1960–68, with Knotts leaving in 1965), was really just a fine-tuned extension of his "nervous man" figure from *The Steve Allen Show* (1956–1961; Knotts left in 1960). Like

Hope, Knotts effectively mixed cowardice and bravado, too. But his frightened saucer-eyes, active Adam's apple, bony body, and squeaky voice had viewers affectionately laughing at him. Whereas with Hope, at least in his young prime, ushered in by *Canary*, one could imagine being him. I am reminded of an article Dick Cavett wrote for *Film Comment* entitled, "I Was Bob Hope."[19] During Cavett's teen years he confessed to doing Hope material in front of a mirror, something this author did, too. But I preferred to mimic Hope's own screen antics before a mirror—lightly patting down the hair, a casual brush of an eyebrow, and that throaty growl of approval for his own reflection. Hope's mix of comedy and good looks is even underlined in *Life* magazine's lengthy 1941 profile of the comedian. Writing about his breakout *Canary* role, the publication stated his "Caspar Milquetoast was never timider in the early scenes, Errol Flynn never braver in the late ones.... Hope emerged as a comic star and matinee idol combined."[20]

A fourth aspect of the Hope persona, which also complemented that common man component, is his breezy casualness—something viewers also like to imagine they possess. *New Yorker* writer John Lahr, son of legendary comedian Bert Lahr (the Cowardly Lion in *The Wizard of Oz*, 1939), noted, "Hope did have one piece of luck: he came into his prime just as the talking pictures and radio were demanding the posture of ease—the illusion of authenticity which was Hope's biggest performing asset."[21] *Canary* was a perfect showcase for this blasé confidence. Hope's carefree manner of not taking things seriously is a perfect marriage for parody's affectionate mocking of a given genre. And while spoof fans tend to gravitate toward the derailing of genres they enjoy, it could be argued that a comic like Hope also allows viewers to savor the trashing of a genre they dislike. *New York Herald Tribune* critic Howard Barnes made just such a point in his review of the *Canary* sequel, *The Ghost Breakers*. Once again a parody of reaffirmation is at work—a mix of serious chills and spoofing comic banter. But Barnes, no friend to horror, finds Hope makes it all palatable: "Whether the star is ignominiously locked up in a trunk or is prowling through a haunted castle in Cuba, the melodrama accents his brash fooling, and his fooling makes the eerie nonsense acceptable."[22]

Given Hope's breezy upbeat manner, one might claim a final key element to his persona as being *modern* and/or future-oriented—keeping up with a fast-paced world. I most relate this modern "with it" trait to his often cocky but comic verbal delivery. Revisionist movie critic Jeffrey Couchman wrote for the May 6, 1979, *New York Times*:

> [Hope's] natural comedic asset is his voice, as distinctive in its twang as the voice of either Groucho or W.C. Fields and well-suited to his clipped, understated delivery.... These sounds are enhanced by a wonderfully mobile face [including] lips which practically curl around his sloped nose in a sneer of contempt or mock ferocity.[23]

In contrast to Hope's modern persona, many of the other comedians focused on in this text are decidedly drawn from an earlier time, with cinema settings often based in the past. And even if the time frame is contemporary, such as Chaplin's *Modern Times* (1936, see chapter 10), the Tramp is overwhelmed by all things current. With Hope's modern mindset and "Rapid Robert" delivery, he is predisposed to cover a great deal

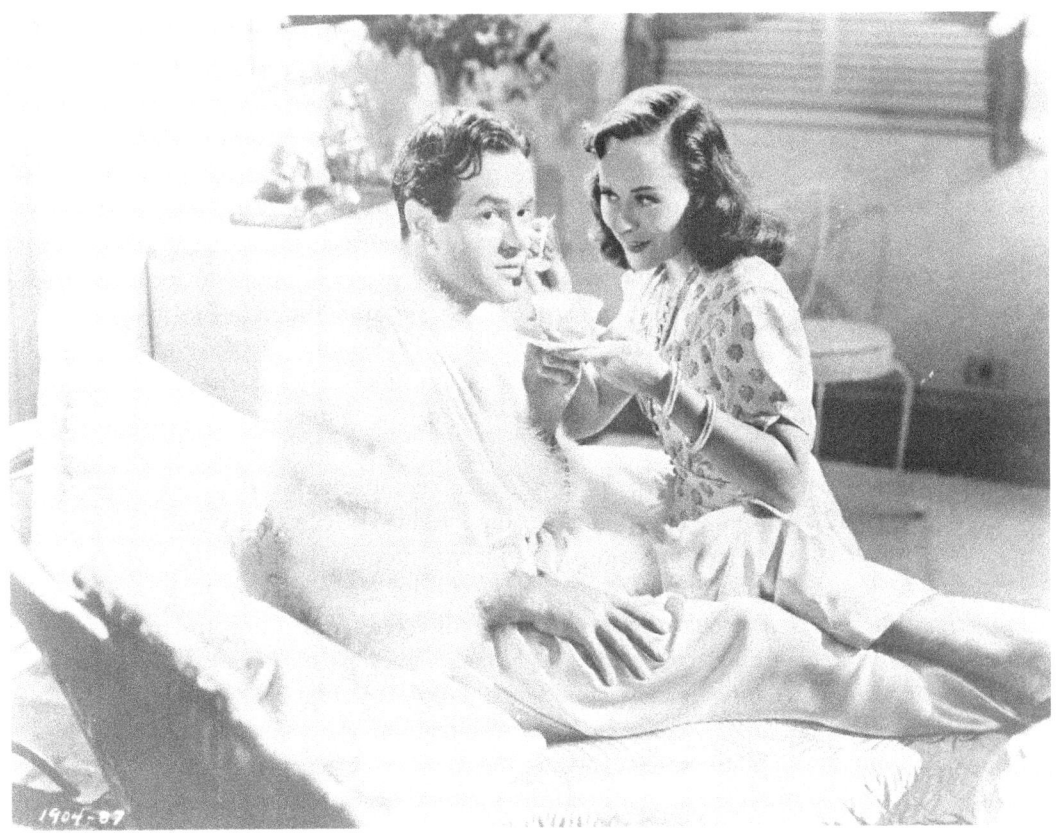

Paulette Goddard takes care of the easily intimidated Bob Hope in *The Ghost Breakers*.

of comedy material. This dovetails into another spoofing characteristic — compounding. While a parody picture keys on a certain type of movie, such as *Canary*'s take-off on horror, the spoof film is frequently peppered with tongue-in-cheek references to other genres and/or popular culture topics in general. For instance, *Canary* even manages to creatively link a political joke to its haunted house narrative. Hope and character actress Nydia Westman, who made a career of playing comic spinsters, investigate the spooky old mansion's cellar. She casually asks him if he believes in reincarnation. When that does not seem to register with Hope, she further elaborates, "You know, the dead come back?"

"Like Republicans?" is the comic's quick reply. As with most examples of compounding, this is a one-shot affair, consistent with parody's tendency to have a scattergun number of potential humor targets. Moreover, it echoes the comic incongruity of the aforementioned light bill joke — the odd juxtapositioning of Republicans and the once dead scoring comic surprise points. Conversely, there is also a darkly amusing slant to the joke. People often characterize politicians (both Democrats and Republicans) as so many dead-like zombies, blindly following their party line.

Be that as it may, Hope's groundbreaking new persona, as demonstrated in *Canary*, was met with almost universal critical praise. Under the review title "*Cat and the Canary* Sparkling Comedy Murder Mystery," *The Hollywood Reporter* stated: "Hope, given the best opportunity he has had to date, is by far the standout in the picture. With excellent material handed him, Hope milked every situation dry, getting a belly laugh at every turn."[24]

Other publications followed this lead, from the *New York World Telegram* calling him a "really amusing wise-cracking hero," to the *Brooklyn Eagle* crediting him with the "best lines he has had on the screen, and Hope makes fine use of them...."[25] *New York Sun* critic Eileen Creelman loved "Mr. Hope's jokes and Mr. Hope's turned-up nose" and as with earlier cited reviews, she found the film "thoroughly scary."[26] But the equally positive *New York Times* critique, by future John Ford scriptwriter Frank S. Nugent, was one of the rare period notices which primarily saw *Canary* as a comedy. With that in mind, Nugent also attempted a comic review, calling the movie "more harebrained than hair-raising," and describing Hope as having a "chin like a forehead and a gag line for every occasion."[27] But the most appreciatively insightful review came from the *New York Post*'s Archer Winsten, the only critic in 1939, of whom I am aware, to fully describe the range of what is now considered Hope's watershed persona: "His characterization vacillates dynamically between [the brave] intrepid pursuit of unknown menaces and being scared stiff."[28]

To further document *Canary*'s immediate hit status, one need only read a late 1939 *Los Angeles Examiner* column by the widely syndicated powerbroker Louella Parsons'— "With *The Cat and the Canary* doing exceptional business all over the country, [producer] Arthur Hornblow wasn't long in getting the idea to reunite Paulette Goddard and Bob Hope is a successor to the chiller-diller."[29] Flash forward to the 1940 release of the sequel, *The Ghost Breakers*, and reviewers invariably sang the praises again of *Canary*. For example, *The Hollywood Reporter* noted, "'Encore' was the cry following the tremendous success of teaming Bob Hope and Paulette Goddard in *The Cat and the Canary*."[30] The *New York Daily News*' Wanda Hale observed, "Having scored a big hit in *The Cat and the Canary*, Bob Hope and Paulette Goddard are teamed again in another spine-chiller ... [which] is spooky, whacky and a lot of fun."[31] And the *PM* critic even predicted a long line of *Canary* sequels: "Bob Hope and Paulette Goddard rang the bell with *The Cat and the Canary*. Now Bob Hope and Paulette Goddard clang the bell with *The Ghost Breakers*. So look for them in a whole bunch of comedy-mysteries in the future...."[32]

This statement might have been prophetic had it not been for the Hope film sandwiched between *Canary* and *Breakers—The Road to Singapore* (1940). This was the beginning of the acclaimed "Road" pictures, which teamed Hope and Bing Crosby (with Dorothy Lamour as the love interest). During the next 22 years there would be six more installments of the series: *Road to Zanzibar* (1941), *Road to Morocco* (1942), *Road to Utopia* (1946), *Road to Rio* (1947), *Road to Bali* (1952), and *Road to Hong Kong* (1962). The "Road" pictures are the most acclaimed "A" comedy series in the history of American movies. As one might assume, given the celebrated nature of these films, the comedy chemistry of the teaming was immediately recognized. The 1940 *Hollywood Reporter* was probably, however, the most perceptive in its praise of the first "Road" movie: "In pairing Bing Crosby and Bob Hope, Paramount has created one of the greatest comedy teams in film history ... a demand for more of the same is an unqualified certainty."[33] There would only be one more Hope and Goddard teaming—the very

Bob Hope (center) and Bing Crosby derailed by yet another pretty girl in *Road to Singapore*.

funny *Nothing But the Truth* (1941, where Bob has to tell the truth for 24 hours, a precursor to Jim Carrey's *Liar, Liar*, 1997).

But one should not bemoan the "Road" pictures derailing a *Canary*-related series. What is often forgotten is that the Bob and Bing "Road" outings are also parodies — the ultimate spoof of the action adventure genre, as well as Hollywood itself. Granted, the "Road" movies are broad spoofs, versus the reaffirmation parodies of *Canary* and *Breakers*. Still, the comedy broadsiding of a specific genre are at the heart of all these films. Hope and Goddard take on horror, while Hope and Crosby have fun at the expense of action adventure. Consequently, one can argue that since Hope's *Canary* role wonderfully demonstrated that his film forte was parody, this movie helped prepare him for the inspired "Road" pictures.

The groundbreaking Hope persona, which film comedy history dates from *Canary* (the cowardly incompetent fluctuating with the smart aleck), is further embellished in his "Road" picture teaming with Crosby. While Hope continues to elicit laughs by bouncing back and forth between these two comedy poles, the duality also defines Bob and Bing — Hope is the antiheroic patsy to Crosby's wise guy. And with Lamour in the middle, the "Road" pictures further tweak Hope's Don Juan delusions, generally resulting in Bing getting Dorothy by the close. Even in a rare exception, like *Road to Utopia*, where Hope and Lamour end up as an old married couple, there is a comic qualifier. The movie's conclusion reveals that their only son is the spitting image of Crosby, and is naturally played by Bing. Hope has been cuckolded. By contrast, Hope wins lovely Goddard by default in *Canary* and *Breakers*, though his romantic posturing is equally self-deprecating. For instance, upon leaving Paulette's boudoir in *Canary*, Hope comically flirts with being gallant: "My mother brought me up never to be caught twice in the same lady's bedroom."

Noted comedy writer Larry Gelbart (from television's *M*A*S*H* to cinema's *Tootsie*, 1982) has amusingly but insightfully observed, "It's no coincidence that Bob Hope's name consists of two verbs."[34] Given "Rapid Robert's" high voltage persona, it is an apt comment. Moreover, given parody's eclectic, anything-goes *compounding* phenomenon — arguably the most scattergun-related comedy genre — it is appropriate that spoofing's greatest ambassador is a two-verb man. With tongue firmly in cheek, one could even comically argue that this double helping of action is fitting for a comedian whose screen character is dual-focused (antiheroic coward/smart aleck). Regardless, Hope's pioneering persona not only had him dominating screen comedy for years, he also influenced an army of significant funnymen, from contemporaries like Red Skelton and Danny Kaye, to modern comedy guru Woody Allen. What is more, the wisecracking antihero remains at center stage in 21st century film comedy, from Luke Wilson's cowardly cowboy in the Western parody *Shanghai Noon* (2000), to Robert Downey, Jr.'s inspiredly flawed but funny detective in the underrated reaffirmation parody of film noir *Kiss Kiss, Bang Bang* (2005).

What was groundbreaking comedy has become comedy's ground floor. And it began with Hope's *Canary*.

Epilogue

During *A Night at the Opera* (1935) Groucho explains to Chico the various taxes to which his protégé will be subject: "You know, there's a federal tax and a state tax and a city tax and a street tax and a sewer tax."
CHICO: "How much does this come to?"
GROUCHO: "Well, I figure if he doesn't sing too often he can break even."

For all the loopiness emblematic of the personality comedian, who can raise funny to the level of fable, there is often an inherent truth (such as the above quote) at the heart of the humor. As Steve Martin's character in *Grand Canyon* (1991) tells a friend, "You haven't seen enough movies. All of life's riddles are answered in the movies." Granted, the surreal does sometime rule, such as Stan Laurel's nonsense axiom from *Way Out West* (1937), "Any bird can build a nest but it isn't everyone that can lay an egg." Still, personality comedy, especially as personified by this text's focus films, is peppered with life lessons among the laughter. The challenge, as *New Yorker* critic Anthony Lane suggests, is to "make an adventure out of a sermon."[1] Through persistence, the genre's most basic component, after comedy itself, these movies are an ongoing showcase for the all-important resilience discussed in the Prologue. While clown comedy can gift us with no greater belief/hope than that of resilience (an especially meaningful message during the Depression), the genre rarely suggests that persistence leads to an easy victory. Screen comedians tend to struggle with life even more than their film fans — which helps fuel the resiliency reflex. That is, if Laurel and Hardy (or the designated comedian of your choice) can somehow muddle through, there is hope for you and me.

Like the populist pictures of directors John Ford and Frank Capra, personality comedians can also embrace unlikely concluding victories — those second chances many deserve but few receive. Thus, when the populist-oriented Will Rogers joined forces with Ford on *Judge Priest* (1934), an improbable feel-good finale was all but guaranteed. But conversely, though there is little that is populist (celebrating the people) about the comedy world of W.C. Fields, his *It's a Gift* (1934) also has the most entertainingly implausible of conclusions. This generally occurs in personality comedies because the genre is all about underdogs eventually winning.[2] In other words, even if it is unlikely that the comedian's persistence/resilience might have resulted in a triumph, in a better world the screen clown (and by extension, the audience) deserves a second chance.

Realist film theorist Siegfried Kracauer goes so far as to celebrate this underdog phenomenon, what he calls the "David-Goliath theme," as one of cinema's most basic motifs.[3] Fittingly, though he does not limit the device to any one genre, his definitive example is the greatest of personality comedians — Charlie Chaplin. Ironically, in Chaplin's *City Lights* (1931), the comedian has even used his screen persona's unique underdog status to suggest the most bittersweet of endings — the former blind flower girl finding her benefactor the Tramp romantically wanting. But as noted earlier by film comedy historian Gerald Mast, maybe the film was never about a potential love story — "Its real subject is what sorts of human actions make human existence possible."[4] For Chaplin's Charlie, the key is sacrifice, even if that means losing the love of one's life.

Though sacrifice and a tattered human dignity are not a perfect fit for all personality comedians, they cast a wider net than one might normally assume. For example, the darkly comic W.C. Fields would, upon first consideration, probably not be included in any sacrificial category. Yet, his inspiringly antiheroic *Gift* character has the patience of a comic Job, enduring the outrageously rude antics of a litany of antagonists, from the most henpecking of wives to the exasperating Baby LeRoy. Consequently, a central reason for viewers to so savor *Gift*'s happy ending is that Fields has comically suffered and sacrificed enough.

Paradoxically, while the Marxes of *Duck Soup* (1933) are the least likely poster people for comic sacrifice and/or victimization (unless one notes Groucho's perennial antiheroic relationship to Chico and Harpo), MGM's makeover of the team for *A Night at the Opera* added — with mixed results — comic vulnerability to their personae. Suddenly the team cared about the happiness of a supporting player just as Laurel and Hardy do everything to help an orphan in *Way Out West*. Though such comic outreach is much more intrinsic to Stanley and Ollie than the brothers Marx, MGM's attempt to homogenize the normally heretical team demonstrates the depths of decency associated with personality comedy.

Most of the clowns featured in the text are on more common ground when one notes another basic component of personality comedy — the often nomadic nature, *à la* the literary links to picaresque figures like Don Quixote and Huck Finn. Obviously, cinema's most acclaimed clown, Chaplin's Charlie, is closely tied to the picaresque, through his identity as a wondering Tramp and the celebrated imagery of him literally shuffling down life's highways — which he does for the last time (with Paulette Goddard's lovely gamin) at the close of *Modern Times* (1936).

There are various comedy reasons for going on the road. The first is that it gives the clown an endless supply of new settings for his comedy. Consequently, after W.C. Fields has exhausted the small town possibilities of his New Jersey home and grocery in *It's a Gift*, the comedian goes on a cross-country Model-T Ford road trip to California. As the inherent comic tendencies of Fields' Ford "Flivver" suggest, the mode of transportation can also become an end in itself. Along similar lines, the Marx Brothers make comic use of an ocean liner in *A Night at the Opera*.

A second reason for travel is that placing a clown in some unlikely setting can be an ongoing joke itself and is often the starting point for parody. For instance, what could be more delightfully incongruous than seeing the traditional garb of Laurel and Hardy as they trek into the cowboy country of *Way Out West*? Conversely, seeing the picaresque prankster in the appropriate garb for some alien activity can also make for entertaining comic incongruity — such as Eddie Cantor in full matador attire battling bulls in *The Kid from Spain*. But probably the most brilliant multi-faceted example of this phenomenon occurs with director Leo McCarey's inspired anti-war finale to *Duck Soup*. The Marx Brothers find themselves in an outpost on the front lines. After each cutaway shot to no-man's-land (the contested space between the opposing armies), McCarey has the Marxes changed to a different type of military uniform — ranging from the elaborate garb of the Napoleonic Wars, to the coonskin cap, buckskin outfit of a Davy Crockett frontiersman. This eclectic march through military uniform history includes the American Civil War (both Union and Confederate garb) and various World War I costumes.

On the surface, seeing the Marxes in the various examples of fighting attire works as simple spoofing incongruity. Like *matador* Cantor in a bull ring, Groucho and company as soldiers is an instant and ongoing comic contradiction. But comedy historian Allen Eyles implies that Groucho's illogical military action in *Duck Soup* becomes a satirical metaphor for the folly of war in general by way of these costume changes: This "retrospective survey of military uniforms ... [suggest] his actions do not apply just to one period...."[5] Eyles' point is well taken, especially when one couples this uniform parade with all the jingoistic patriotism used to elicit support for questionable wars, such as *Duck Soup*'s satirically upbeat musical number "The Country's Going to War." Naturally, Groucho further fuels this satire quotient by the comic paranoia he brings to his militaristic leader in *Duck Soup*, anticipating by decades General Jack D. Ripper's (Sterling Hayden) psychotic obsession that the Soviets are about to overrun America in *Dr. Strangelove: Or, How I Learned to Stop Worrying and Love the Bomb* (1964).[6]

A third reason for screen clown travel is that it justifies introducing a broad cross-section of supporting comedy characters, such as Laurel and Hardy's misadventures with a crooked saloon owner, a voluptuous saloon girl, and a no-nonsense sheriff in *Way Out West*. Eddie Cantor's sojourn to Mexico in *The Kid from Spain* has him interacting with a host of stereotypically entertaining figures, including a sexy señorita, a goofy border guard, and a political bandito. Bob Hope's *Cat and the Canary* trip to the spooky old Louisiana bayou has a haunted house collection of potential comic types, starting with the creepy medium-like housekeeper. Even in the modest treks of Chaplin's Charlie around two urban settings, in *City Lights* and *Modern Times*, the Tramp has comic encounters with a plethora of big city characters — crooks, cops, bums, boxers, prison inmates, various blue-collar figures, and a forgetful millionaire.

A final justification for clown travel is that it often segues into what *moving* pictures do best — the chase. "Picaresque comedian" is often an artsy way of saying "funny person on the run." Cantor is on the lam from the law throughout *The Kid from Spain*. Conversely, both Joe E. Brown's title character in *Alibi Ike* and Laurel and Hardy's wannabe cowboys in *Way Out West* are being chased by bad guys. Bob Hope is constantly on the run from things that go bump in the *Cat and the Canary* night, while Chaplin's Tramp has more traditional pursuit problems from the police in *City Lights* and *Modern Times*. And Groucho is at odds with the authorities over his ocean liner stowaway brothers in *A Night at the Opera*.

Beyond the fundamental personality comedy component of a consistent persona and related shtick, which has been mapped out in the proceeding chapters, there is a final common clown characteristic — the tendency for a team-like interaction. That is, even solo comedians need someone off whom to bounce their humor (or, in the case of Mae West, sexual innuendo). Moreover, while little needs to be said about most acknowledged comedy teams like Laurel and Hardy, the Marx Brothers are better understood by way of the teams within the team, such as Groucho and Chico. Or Harpo and Chico. When examined along these lines, the less celebrated, ethnic-driven Chico actually becomes the indispensable one, either through maintaining comedy lines of communication (especially acting as the interpreter for the mad mute Harpo), or simply as the catalyst for team action itself. When all the Marxes are together on screen, translator Chico is even more indispensable. The main exception to this is still another popular Marx Brothers duo — Groucho and Margaret Dumont, with the actress sometimes referred to as the "fifth Marx Brother." (Zeppo's appearances — he retired after *Duck Soup*—were generally in modest support of Groucho.)

Unofficial teamings are often less apparent because the supporting member is neither a star nor a regular repeater, although the comedy type is. For example, W.C. Fields' antiheroic humor is frequently in need of a nagging wife and/or standard comic female busybody, as are Laurel and Hardy. Through the years a number of women nicely essayed the part opposite Fields, though *It's a Gift* repeater Kathleen Howard is the best. Plus, Fields constantly peopled his movies with additional comedy nemeses, such as the problem *Gift* customers: the cane-swinging blind detective, Mr. Muckle, and the man demanding kumquats.

Maybe the most interesting unofficial teaming of the pantheon pictures in this text occurs with the *Modern Times* duo of Chaplin's Tramp and Paulette Goddard's gamin. Reminiscent of the pairing of Charlie and little Jackie Coogan's title character in *The Kid* (1921), the gamin (like Coogan) is a younger, streetwise version of Charlie. This gives the viewer an amusing dual focus narrative — the beloved Tramp in visual stereo. And unlike in *The Kid*, the aging *Modern Times* Charlie needs a younger alter ego to energize him.

Another memorial unofficial teaming herein involves *Judge Priest*'s Will Rogers and Stepin Fetchit (Lincoln Perry). Like many maverick heroes in American popular culture, Rogers' metaphorical outsider status is reinforced by his close relationship with his minority sidekick. Similar examples would range from Huck Finn and Jim to the Lone Ranger and Tonto. The justice served by all these duos is an extension of the liberalness inherent to any bi-racial team. As noted earlier in the text, Fetchit knowingly observed, "When people saw me and Will Rogers like brothers, that said something to them."[7]

Beyond all these common clown components, of course, it should go without saying that they share one more trait from which all others emanate — they make us laugh, a commonality about which there is nothing common. While this study's comedians produced laughter for a Depression audience, their artistry lives on today as an antidote for various modern forms of "depression." To the fan of funny, they are a comedy communion. We cherish their slapstick dance on the *edge* of the abyss, deflating our fears with their fun. (Plus, as dark comedy novelist Kurt Vonnegut, Jr., reminds us, "Out on the edge you see all kinds of things you can't see from the center.") And if "All of life's riddles are answered in the movies," this is especially true of the funny ones.

The opening of Chaplin's *City Lights* was arguably the most anticipated kick-off of any comedy featured in this text. No less a critic and period personality than Alexander Woollcott* stated, "A Couple of our [Depression] banks had closed their doors and a few of our judges were hastily leaving town but as men met on the street the first word between them would be 'Have you seen it?' And the question needed no elaboration."[8] Yet, for today's student of film comedy, each of the movies examined herein could now be said to generate that potential.

In the 1930s, Depression America went off the gold standard but gold resurfaced in the decade's film comedy, from W.C. Fields — truth with a potato nose — to the leader of America's own particular brand of Marxism — Groucho. This duo, and the rest of their '30s comedy colleagues, remind us, if truth be told, we all live in a comic way. Comedy, like cataract surgery, helps one see. Entertainment derived from that comic reality represents a personal outpost of freedom and sanity in a world too often ruled by the humor impaired. Long live comedy's inherent irreverence!

When Chaplin released a reedited version of The Gold Rush *(1925) in 1942, which also included his narration and music, the movie included a special dedication to Woollcott. The writer had been a long time champion of Chaplin.*

Filmography

1931 *City Lights* (United Artists, 87 minutes).
    Director: Charles Chaplin. Story-Screenplay: Chaplin. Stars: Chaplin, Virginia Cherrill, Harry Myers, Hank Mann, Allan Garcia, Florence Lee, Henry Bergman, Albert Austin, John Rand, James Donnelly, Robert Parrish.

1932 *The Kid from Spain* (Goldwyn-United Artists, 96 minutes).
    Director: Leo McCarey. Screenplay: William Anthony McGuire, Bert Kalmar, and Harry Ruby, from a McCarey story (songs by Kalmar and Ruby). Stars: Eddie Cantor, Lyda Roberti, Robert Young, Ruth Hall, John Miljan, Noah Beery.

1933 *She Done Him Wrong* (Paramount, 66 minutes).
    Director: Lowell Sherman. Screenplay: Harvey Thew and John Bright, adapted from Mae West's play *Diamond Lil* (music and lyrics for *She Done Him Wrong*, Ralph Rainger). Stars: West, Cary Grant, Gilbert Roland, Noah Beery, Rafaela Ottiano, David Landau, Rochelle Hudson, Owen Moore, Fuzzy Knight, Tammany Young, Dewey Robinson, Grace LaRue, Robert E. Homans, Louise Beavers, Wade Boteler, Aggie Herring.

1933 *Duck Soup* (Paramount, 70 minutes).
    Director: Leo McCarey. Screenplay: Bert Kalmar and Harry Ruby, additional dialogue by Arthur Sheekman and Nat Perrin, uncredited added material by McCarey (songs by Kalmar and Ruby). Stars: The Marx Brothers, Margaret Dumont, Louis Calhern, Edgar Kennedy, Raquel Torres, Verna Hillie.

1933 *Sons of the Desert* (Roach-MGM, 68 minutes).
    Director: William A. Seiter. Story-Screenplay: Frank Craven, continuity Byron Morgan, uncredited additional material by Stan Laurel. Stars: Laurel and Hardy, Mae Busch, Dorothy Christy, Charley Chase, Lucien Littlefield.

1934 *Judge Priest* (Fox, 80 minutes).
    Director: John Ford. Screenplay: Dudley Nichols and Lamar Trotti, adapted from stories by Irvin S. Cobb. Stars: Will Rogers, Tom Brown, Anita Louise, Henry B. Walthall, Stepin Fetchit, Hattie McDaniel, David Landau, Rochelle Hudson, Berton Churchill, Francis Ford.

1934 *It's a Gift* (Paramount, 68 minutes).
    Director: Norman Z. McLeod. Screenplay: Jack Cunningham, from a Charles Bogle (W. C. Fields) story, which incorporates various Fields-copyrighted sketches, and material from J. P. McEvoy's comedy revue *The Comic Supplement*. Stars: Fields, Kathleen Howard,

Jean Rouveral, Julian Madison, Tom Bupp, Baby LeRoy, Tammany Young, Morgan Wallace, Charles Sellon, Josephine Whittell, Diana Lewis, T. Roy Barnes, Spencer Charters, Del Henderson.

1935 *Alibi Ike* (Warner Bros., 73 minutes).
Director: Ray Enright. Screenplay: William Wister Haines, from the Ring Lardner story. Stars: Joe E. Brown, Olivia de Havilland, Ruth Donnelly, Roscoe Karns, William Frawley.

1935 *A Night at the Opera* (MGM, 92 minutes).
Director: Sam Wood. Screenplay: George S. Kaufman and Morrie Ryskind, additional material by Al Boasberg, from a James Kevin McGuinness story. Stars: Groucho Marx, Chico Marx, Harpo Marx, Kitty Carlisle, Allan Jones, Walter Woolf King, Sig Rumann, Margaret Dumont, Edward Keane, Robert Emmet O'Connor, Billy Gilbert.

1936 *Modern Times* (United Artists, 85 minutes).
Director: Charles Chaplin. Story-Screenplay: Chaplin. Stars: Chaplin, Paulette Goddard, Henry Bergman, Chester Conklin, Stanley J. Stanford, Hank Mann, Louis Netheau, Allen Garcia.

1937 *Way Out West* (Roach — MGM, 65 minutes).
Director: James W. Horne. Screenplay: Charles Rogers, Felix Adler, and James Parrott, uncredited additional material by Stan Laurel, from a Jack Jevne and Charles Rogers story. Stars: Laurel and Hardy, Sharon Lynne, James Finlayson, Rosina Lawrence, Stanley Fields, Vivien Oakland, Chill Wills and the Avalon Boys.

1939 *The Cat and the Canary* (Paramount, 74 minutes).
Director: Elliott Nugent. Screenplay: Walter DeLeon and Lynn Starling, adapted from the John Willard play. Stars: Bob Hope, Paulette Goddard, John Beal, Douglass Montgomery, Gale Sondergaard, Elizabeth Patterson, Nydia Westman, George Zucco, John Wray, George Regas, Willard Robertson.

Chapter Notes

Preface

1. Peter Novick, *The Noble Dream: The "Objectivity Question" and the American Historical Profession* (Cambridge: Cambridge University Press, 1988): 7.
2. Peter Schjeldahl, "Rule Like an Egyptian," *The New Yorker* (April 3, 2006): 86.

Introduction

1. Robert Benchley, *After 1903—What?* (New York: Harper & Brothers, 1938): 42.
2. American Film Institute (with Duane Byrge), *Private Screenings: Insiders Share a Century of Great Movie Moments* (Atlanta: Turner Publishing, 1995): 107.
3. See the author's *Laurel & Hardy: A Bio-Bibliography* (Westport, Connecticut: Greenwood Press, 1990).
4. See the author's *The Marx Brothers: A Bio-Bibliography* (Westport, Connecticut: Greenwood Press, 1987), *Groucho & W. C. Fields: Huckster Comedians* (Jackson: University Press of Mississippi, 1994), and *Leo McCarey: From Marx to McCarthy* (Lanham, Maryland: Scarecrow Press, 2005).
5. Gerald Clark, "She Was What She Was: Mae West, 1893–1980," *Time* (December 1, 1980): 80.
6. Neil Schmitz, *Of Huck and Alice: Humorous Writing in American Literature* (Minneapolis: University of Minnesota Press, 1983): 15.

Chapter 1: Charlie Chaplin's *City Lights* (1931)

1. Charlie Chaplin, "Pantomime and Comedy," *New York Times* (January 23, 1931): Section 8: 6.
2. Arthur Knight, "One Man's Movie," *Saturday Review* (May 6, 1972): 14.
3. James Agee, "Comedy's Greatest Era," *Life* (September 3, 1949).
4. Peter Bogdanovich, "Modern Screen," *New York Observer* (March 6, 2000): 23.
5. Robert F. Moss, *Charlie Chaplin* (1975; rpt. New York: Harcourt Brace Jovanovich, 1977): 101.
6. See Gladys Hall's "Charlie Chaplin Attacks the Talkies," *Motion Pictures* (May 1929): 28+; Chaplin, "Pantomime and Comedy."
7. Kevin Brownlow, *The Parades Gone By...* (1968; rpt. New York: Ballantine Books, 1970): 667.
8. Louella O. Parsons, "Chaplin to Take *City Lights* to Europe, Being Only Actor Who Can Show Original Film" (syndicated), *New York American* (February 5, 1931): 19.
9. "A Voiceless Chaplin," *New York Times* (January 11, 1931): Section 8: 6.
10. Charles Chaplin, Jr. (with N. and M. Rau), *My Father, Charlie Chaplin* (New York: Random House, 1960): 42.
11. Arthur Knight, *The Liveliest Art: A Panoramic History of the Movie* (New York: Macmillan, 1978): 123.
12. Lewis Jacobs, *The Rise of the American Film: A Critical History* (1939; rpt. New York: Teachers College Press, Columbia University, 1971): 334.
13. Jerry Tallmer, "Book and Author: Robert Parrish," *New York Post* (May 29, 1976): 33.
14. Charles Chaplin, *My Autobiography* (1964; rpt. New York: Pocket Books, 1966): 353.
15. "Hails Chaplin Aid to Blind," *New York Times* (February 23, 1931): 5.
16. Chaplin, *My Autobiography*: 353.
17. Georgia Hale (edited by Heather Kiernan), *Charlie Chaplin: Intimate Close-Ups* (1995; rpt. Lanham, Maryland: Scarecrow Press, 1999): 114.
18. Mark Twain, *Huckleberry Finn* (1885; rpt. New York: W. W. Norton, 1962): 1.
19. Walter Kerr, *The Silent Clowns* (New York: Alfred A. Knopf, 1975): 346.
20. Jerry Lewis and James Kaplan, *Dean & Me: A Love Story* (New York: Doubleday, 2005): 211.
21. *Ibid.*
22. Theodore Huff, *Charlie Chaplin* (1951; rpt. New York: Henry Schuman, 1972): 49.
23. Carl Sandburg, "Carl Sandburg Says Chaplin Could Play Drama" (1921), in *Authors on Film*, ed. Harry M. Geduld (Bloomington: Indiana University Press, 1972): 264.

24. Huff, *Charlie Chaplin*: 50.
25. Isabel Quigly, *Charlie Chaplin: Early Comedies* (London: Studio Vista, 1968): 75.
26. Wes D. Gehring, *Charlie Chaplin: A Bio-Bibliography* (Westport, Connecticut: Greenwood Press, 1983).
27. Richard Meryman, "Ageless Master's Anatomy of Comedy: Chaplin, An Interview," *Life* (March 10, 1967): 82+.
28. André Bazin, "The Virtues and Limitations of Montage," in *What Is Cinema? Vol. 1*, selected and translated by Hugh Gray (1958; rpt. Los Angeles: University of California Press, 1967).
29. "*City Lights* A Cinch For Big Money Everywhere," *Hollywood Reporter* (January 30, 1931): 3.
30. John S. Cohen, Jr., "Chaplin Triumphs Anew in *City Lights*," *New York Sun* (February 7, 1931): 6; Richard Watts, Jr., "Charlie Chaplin in *City Lights*," *New York Herald Tribune* (February 7, 1931): 8.
31. Gerald Mast, *The Comic Mind: Comedy and the Movies* (Indianapolis: Bobbs-Merrill, 1973): 106.
32. Henri Bergson, "Laughter" (1900), in *Comedy*, ed. Wylie Sypher (Garden City, New York: Doubleday Anchor Books, 1956): 66–67.
33. Siegfried Kracauer, *Theory of Film: The Redemption of Physical Reality* (New York: Oxford University Press, 1960): 107–08.
34. *City Lights* review, *Variety* (February 11, 1931).
35. Mordaunt Hall, "Chaplin Hilarious In His *City Lights*," *New York Times* (February 7, 1931): 11.
36. Lita Grey Chaplin (with Morton Cooper), *My Life with Chaplin* (New York: Bernard Geir Associates, 1966): 143.
37. John McCabe, *Charlie Chaplin* (Garden City, New York: Doubleday, 1978): 174.
38. David Robinson, *Chaplin: His Life and Art* (New York: McGraw-Hill, 1985): 140.
39. "Thomas J. McCarey," *New York Times* (February 2, 1936): Section 2: 8.
40. Conversation with John Hampton, silent film collector and original owner-operator of Los Angeles' Silent Movie Theatre, author's files (June 1975).
41. Edward Murray, *Fellini the Artist* (New York: Frederick Ungar, 1976): 32.
42. *Ibid.*: 83.
43. Cohen, "Chaplin Triumphs Anew in *City Lights*."
44. Thornton Delehanty, "Charles Chaplin Contributes a Generous Sample of His Genius in *City Lights*," *New York Post* (February 7, 1931): Section 4: 3.
45. James Gow, "Art Without Words," *New York World* (February 7, 1931): 11.
46. Hall, "Chaplin Hilarious In His *City Lights*."
47. Watts, "Charlie Chaplin, in *City Lights*."
48. "London in Raptures at Chaplin Movie," *New York Times* (February 28, 1931): 22.
49. For example, see Cohen, "Chaplin Triumphs Anew in *City Lights*" and, Watts, "Charlie Chaplin, in *City Lights*."
50. "Old Chaplin Dead? Say It's Not True, Charlie: Cane, Derby and Mustache Doomed If He Enters Talkies," *New York American* (February 5, 1931): 17.

51. *Ibid.*
52. "Charlie Chaplin Comes to Town," uncited New York newspaper (February 4, 1931), in the *City Lights* file, Performing Arts Library, New York Public Library at Lincoln Center.
53. "Einstein Waves Aside Luring Movie Offers," *New York Times* (January 11, 1931): Section 2: 2.
54. Chaplin, *My Autobiography*: 359.
55. "Chaplin and Movie Hailed by Broadway," *New York World* (February 7, 1931): 11.
56. Regina Crewe, "Chaplin Film Test Tonight of Silent Versus the Talkies," *New York American* (February 6, 1931): 18.
57. Rose Pelswick, "Rose Pelswick Reviews Chaplin Premiere," *New York Evening Journal* (February 7, 1931): 12.
58. "$650,000 Radio Offer Refused by Chaplin," *New York Times* (February 12, 1931): 13.
59. "Big Deal for London," *Hollywood Reporter* (December 19, 1930): 1.
60. "Paris Hails Chaplin with Delirious Joy," *New York Times* (March 23, 1931): 24.
61. "Chaplin Gets Legion of Honor, First For Foreign Film Actor," *New York Times* (March 28, 1931): 1.
62. "Prague Angry At Chaplin," *New York Times* (June 14, 1931): 14.
63. Mast, *The Comic Mind: Comedy and the Movies*: 109.
64. Anthony Lane, "Looking For Heroes," *The New Yorker* (June 6, 2005): 106.

Chapter 2: Eddie Cantor's *The Kid from Spain* (1932)

1. David Thomson, *The New Biographical Dictionary of Film* (New York: Alfred A. Knopf, 2003): 131.
2. Harrison B. Summers (ed.), *A Thirty-Year History of Programs Carried on National Radio Networks in the United States, 1926–1956* (New York: Arno Press, 1971): 25.
3. *Ibid.*, 31, 37; Arthur Frank Wertheim, *Radio Comedy* (New York: Oxford University Press, 1979): 89.
4. Cobbett Steinberg, *Reel Facts: The Movie Book of Records* (New York: Vintage Books, 1978): 404.
5. Janet Maslin, "Nothing Stands in the Way of a Laugh," *New York Times* (September 23, 1992).
6. Henry Jenkins, *What Made Pistachio Nuts? Early Sound Comedy and the Vaudeville Aesthetic* (New York: Columbia University Press, 1992): 227–28.
7. Steve Allen, *The Funny Men* (New York: Simon and Schuster, 1956): 125.
8. Jenkins, *What Made Pistachio Nuts? Early Sound Comedy and the Vaudeville Aesthetic*: 172.
9. Joe Franklin, *Joe Franklin's Encyclopedia of Comedians* (Secaucus, New Jersey: Citadel Press, 1979): 90.
10. "Rogue's Progress," *Newsweek* (January 6, 1947): 19.

11. Eddie Cantor (with Jane Kesner Ardmore), *Take My Life* (Garden City, New York: Doubleday, 1957): 140.
12. "Leo McCarey Oral History," American Film Institute (Los Angeles), 1972, originally conducted by Peter Bogdanovich, 1968–69, 60.
13. Cantor, *Take My Life*: 158.
14. See the author's *Leo McCarey: From Marx to McCarthy* (Lanham, Maryland: Scarecrow Press, 2005).
15. Thomson, *The New Biographical Dictionary of Film*: 132.
16. John S. Cohen, Jr., "*The Kid from Spain*, or Bullfights with Eddie Cantor and Sidney Franklin," *New York Sun* (November 18, 1932): 27.
17. "Cantor for Vaude Tour," *Hollywood Reporter* (October 6, 1932): 2.
18. Thornton Delehanty, "*The Kid from Spain*, Starring Eddie Cantor, Inaugurates New Policy at the Palace," *New York Post* (November 18, 1932): 22.
19. "*The Kid from Spain* a Hit; Gay Gorgeous Production," *Hollywood Reporter* (October 20, 1932): 3.
20. Irene Thirer, "*Kid from Spain* Mirth Film," *New York Daily News* (November 18, 1932): 54.
21. Ernest Hemingway, *Death in the Afternoon* (New York: Scribner, 1932).
22. Regina Crewe, "*Kid from Spain*, Shown at Palace, Gay and Tuneful," *New York American* (November 18, 1932): 10.
23. Mordaunt Hall, "Eddie Cantor in an Uproaring Farce with Interludes of Singing and Dancing," *New York Times* (November 18, 1932): 23.
24. Cohen, "*The Kid from Spain*, or Bullfights with Eddie Cantor and Sidney Franklin."
25. Serge Daney and Jean-Louis Noames, "Taking Chances: Interview with Leo McCarey," *Cahiers du cinema in English* (January 1967): 48.
26. *Ibid*.: 49.
27. Cantor, *Take My Life*: 157.
28. *Kid from Spain* review, *Variety* (November 22, 1932).
29. Rose Pelswick, "Eddie Cantor Film Inaugurates Straight Movie Policy For Palace Theatre," *New York Evening Journal* (November 18, 1932): 24.
30. Sidney Franklin, *Bullfighter from Brooklyn* (New York: Prentice Hall, 1952): 212.
31. For more on Goldwyn's decision, see: "Goldwyn to Hit #2 Spots with Cantor," *Hollywood Reporter* (September 23, 1932): 1.
32. *Kid from Spain* review, *Variety*.
33. Steinberg, *Reel Facts: The Movie Book of Records*: 368.
34. Cantor, *Take My Life*: 158.
35. A Scott Berg, *Goldwyn: A Biography* (New York: Riverhead Books, 1989): 227.

Chapter 3: Mae West's *She Done Him Wrong* (1933)

1. Mae West, *Goodness Had Nothing to Do with It* (1959; rpt. New York: Macfadden-Bartell, 1970): 110.
2. Jill Watts, *Mae West: An Icon in Black and White* (New York: Oxford University Press, 2001): 98.
3. George Eells and Stanley Musgrove, *Mae West: A Biography* (New York: Morrow, 1982): 68.
4. John Mason Brown, "Mae West As An Actress On the Stage and Screen — Her Performance in *She Done Him Wrong*," *New York Post* (March 25, 1933): Section 2: 4.
5. Rose Pelswick, "Mae West Film Rich in Slang and Humor," *New York Evening Journal* (February 10, 1933): 13.
6. See the author's *Parody as Film Genre: "Never Give a Saga an Even Break"* (Westport, Connecticut: Greenwood Press, 1999).
7. Author's correspondence with William Goldman (October 5, 1980): 1.
8. *She Done Him Wrong* review, *London Times* (April 3, 1933).
9. William Boehnel, "*She Done Him Wrong* Crisp Picture of the '90s," *New York World Telegram* (February 10, 1933): 18; Martin Dickstein, "Mae West Adorns the Brooklyn Paramount's Screen in *She Done Him Wrong*," *Brooklyn Daily Eagle* (February 24, 1933).
10. Thornton Delehanty, "Mae West in *She Done Him Wrong* As Shown on the Paramount Screen," *New York Post* (February 10, 1933).
11. Pare Lorentz, *She Done Him Wrong* review, *Vanity Fair* (March 1933).
12. George Kent, "The Mammy and Daddy of Us All," *Photoplay* (May 1934): 32–33, 100–03.
13. Finley Peter Dunne, *The World of Mr. Dooley*, ed., Louis Filler (New York: Collier Books, 1962): 29.
14. Leo McCarey, "Mae West Can Play Anything," *Photoplay* (June 1935): 126.
15. Jon Tuska, *The Films of Mae West* (Secaucus, New Jersey: Citadel Press, 1973): 69.
16. West, *Goodness Had Nothing to Do with It*: 151.
17. Geoffrey Wansell, *Haunted Idol: The Story of the Real Cary Grant* (New York: William Morrow and Company, Inc., 1983): 90.
18. Leonard Maltin, *The Great Movie Comedians: From Charlie Chaplin to Woody Allen* (New York: Crown Publishers, Inc., 1978): 154.
19. Cobbett Steinberg, *Reel Facts: The Movie Book of Records* (New York: Vintage Books, 1978): 368.
20. "Comic Relief," *The New Yorker* (February 18, 1933).
21. Richard Watts, Jr., "*She Done Him Wrong*— Paramount," *New York Herald Tribune* (February 10, 1933): 11.
22. Lorentz, *She Done Him Wrong* review.
23. Pelswick, "Mae West Film Rich in Slang and Humor."
24. *She Done Him Wrong* review, *London Times*.
25. Stark Young, *Diamond Lil* review, *New Republic* (June 27, 1928): 145–46.
26. "So Mae West's Slipping? Not So She Can Notice It!" *Los Angeles Times* (May 20, 1934): Section 2: 3.
27. *Ibid*.
28. Brown, "Mae West as an Actress on the Stage

and Screen — Her Performance in *She Done Him Wrong*."
29. Watts, "*She Done Him Wrong*— Paramount."
30. Leonard J. Leff and Jerold L. Simmons, *The Dame in the Kimono: Hollywood, Censorship, and the Production Code* (Lexington: University Press of Kentucky, 2001): 31.
31. "Para's *She Done Him Wrong* Bawdy but Plenty Funny," *Hollywood Reporter* (January 10, 1933): 3.
32. *Ibid.*
33. Gerald Weales, *Canned Goods as Caviar: American Film Comedy of the 1930s* (Chicago: University of Chicago Press, 1985): 49.
34. *Ibid.*: 39.
35. Andre Sennwald, "Lines For a Mae West Scrapbook," *New York Times* (September 30, 1934): Section 9: 4.
36. Otis Ferguson, *The Film Criticism of Otis Ferguson*, ed. Robert Wilson (Philadelphia: Temple University Press): 53.
37. Lewis Jacobs, *The Rise of the American Film: A Critical History* (1939; rpt New York: Teachers College Press, Columbia University, 1971): 532–33.
38. As quoted in Jacobs' *The Rise of the American Film: A Critical History*: 533.
39. Eells and Musgrove, *Mae West: A Biography*: 138.

Chapter 4: The Marx Brothers' *Duck Soup* (1933)

1. Numerous listings can be found for the date of Chico's (Leonard) birth but August 1887 seems the most likely. See the author's *The Marx Brothers: A Bio-Bibliography* (Westport, Connecticut: Greenwood Press, 1987) and *Groucho & W. C. Fields: Huckster Comedians* (Jackson: University Press of Mississippi, 1994).
2. Joe Adamson, *Groucho, Harpo, Chico and Sometimes Zeppo* (New York: Simon and Schuster, 1973).
3. See especially the Salvador Dalí article "Surrealism in Hollywood," *Harper's Bazaar* (June 1937): 68–69, 132.
4. Louis Chavance, "The Four Marx Brothers As Seen by a Frenchman," *The Canadian Forum* (February 1933): 175.
5. Maxine Marx, *Growing Up with Chico* (Englewood Cliffs, New Jersey: Prentice-Hall, 1980): 60.
6. Ronald J. Fields (ed.), *W. C. Fields by Himself: His Intended Autobiography* (Englewood Cliffs, New Jersey: Prentice-Hall, 1973): 481.
7. Arthur Marx, *Life with Groucho: A Son's-Eye View* (New York: Simon and Schuster, 1954): 173.
8. Jay Carr, *The A List: The National Society of Film Critics' 100 Essential Films* (Cambridge, Massachusetts: Da Capo Press, 2002): 100.
9. See the author's *Dark Comedy: Beyond Satire* (Westport, Connecticut: Greenwood Press, 1996), 54, 60, 61.
10. "Marx Break Reported," *New York Times* (March 10, 1933): 18.
11. Richard Barrios, *A Song in the Dark: The Birth of the Musical Film* (New York: Oxford University Press, 1995): 255.
12. For example, see John S. Cohen, "*Let's Go Native*, Wherein Jack Oakie and Others Spread Mirth on a Tropical Island," *New York Sun* (August 30, 1930): 4.
13. Adamson, *Groucho, Harpo, Chico and Sometimes Zeppo*: 217.
14. Allen Eyles, *The Marx Brothers: Their World of Comedy* (New York: Paperback Library, 1971): 104.
15. Charles Silver, "Leo McCarey: From Marx to McCarthy," *Film Comment* (September 1973): 9.
16. Edward Dmytryk, *It's a Hell of a Life but Not a Bad Living* (New York: Time Books, 1978): 37.
17. *Ibid.*: 35.
18. Leo McCarey, "The Audience Must Go On," *Hollywood Reporter* (November 2, 1943 — Thirteenth Anniversary Issue).
19. Sidney Carroll, "Everything Happens to McCarey: During those sparse times when he isn't breaking his valuable neck, Leo McCarey does direct some extraordinary pictures," *Esquire* (May 1943): 57, 140–42.
20. See the author's *Leo McCarey: From Marx to McCarthy* (Lanham, Maryland: Scarecrow Press, 2005).
21. See the author's *The Marx Brothers: A Bio-Bibliography*; *Groucho & W. C. Fields: Huckster Comedians*.
22. Eyles, *The Marx Brothers: Their World of Comedy*: 106.
23. Serge Daney and Jean-Louis Noames, "Taking Chances: Interview with Leo McCarey," *Cahiers du cinema in English* (January 1967): 49.
24. Groucho Marx and Richard J. Anobile, *The Marx Brothers Scrapbook* (New York: Grosset & Dunlap, 1974): 149.
25. Gerald Weales, *Canned Goods as Caviar: American Film Comedy of the 1930s* (Chicago: University of Chicago Press, 1985): 72.
26. Daney and Noames, "Taking Chances": 49.
27. Marx and Anobile, *The Marx Brothers Scrapbook*: 150.
28. Hector Arce, *Groucho* (New York: Putnam, 1979): 212.
29. Marx and Anobile, *The Marx Brothers Scrapbook*: 148.
30. Adamson, *Groucho, Harpo, Chico and Sometimes Zeppo*: 224.
31. Andrew Bergman, *We're in the Money: Depression America and Its Films* (New York: Harper and Row, 1972): 37.
32. Robert S. McElvaine, *The Depression and the New Deal: A History in Documents* (New York: Oxford University Press, 2000): 153.
33. Edward Watz, *Wheeler & Woolsey: The Vaudeville Comic Duo and Their Films, 1929–1937* (1994; rpt. Jefferson, North Carolina: McFarland, 2001): 189–90.

34. "Wheeler and Woolsey in New Film at RKO Roxy," *New York Post* (May 1, 1933): 12.
35. Regina Crewe, "Wheeler, Woolsey In *Diplomaniacs* at the RKO — Roxy," *New York American* (May 2, 1933).
36. Richard Watts, Jr., "*Duck Soup*— Rivoli," *New York Herald Tribune* (November 23, 1933): 15.
37. See the author's *Dark Comedy: Beyond Satire* (Westport, Connecticut: Greenwood Press, 1996).
38. Jim Knipfel, *Slackjaw* (1999; rpt. New York: Berkley Books, 2000): 180.
39. Harpo Marx (with Rowland Barber), *Harpo Speaks!* (1961; rpt. New York: Freeway Press, 1974): 27.
40. *Ibid.*: 38.
41. *Duck Soup* review, *Variety* (November 28, 1933).
42. Kate Cameron, "Marx Brothers Full of Fun in *Duck Soup*," *New York Daily News* (November 23, 1933): 44.
43. *Duck Soup* review, *Newsweek* (December 2, 1933): 33.
44. "*Duck Soup* Typical Marx Whirligig of Laughter," *The Hollywood Reporter* (November 2, 1933): 3.
45. Cameron, "Marx Brothers Full of Fun in *Duck Soup*."
46. Marx and Anobile, *The Marx Brothers Scrapbook*: 80.
47. Harpo Marx, *Harpo Speaks!*: 24.

Chapter 5: Laurel and Hardy's *Sons of the Desert* (1933)

1. Gerald Mast, *The Comic Mind: Comedy and the Movies* (Indianapolis: Bobbs-Merrill, 1973): 191.
2. Kurt Vonnegut, *Slapstick* (New York: Delacorte Press/Seymour Lawrence, 1976): 1–19.
3. See the author's *Laurel & Hardy: A Bio-Bibliography* (Westport, Connecticut: Greenwood Press, 1990).
4. See the author's two books on McCarey: *Leo McCarey and the Comic Anti-Hero in American Film* (New York: Arno Press, 1980); *Leo McCarey: From Marx to McCarthy* (Lanham, Maryland: Scarecrow Press, 2005).
5. The author has written extensively on the subject, starting with these two articles: "The Comic Anti-Hero in American Fiction: Its First Full Articulation," *Thalia: Studies in Literary Humor* (Winter 1979–80): 11–14; "Film's First Comic Anti-Heroes: Leo McCarey's Laurel & Hardy," *Ball State University Forum* (Autumn 1979): 46–56.
6. Hamlin Hill, "Modern American Humor: The Janus Laugh," *College English* (December 1963): 174.
7. Gerald Mast, *A Short History of the Movies* (1971; rpt. Indianapolis: Bobbs-Merrill, 1981): 76–92.
8. Robert Benchley, *From Bed to Worse: Or Comforting Thoughts About the Bison* (New York: Harper & Brothers, 1934): 255.
9. Graham Greene, *A Chump at Oxford* review, *Spectator* (February 23, 1940): 248.
10. John McCabe, *The Comedy World of Stan Laurel* (Garden City, New York: Doubleday, 1974): 64.
11. For example, see *Sons of the Desert* review, *Variety* (January 9, 1934).
12. Alan Dale, *Comedy Is a Man in Trouble: Slapstick in American Movies* (Minneapolis: University of Minnesota Press, 2000): 9.
13. Leo McCarey, "The Could-Be Quality," *The Hollywood Reporter* (October 28, 1939) — 9th Anniversary Issue.
14. Donald W. McCaffrey, *The Golden Age of Sound Comedy: Comic Films and Comedians of the Thirties* (New York: A. S. Barnes, 1973): 92.
15. Randy Skretvedt, *Laurel and Hardy: The Magic Behind the Movies* (Beverly Hills, California: Moonstone Press, 1987): 201.
16. *Sons of the Desert* review, *New York Post* (January 9, 1934).
17. Cobbett Steinberg, *Reel Facts: The Movie Book of Records* (New York: Vintage Books, 1978): 339.
18. "New Laurel and Hardy Feature Is Good Fun," *Hollywood Reporter* (November 10, 1933): 3.
19. Andre Sennwald, *Sons of the Desert* review, *New York Times* (January 12, 1934): 29.
20. *Sons of the Desert* review, *Newsweek* (January 20, 1934): 35; "Laurel and Hardy Film Farce Seen at Loew's Metropolitan," *New York American* (January 8, 1934).
21. John S. Cohen, Jr., "*Sons of the Desert*, with Laurel and Hardy, at the Rialto," *New York Sun* (January 1, 1934).
22. Wanda Hale, "Laurel and Hardy Okay in *Sons of the Desert*," *New York Daily News* (January 12, 1934): 54.
23. *Sons of the Desert* review, *Liberty Magazine* (February 17, 1934).
24. *Ibid.*
25. Mel Watkins, "Richard Pryor, Who Turned Ghetto Humor Into Biting Social Satire, Dies at 65," *New York Times* (December 11, 2005): 42.

Chapter 6: Will Rogers' *Judge Priest* (1934)

1. Will Rogers, *Letters of a Self-Made Diplomat to His President* (New York: Albert & Charles Boni, 1926).
2. An uncredited *They Had to See Paris* review cited by Ben Yagoda, *Will Rogers: A Biography* (1993; rpt. New York: HarperCollins, 1994): 259.
3. Cobbett Steinberg, *Reel Facts: The Movie Book of Records* (New York: Vintage Books, 1978): 404.
4. George McKenna, ed., *American Populism* (New York: G. P. Putnam's, 1974): xii.
5. See the author's populism books: *Populism and the Capra Legacy* (Westport, Connecticut: Greenwood Press, 1995); *Mr. Deeds Goes to Yankee Stadium: Baseball Films in the Capra Tradition* (Jefferson, North Carolina: McFarland, 2004).
6. Roger Butterfield, "The Legend of Will Rogers," *Life* (July 1949): 92, 94.

7. Walter Blair, *Horse Sense in American Humor* (Chicago: University of Chicago Press, 1942): vii.

8. James Russell Lowell, "The Biglow Papers: Second Series," in *The Complete Poetical Works of James Russell Lowell*, ed. Horace E. Scuddler (1894; rpt. Cambridge, Massachusetts: Riverside Press, 1924): 237.

9. Richard Hofstadter, "North America," in *Populism: Its Meanings and National Characteristics*, eds. Ghita Ionescu and Ernest Gellner (London: Weidenfeld and Nicholson, 1969): 17.

10. Rogers, *Letters of a Self-Made Diplomat to His President*: 234.

11. *Judge Priest* press release (Fox, 1934), in the Will Rogers file, Margaret Herrick Library, Academy of Motion Picture Arts and Sciences (Beverly Hills, California).

12. Scott Eyman, *Print the Legend: The Life and Times of John Ford* (Baltimore: John Hopkins University Press, 1999): 146.

13. Mark Spragg, *An Unfinished Life* (2004; rpt. New York: Vintage Contemporaries, 2005).

14. Irvin S. Cobb, *Exit Laughing* (1941; rpt. Garden City, New York: Garden City Publishing, 1942): 340.

15. Elizabeth Cobb, *My Wayward Parent: A Book About Irwin S. Cobb* (Indianapolis: Bobbs-Merrill Company, 1945): 162.

16. *Ibid.*: 163.

17. McKenna, ed., *American Populism*: 3.

18. Rose Pelswick, "Rogers Brings Fine Humor to Judge's Role," *New York Evening Journal* (October 12, 1934): 19.

19. William Boehnel, "Irvin Cobb's Old South Seen in Rogers Comedy," *New York World Telegram* (October 12, 1934): 25.

20. Hilton Als, "Mammy for the Masses," *The New Yorker* (September 26, 2005): 148–51.

21. Mel Watkins, *Stepin Fetchit: The Life & Times of Lincoln Perry* (New York: Pantheon Books, 2005): Dedication.

22. Als, "Mammy for the Masses": 150.

23. Eyman, *Print the Legend: The Life and Times of John Ford*: 147.

24. Ben Yagoda, *Will Rogers: A Biography* (1993; rpt. New York: Harper Collins, 1994): 312.

25. Rochelle Hudson (as told to Reginald Taviner), "On the Set with Will Rogers," *Photoplay* (August 1935): 108.

26. *Ibid.*: 106.

27. Bryan B. Sterling, ed., *The Will Rogers Scrapbook* (New York: Grosset & Dunlap, 1976): 175.

28. "Rogers' Kindness Recalled by Cobb," *Philadelphia Bulletin* (August 22, 1935).

29. Bryan B. Sterling and Frances N. Sterling, *Will Rogers in Hollywood* (New York: Crown Publishers, 1984): 152.

30. Irvin S. Cobb, "Irvin Cobb Recalls His Pal Bill," *Los Angeles Examiner* (August 17, 1935).

31. Seba Smith, *The Life and Writings of Major Jack Downing* (1833; rpt. New York: AMS Press, 1973): 226.

32. Will Rogers, *There's Not a Bathing Suit in Russia & Other Bare Facts* (New York: Albert & Charles Boni, 1927): 136.

33. Jack Lait, ed., *Will Rogers: Wit and Wisdom* (New York: Frederick A. Stokes Company, 1936): 55, 65.

34. Yagoda, *Will Rogers: A Biography*: 292.

35. Eyman, *Print the Legend: The Life and Times of John Ford*: 148.

36. Steinberg, *Reel Facts: The Movie Book of Records*: 339.

37. Andre Sennwald, *Judge Priest* review, *New York Times* (October 12, 1934): 33.

38. *Judge Priest* review, *Variety* (October 16, 1934).

39. John Scott, "*Judge Priest* Scores in Studio's Preview Showing," *Los Angeles Times* (September 14, 1934), and "Star Scores Screen Hit," *Los Angeles Times* (September 28, 1934): Section 1: 13.

40. "John Ford Re-joins Fox," *Los Angeles Times* (September 15, 1934): Section 1: 4.

41. *Judge Priest* "subpoena" invitation, in the *Judge Priest* file, Performing Arts Library, New York Public Library at Lincoln Center (New York).

42. Eileen Creelman, *Judge Priest* review, *New York Sun* (October 12, 1934): 27.

43. Regina Crewe, "Will Rogers Acts One of Best Roles As *Judge Priest*," *New York American* (October 12, 1934): 30.

44. Rose Pelswick, "Rogers Brings Fine Humor to Judge's Role."

45. Richard Watts, Jr., "*Judge Priest*: Radio City Music Hall," *New York Herald Tribune* (October 12, 1934): 27.

46. "New York Reviews: *Judge Priest*," *Hollywood Reporter* (October 20, 1934): 2.

47. Will Rogers, "Rogers Gets a History Lesson" (June 24, 1934), in *Will Rogers' Weekly Articles: The Roosevelt Years, 1933–1935*, ed. Steven K. Gragert (Stillwater: Oklahoma State University Press, 1982): 128.

48. *Ibid.*: 130.

49. Will Rogers, "Good Sportsmanship Among the Movie Actors" (July 1, 1934), in *Will Rogers Weekly Articles: The Roosevelt Years, 1933–1935*, ed. Steven K. Gragert (Stillwater: Oklahoma State University Press, 1982): 131.

50. "John Ford Gives Old-Timers Chance for a Film Comeback," *New York World Telegram* (May 6, 1933): 9.

51. Scott Eyman, *John Ford: The Searcher, 1894–1973* (Los Angeles: Taschen, 2004): 86.

52. Eyman, *Print the Legend: The Life and Times of John Ford*: 146.

53. Margo Jefferson, "A Serious Look at a Humorous Man," *New York Times* (September 29, 1993): C-20.

54. *Judge Priest* print ad, *Los Angeles Times* (September 27, 1934): Part 1: 13.

55. Jim Kitses, *Horizons West* (Bloomington: Indiana University Press, 1969): 103.

56. As quoted in Peter C. Rollins' "Will Rogers: Symbolic Man and Film Image," *Journal of Popular Film* (Fall 1973): 331.

Chapter 7: W.C. Fields' *It's a Gift* (1934)

1. See the author's *W. C. Fields: A Bio-Bibliography* (Westport, Connecticut: Greenwood Press, 1984); *Groucho & W. C. Fields: Huckster Comedians* (Jackson: University Press of Mississippi, 1994).
2. *Poppy* review, *London Times* (July 13, 1936).
3. Walter Blair, *Native American Humor* (1937; rpt. Scranton, Pennsylvania: Chandler Publishing, 1960): 86.
4. "W. C. Fields Stars in Hilarious Film at the Paramount," *New York American* (July 14, 1934): 9.
5. William Boehnel, "Horseplay's the Thing in New Fields Picture," *New York World Telegram* (July 14, 1934): 9.
6. See the author's "W. C. Fields: The Copyrighted Sketches," *Journal of Popular Film & Television* (Summer 1986): 65–75.
7. W. C. Fields, "The Family Ford," in the "W. C. Fields Papers" (copyrighted October 16, 1919 — first of three versions), Library of Congress: 6.
8. Floyd Clymer, *Those Wonderful Old Automobiles* (New York: Bonanza Books, 1953): 151.
9. Anthony Channell Hilfer, *The Revolt from the Village: 1915–1930* (Chapel Hill: University of North Carolina, 1969): 5.
10. Carl Van Doren, "The Revolt from the Village," *Nation* (October 12, 1921): 407.
11. Carlotta Monti (with Cy Rice), *W. C. Fields & Me* (1971; rpt. New York: Warner Books, 1973): 48.
12. Edgar Lee Masters, "Deacon Taylor," in *Spoon River Anthology* (1915; rpt. New York: Collier Books, 1962): 80.
13. Van Doren, "Revolt from the Village,": 410.
14. Sinclair Lewis, *Babbitt* (1922; rpt. New York: Signet Classic, 1980): 6–7.
15. Jack Grant, "That Nose of W. C. Fields," *Movie Classic* (February 1935): 60.
16. Maude Cheatham, "Juggler of Laughs," *Silver Screen* (April 1935): 30.
17. Mary B. Mullett, "Bill Fields Disliked His Label, So He Laughed It Off," *American Magazine* (January 1926): 19.
18. Dunham Tharp, "The Up-To-Date Old Timer," *Motion Picture Classic* (September 1926): 39.
19. Ibid.
20. Sara Redway, "W. C. Fields Pleads For Rough Humor," *Motion Picture Classic* (September 1925): 33.
21. *It's a Gift* review, *Literary Digest* (January 19, 1935): 30.
22. James Curtis, *W. C. Fields: A Biography* (New York: Alfred A. Knopf, 2003): 305.
23. Redway, "W. C. Fields Pleads for Rough Humor": 32.
24. Andre Sennwald, *It's a Gift* review, *New York Times* (January 5, 1935): 20.
25. Robert Benchley, "Kiddie-Kar Travel," in *Pluck and Luck* (New York: Henry Holt and Company, 1925): 6.
26. W. C. Fields, "Life Begins at 20 — Says W. C. Fields," *Motion Picture* (September 1935): 71.
27. Simon Louvish, *Man on the Flying Trapeze: The Life and Times of W. C. Fields* (New York: W. W. Norton & Company, 1997): 387.
28. *It's a Gift* review, *Variety* (January 8, 1935).
29. Will Rogers, "All I Know Is What They Say in Their Wires" (June 3, 1934), in *Will Rogers' Weekly Articles: The Roosevelt Years, 1933–1935*, ed. Steven K. Gragert (Stillwater: Oklahoma State University Press, 1982): 124.
30. Richard Watts, Jr., "*It's a Gift* — Roxy," *New York Herald Tribune* (January 5, 1935): 10.
31. William Boehnel, "Lively Screen Infants Greet the New Year," *New York World Telegram* (January 5, 1935): 18.
32. *It's a Gift* review, *Literary Digest*.
33. "*It's a Gift* (Paramount)," *Time* (January 14, 1935): 34, 36.
34. *It's a Gift* review, *London Times* (December 31, 1934).
35. *It's a Gift* capsule review, *Film Comment* (May/June 1983).
36. Andre Sennwald, "W. C. Fields Buffoon," *New York Times* (January 13, 1935): Section 9: 5.
37. "Sennwald's Death Laid to Gas Fumes," *New York Times* (January 13, 1936): 18.
38. Ibid.
39. Steve Seidman, *Comedian Comedy: A Tradition in Hollywood* (Ann Arbor: University of Michigan Research Press, 1981): 153.
40. See James Thurber's *The Owl in the Attic* (1931; rpt. New York: Harper & Row, 1965).

Chapter 8: Joe E. Brown's *Alibi Ike* (1935)

1. Joe E. Brown (with Margaret Lee Runbeck), *Your Kids and Mine* (Garden City, New York: Doubleday, Doran and Co., Inc., 1944): 12.
2. Bosley Crowther, *Earthworm Tractors* review, *New York Times* (July 25, 1936): 16.
3. Joe E. Brown (as told to Ralph Hancock), *Laughter Is a Wonderful Thing* (New York: A. S. Barnes and Company, 1956): 222.
4. "Sporting Life," *Time* (April 27, 1953).
5. Lowell Reidenbaugh, *Baseball's Hall of Fame: Cooperstown: Where the Legends Live Forever* (1983; New York: Crescent Books, 1997): 52.
6. Nicholas Dawidoff (ed.), *Baseball: A Literary Anthology* (New York: Library of America, 2002): 1.
7. John Bowman and Zoel Zoss, *Diamonds in the Rough: The Untold History of Baseball* (New York: Macmillan, 1989): 3.
8. "Sporting Life."
9. "*Fireman* Corking Comedy," *The Hollywood Reporter* (January 27, 1932): 3.
10. Mordaunt Hall, "Joe E. Brown and Patricia Ellis in a Film of a Baseball Comedy by Ring Lardner," *New York Times* (May 26, 1933): 24.
11. Bland Johaneson, *Alibi Ike* review, *New York Daily Mirror* (July 17, 1935).

12. Joe E. Brown, "The Role I Liked Best..," *Saturday Evening Post* (November 9, 1946).
13. Leonard Maltin, *The Great Movie Comedians: From Charlie Chaplin to Woody Allen* (New York: Crown Publishers, Inc., 1978): 125.
14. "Japanese Captives Wanted Baseball Talk," *New York Times* (April 25, 1943): Section 1: 13.
15. Carl Erskine, "Foreword," in the author's *Mr. Deeds Goes to Yankee Stadium: Baseball Films in the Capra Tradition* (Jefferson, North Carolina: McFarland, 2004): 10.
16. Brown, *Your Kids and Mine*: 100.
17. "Wife Leaves for East to Greet Joe E. Brown," *Hollywood Citizen-News* (February 11, 1944).
18. "Baseball Post to Joe E. Brown," *New York Times* (April 1, 1953): 38.
19. Sheila Wolfe, "Joe E. Brown Grins, Waits for Surgery," *Chicago Tribune* (April 16, 1965): Section 1: 3.
20. "Ricky Successor Pledges Pennant," *New York Times* (October 26, 1955): 36.
21. Brown, *Laughter Is a Wonderful Thing*: 225.
22. See the author's *Mr. Deeds Goes to Yankee Stadium: Baseball Films in the Capra Tradition*.
23. Brown, "The Role I Liked Best ..."
24. Ring Lardner, *You Know Me Al: A Busher's Letters* (1914; rpt. New York: Collier Books, 1991).
25. See especially Walter Blair's *Native American Humor* (1937; rpt. Scranton, Pennsylvania: Chandler Publishing, 1960).
26. For example, see Richard Watts, Jr., *Fireman, Save My Child* review, *New York Herald Tribune* (February 19, 1932): 12; *Fireman, Save My Child* review, *New York Sun* (February 20, 1932): 6.
27. "Joe Brown Wants To Play Rube Waddell," *Hollywood Reporter* (December 28, 1942): 3.
28. *Fireman, Save My Child* review, *Variety* (February 23, 1932).
29. "*Fireman* Corking Comedy," *The Hollywood Reporter* (January 27, 1932): 3.
30. Cobbett Steinberg, *Reel Facts: The Movie Book of Records* (New York: Vintage Books, 1978): 403.
31. Lucius Beebe, "*Elmer the Great*—Radio City Music Hall," *New York Herald Tribune* (May 26, 1933): 18; "*Elmer the Great* Gives Plenty of Belly-Laughs," *The Hollywood Reporter* (March 23, 1933): 3.
32. Mordaunt Hall, "Joe E. Brown and Patricia Ellis in a Film of a Baseball Comedy by Ring Lardner," *New York Times* (May 26, 1933): 24.
33. *Elmer the Great* review, *New York Sun* (May 27, 1933): 27.
34. William Dabb, *Elmer the Great* mini-review, *Motion Picture Herald* (May 13, 1933): 53.
35. Carl Veseth, *Elmer the Great* mini-review, *Motion Picture Herald* (July 22, 1933): 69.
36. Ring Lardner, "Alibi Ike," in "*Haircut*" *and Other Stories* (1922; New York: Charles Scribner's Sons, 1954): 36.
37. Mitchell Woodbury, "Strolling Around [Series Trophies Given Joe Brown]," *Toledo Times* (October 14, 1934): 5-D.
38. "Me 'n Paul" (cover story), *Time* (April 15, 1935): 52.
39. Regina Crewe, "*Alibi Ike*, Amusing Ring Lardner Tale, Stars Joe Brown," *New York American* (July 17, 1935); "*Alibi Ike* Comedy Home Run," *The Hollywood Reporter* (June 8, 1935): 3.
40. Richard Watts, Jr., *Alibi Ike* review, *New York Herald Tribune* (July 17, 1935): 10.
41. Lardner, *You Know Me Al: A Busher's Letters*: 46.
42. *Ibid.*, 72.
43. Brown, *Laughter Is a Wonderful Thing*: 213.
44. Lardner, *You Know Me Al: A Busher's Letters*: 45.
45. Reidenbaugh, *Baseball's Hall of Fame: Cooperstown, Where the Legends Live Forever*: 193.
46. "Lusty Shake: Joe Brown's Grip May Have Cost Game," *Toledo Times* (October 9, 1934): 2.
47. Will Rogers, "Mr. Rogers Makes His Official Report on World Series Finale and The Riot" (October 10, 1934, syndicated daily newspaper telegram), in *Will Rogers' Daily Telegrams, vol. 4, The Roosevelt Years: 1933–1935*, ed. James M. Smallwood (Stillwater: Oklahoma State University Press, 1979): 228.
48. *Alibi Ike* review, *Los Angeles Times* (June 7, 1935).
49. John Thorn and Pete Palmer, eds., *Total Baseball* (New York: Warner Books, 1989): 261.
50. "*Alibi Ike* Comedy Home Run," *The Hollywood Reporter*.
51. "Ring Lardner Story Offers Joe Brown Familiar Material," *New York Post* (July 17, 1935).
52. "Joe E. Brown Returns in a Merry Film Version of Ring Lardner's *Alibi Ike*, at the Cameo," *New York Times* (July 17, 1935): 22.
53. Rose Pelswick, "Joe E. Brown Amusingly Plays Goofy Pitcher in Baseball Classic," *New York Evening Journal* (July 17, 1935).
54. Eileen Creelman, "Joe E. Brown as a Ring Lardner Ball Player in *Alibi Ike*," *New York Sun* (July 17, 1935).
55. Wanda Hale, "*Alibi Ike* Cheers Joe E. Brown Fans," *New York Daily News* (July 17, 1935).
56. Brown, "The Role I Liked Best..."; David Condon, "The Hand That Still Grips Joe E. Brown," *Chicago Tribune* (June 15, 1963).
57. "Then Joe Brown Ducked," uncredited newspaper story (October 23, 1930), in the Joe E. Brown file, National Baseball Hall of Fame and Museum (Cooperstown, New York).
58. Sandy Grady, "The Forum," *USA Today* (August 22, 2002): 12-A.
59. Paul Dickson, *Baseball's Greatest Quotations* (New York: HarperCollins, 1991): 148.

Chapter 9: The Marx Brothers' *A Night at the Opera* (1935)

1. See the author's *The Marx Brothers: A Bio-Bibliography* (Westport, Connecticut: Greenwood Press, 1987); *Groucho & W. C. Fields: Huckster Comedians* (Jackson: University Press of Mississippi, 1994).

2. "Classic Scene: *A Night at the Opera*," *Premiere* (November 1996): 115.
3. Groucho Marx, *Groucho and Me* (1959; rpt. New York: Manor Books, 1974): 234–35.
4. Francis Birrell, "The Marx Brothers," *New Statesman and Nation* (October 1, 1932): 374.
5. Teet Carle, "Laughing Stock: Common and Preferred," *Stage* (March 1937): 50.
6. Arthur Marx, *Life with Groucho* (New York: Simon and Schuster, 1954): 198.
7. See the author's *Leo McCarey: From Marx to McCarthy* (Lanham, Maryland: Scarecrow Press, 2005).
8. See the author's *Irene Dunne: First Lady of Hollywood* (Lanham, Maryland: Scarecrow Press, 2003).
9. For example, see Alva Johnston's "The Scientific Side of Lunacy," *Woman's Home Companion* (September 1936): 12.
10. Harpo Marx (with Rowland Barber), *Harpo Speaks!* (1961; rpt. New York: Freeway Press, 1974): 375.
11. Lillian Roth (with Mike Connolly and Gerald Frank), *I'll Cry Tomorrow* (New York: Frederick Fell, 1954): 85.
12. Otis Ferguson, "The Marxian Epileptic," *The New Republic* (December 11, 1935): 130.
13. "*It's a Gift* Grand Nonsense," *The Hollywood Reporter* (November 8, 1934): 3.
14. "Testing a Film—for Laughs," *Brooklyn Eagle* (December 10, 1935).
15. "*A Night at the Opera* Will Win Converts to Marxism," *Newsweek* (November 23, 1935): 29.
16. Johnston, "The Scientific Side of Lunacy": 12.
17. *A Night at the Opera* ad, *New York American* (December 6, 1935): 17.
18. *Ibid.*
19. Carle, "Laughing Stock: Common and Preferred."
20. Clifton Fadiman, "A New High in Low Comedy," *Stage* (January 1936).
21. James Thurber, *My Life and Hard Times* (1933; rpt. New York: Bantam Books, 1947): 52–53.
22. James Thurber, "James Thurber Presents *Der Tag Aux Courses*," *Stage* (March 1937): 49.
23. Antonin Artaud, "Les Frères Marx au Cinéma du Panthéon," *Nouvelle Revue Française* (January 1, 1932).
24. Joseph Alsop, Jr., "Surrealism Beaten at Its Own Game," *New York Herald Tribune* (December 15, 1935).
25. E. H. Gombrich, *The Story of Art* (1950; rpt. and enlarged. New York: Phaidon Press, 1975): 472.
26. See the author's *American Dark Comedy: Beyond Satire* (Westport, Connecticut: Greenwood Press, 1996).
27. Max Schultz, *Black Humor Fiction of the Sixties* (Athens: Ohio University Press, 1973): 71.
28. Blake Bailey, "Proto Beat," *New York Times* (January 29, 2006): Book Review section: 12.
29. Salvador Dalí, "Surrealism in Hollywood," *Harper's Bazaar* (June 1937): 68.
30. Marie Seton, "S. Dalí + 3 Marxes = ," *Theatre Arts* (October 1939): 734–40.
31. Robert Goff, *The Essential Salvador Dalí* (New York: Wonderland Press, 1998): 66.
32. "The Marx Brothers in *A Night at the Opera*, a Mad, Merry Comedy, at the Capitol," *New York Sun* (December 7, 1935): 10.
33. Gilbert Seldes, *The Movies Come from America* (New York: Charles Scribner's Sons, 1937): 44.
34. Thornton Delehanty, "The Marx Brothers At the Capitol," *New York Post* (December 7, 1935).
35. William Boehnel, "*A Night at the Opera* Causes Jaws to Ache," *New York World Telegram* (December 7, 1935): 21; Kate Cameron, "Marx Brothers in Hilarious Comedy," *New York Daily News*.
36. Rose Pelswick, "Hilarious Lunacy Marks Marx Film—Diverting Comedy at Roxy," *New York Evening Journal* (December 7, 1935): 8.
37. Richard Watts, Jr., "*A Night at the Opera*—Capitol," *New York Herald Tribune* (December 7, 1935): 10.
38. Fadiman, "A New High in Low Comedy."
39. *Ibid.*
40. Read Kendall, "Around and About in Hollywood," *Los Angeles Times* (November 2, 1934): Section 1: 15.
41. "Marx Brothers Plans Unusual," *Los Angeles Times* (November 15, 1934): Section 1: 13.
42. Kendall, "Around and About in Hollywood."
43. See the author's *Screwball Comedy: A Genre of Madcap Romance* (Westport, Connecticut: Greenwood Press, 1986); *Romantic vs. Screwball Comedy: Charting the Difference* (Lanham, Maryland: Scarecrow Press, 2002).
44. Kate Cameron, "Babies, Just Babies, on Music Hall Screen," *New York Daily News* (March 4, 1938): 46.
45. Otis Ferguson, "While We Were Laughing" (1940), in *The Film Criticism of Otis Ferguson*, ed. Robert Wilson (Philadelphia: Temple University Press, 1971): 24.
46. Philip K. Scheuer, "Barrymore Has Acting Holiday," *Los Angeles Times* (May 1934).
47. *My Man Godfrey* review, *Variety* (September 23, 1936).
48. Jim Knipfel, *Quitting the Nairobi Trio* (2000; rpt. New York: Berkley Books, 2001): 277.
49. Alan Alda, *Never Have Your Dog Stuffed and Other Things I've Learned* (New York: Random House, 2005): 157.

Chapter 10: Charlie Chaplin's *Modern Times* (1936)

1. "Chaplin: A Bewildered 'Little Feller' Bucking Modern Times," *Newsweek* (February 8, 1936): 19.
2. *Ibid.*
3. John McCabe, *Charlie Chaplin* (Garden City, New York: Doubleday, 1978): 182.
4. Charles Chaplin, *My Autobiography* (1964; rpt. New York: Pocket Books, 1966): 415.
5. David Robinson, *Chaplin: His Life and Art* (New York: McGraw-Hill, 1985): 474.

6. Charlie Chaplin, *A Comedian Sees the World* (New York: Crowell, 1933).

7. "Chaplin to Direct the 'Perfect' Talkie," *The Hollywood Reporter* (August 25, 1932): 1.

8. Charles Maland, *Chaplin and American Culture: The Evolution of a Star Image* (Princeton, New Jersey: Princeton University Press, 1989): 143–44.

9. "Chaplin Set on All Silent for Next," *The Hollywood Reporter* (January 26, 1934): 1.

10. "Chaplin Will Talk In Production No. 5," *The Hollywood Reporter* (October 13, 1934): 1.

11. Robert Forsythe, *Modern Times* review, *New Masses* (February 18, 1936).

12. *Ibid.*

13. See the author's "Chaplin and the Progressive Era: The Neglected Politics of a Clown," *Indiana Social Studies Quarterly* (Autumn 1981): 10–18. The subject is also addressed in the author's *Charlie Chaplin: A Bio-Bibliography* (Westport, Connecticut: Greenwood Press, 1983).

14. Robert Warshow, "*Monsieur Verdoux*," in *The Immediate Experience* (1962; rpt. New York: Antheneum, 1972): 208.

15. Otis Ferguson, *Modern Times* review, *The New Republic* (February 19, 1936).

16. Theodore Huff, *Charlie Chaplin* (1951; rpt. New York: Arno Press and the New York Times, 1972): 258.

17. George Orwell, *1984* (1949; rpt. New York: Signet Classic, 1961).

18. Michael Shelden, *Orwell: The Authorized Biography* (New York: HarperCollins, 1991): 325.

19. Rose Pelswick, "Chaplin Returns in Old Role but Brings New Laughs and Sings to Film Fans," *New York Evening Journal* (February 6, 1936): 16.

20. Campbell Dixon, "New Triumph by Chaplin," *London Daily Telegraph* (February 12, 1936).

21. Béla Balázs, *Theory of the Film*, trans. Edith Bone (1952; rpt. New York: Dover, 1970): 237.

22. Robert Payne, *The Great God Pan: A Biography of the Tramp Played by Charles Chaplin* (New York: Hermitage House, 1952).

23. Lillian Ross, *Moments with Chaplin* (New York: Dodd, Mead, 1980): 59, 61.

24. Walter Kerr, *The Silent Clowns* (New York: Alfred A. Knopf, 1975): 358.

25. Huff, *Charlie Chaplin*: 257.

26. Charles Chaplin, Jr. (with N. and M. Rau), *My Father, Charlie Chaplin* (New York: Random House, 1960): 113.

27. Balázs, *Theory of the Film*: 284–85.

28. Gene Siskel, "Woody Allen, A Joker More Mild Than Wild," *Chicago Tribune* (September 24, 1978): Section 6: 3.

29. Frank S. Nugent, "Heralding the Return, After an Undue Absence, of Charlie Chaplin in *Modern Times*," *New York Times* (February 6, 1936): 23.

30. Mark Van Doren, "Charlie Chaplin," *Nation* (February 19, 1936): 232.

31. *Modern Times* review, *Variety* (February 12, 1936).

32. Dixon, "New Triumph by Chaplin."

33. William Boehnel, "Chaplin Still Supreme in His *Modern Times*," *New York World Telegram* (February 6, 1936): 27.

34. Frank S. Nugent, "The Reign of Good King Charlie," *New York Times* (February 9, 1936): Section 10: 5.

35. Winston Burdett, "*Modern Times*, With Charlie Chaplin, Opens at the Rivoli," *Brooklyn Eagle* (February 6, 1936).

36. "*Modern Times* at the Rivoli," *New York Daily Mirror* (February 7, 1936).

37. Otis Ferguson, *Modern Times* review, *New Republic* (February 19, 1936).

38. John McCabe, *Charlie Chaplin*: 186.

39. "Reich Has Yet to Act on New Chaplin Film," *New York Times* (February 18, 1936): 8.

40. "Vienna Won't Let Chaplin Wave Red Flag in Picture," *New York Times* (April 3, 1936): 27.

41. Chaplin, *My Autobiography*: 420.

42. Huff, *Charlie Chaplin*: 253.

43. "Charlie Chaplin," in *Current Biography 1940*, ed. Maxine Block (New York: H. H. Wilson, 1940): 158.

Chapter 11: Laurel and Hardy's *Way Out West* (1937)

1. Will Rogers, "Some Vivas for Mexico" (November 15, 1931), in *Will Rogers' Weekly Articles: The Hoover Years: 1931–1933*, ed. Steven K. Gragert (Stillwater: Oklahoma State University Press, 1982): 87.

2. Leonard Maltin, *The Great Movie Comedians: From Charlie Chaplin to Woody Allen* (New York: Crown Publishers, Inc., 1978): 103.

3. Basil Wright, "Blest Pair of Sirens," *World Film News* (June 1937): 3.

4. *Ibid.*

5. John Grierson, "The Logic of Comedy" (1935), in *Grierson on Documentary*, ed. Forsyth Hardy (New York: Praeger Publishers, 1971): 51.

6. See the author's *Parody as Film Genre: "Never Give a Saga an Even Break"* (Westport, Connecticut: Greenwood Press, 1999).

7. *Way Out West* review, *Variety* (May 5, 1937): 16.

8. See the author's *Laurel & Hardy: A Bio-Bibliography* (Westport, Connecticut: Greenwood Press, 1990).

9. John McCabe, *Laurel & Hardy*, ed. Al Kilgore (1975; rpt. New York: Ballantine Books, 1976): 347.

10. Siegfried Kracauer, *Theory of Film: The Redemption of Physical Reality* (1960; rpt. New York: Oxford University Press, 1971): 107.

11. Leo McCarey, "The Could-Be Quality," *The Hollywood Reporter* (October 28, 1939)—9th Anniversary Issue.

12. "1937—An Interview with L & H," discovered and prefaced by Eldon K. Everett, *Classic Film Collector* (1976)—see the author's *Laurel & Hardy: A Bio-Bibliography*: 227.

13. W. H. Mooring, "With MacLaurel & MacHardy in Bonnie Scotland," *Film Weekly* (June 28, 1935): 8, 9, 28.
14. Frank Capra, *The Name Above the Title* (New York: Macmillan, 1971): 64.
15. Dorothy Masters, "Laurel-Hardy Comedy Jeopardizes Theatre," *New York Daily News* (May 4, 1937).
16. Archer Winsten, "Laurel and Hardy Panic Rialto with Their Act," *New York Post* (May 4, 1937).
17. *Ibid.*
18. Frank S. Nugent, *Way Out West* review, *New York Times* (May 4, 1937): 29.
19. William Boehnel, "Laurel and Hardy in Lively Comedy," *New York World Telegram* (May 4, 1937).
20. *Way Out West* review, *London Times* (May 3, 1937).
21. Randy Skretvedt, *Laurel and Hardy: The Magic Behind the Movies* (Beverly Hills, California: Moonstone Press, 1987): 323.
22. John Lahr, "Bring Me Sunshine," *The New Yorker* (January 21, 2002): 84.
23. William Paul, *Way Out West* (January 29, 1970): 58.

Chapter 12: Bob Hope's *The Cat and the Canary* (1939)

1. Bob Hope and Bob Thomas, *The Road to Hollywood: My 40-Year Love Affair with the Movies* (Garden City, New York: Doubleday & Company, 1977): 31.
2. Bob Hope, *They Got Me Covered* (Hollywood, California: no publisher credited, 1941). This short paperback (95 pages) is seldom listed among Hope's many books and appears to have been privately published.
3. Eric Lax, *Woody Allen: A Biography* (New York: Alfred A. Knopf, 1991): 25.
4. Harrison B. Summers (ed.), *A Thirty-Year History of Programs Carried on National Radio Networks in the United States, 1926–1956* (New York: Arno Press, 1971): 83.
5. William Robert Faith, *Bob Hope: A Life in Comedy* (New York: G. P. Putnam's Sons, 1982): 140.
6. See the author's *Parody as Film Genre: "Never Give a Saga an Even Break"* (Westport, Connecticut: Greenwood Press, 1999).
7. *Cat and the Canary* review, *Variety* (November 1, 1939).
8. Howard Rushmore, "Horror Stuff, but Pleasant, at Paramount," *New York Daily Worker* (November 23, 1939).
9. Robert Coleman, "*Cat and Canary* Film Outdoes Stage Play," *New York Daily Mirror* (November 23, 1939).
10. Rose Pelswick, "*Cat and the Canary* Opens at Paramount," *New York Journal American* (November 24, 1939): 14.
11. Kate Cameron, "*Cat and the Canary* a Wow at Paramount," *New York Daily News* (November 23, 1939): 52.
12. Archer Winsten, "*The Cat and the Canary* Opens at the Paramount," *New York Post* (November 24, 1939): 13.
13. "Red Skelton Scores in First Starring Role," *New York Morning Telegram* (August 28, 1941).
14. "Radio Poll," *The Hollywood Reporter* (December 21, 1941): 1.
15. "Top Male Stars," *The Hollywood Reporter* (October 31, 1941).
16. *The Ghost Breakers* review, *New York Post* (July 5, 1940): 8.
17. Todd S. Purdum, "Bob Hope, Before He Became the Comedy Establishment," *New York Times* (April 20, 2003): Section 2: 7.
18. Brooks Riley, "Words of Hope," *Film Comment* (May/June 1979): 21.
19. Dick Cavett, "I Was Bob Hope," *Film Comment* (May/June 1979): 18–19.
20. Alva Johnston, "Close-Up: Bob Hope," *Life* (October 27, 1941): 112.
21. John Lahr, "The C. E. O. of Comedy," *The New Yorker* (December 21, 1998): 72.
22. Howard Barnes, "*The Ghost Breakers*—Paramount," *New York Herald Tribune* (July 4, 1940): 6.
23. Jeffrey Couchman, "Bob Hope: More Than a Gagster?," *New York Times* (May 6, 1979): Section 2: 1,15.
24. "*Cat and Canary* Sparkling Comedy Murder Mystery," *The Hollywood Reporter* (October 25, 1939): 3.
25. "At the Paramount," *New York World Telegram* (November 24, 1939): 28; Herbert Cohn, "Hope in Top Form in *Cat and Canary*," *Brooklyn Eagle* (November 23, 1939).
26. Eileen Creelman, "Five Pictures, Melodrama and Comedy, Open on the Holidays," *New York Sun* (November 24, 1939): 30.
27. Frank S. Nugent, *The Cat and the Canary* review, *New York Times* (November 23, 1939): 38.
28. Winsten, "*The Cat and the Canary* Opens at the Paramount."
29. Louella Parsons, "Paulette Goddard and Bob Hope Scheduled For Another Thriller, *The Ghost Breakers*," *Los Angeles Examiner* (November 22, 1939): Section 1: 17.
30. "*Ghost Breakers* Riotous...," *The Hollywood Reporter* (June 6, 1940): 3.
31. Wanda Hale, "*The Ghost Breakers* A Mirthful Thriller," *New York Daily News* (July 4, 1940): 22.
32. "*Ghost Breakers* at the Paramount," *PM* (July 4, 1940).
33. "*Road to Singapore* Swell; Crosby and Hope Fine Team," *The Hollywood Reporter* (February 21, 1940): 3.
34. Larry Gelbert, *Laughing Matters* (New York: Random House, 1998): 71.

Epilogue

1. Anthony Lane, "Looking For Heroes," *The New Yorker* (June 6, 2005): 106.
2. See the author's *Personality Comedians as Genre: Selected Players* (Westport, Connecticut: Greenwood Press, 1997).
3. Siegfried Kracauer, *Theory of Film: The Redemption of Physical Reality* (New York: Oxford University Press, 1960): 272.
4. Gerald Mast, *The Comic Mind: Comedy and the Movies* (Indianapolis: Bobbs-Merrill, 1973): 109.
5. Allen Eyles, *The Marx Brothers: Their World of Comedy* (New York: Paperback Library, 1971): 109.
6. See the author's *America Dark Comedy: Beyond Satire* (Westport, Connecticut: Greenwood Press, 1996).
7. Scott Eyman, *Print the Legend: The Life and Times of John Ford* (Baltimore: John Hopkins University Press, 1999): 147.
8. Alexander Woollcott, *While Rome Burns* (New York: Grosset and Dunlap, 1934): 268–269.

Bibliography

Books

Adamson, Joe. *Groucho, Harpo, Chico and Sometimes Zeppo.* New York: Simon and Schuster, 1973.

Alda, Alan. *Never Have Your Dog Stuffed: And Other Things I've Learned.* New York: Random House, 2005.

Allen, Steve. *The Funny Men.* New York: Simon and Schuster, 1956.

American Film Institute (with Duane Byrge). *Private Screenings: Insiders Share a Century of Great Movie Moments.* Atlanta: Turner Publishing, 1995.

Arce, Hector. *Groucho.* New York: Putnam, 1979.

Balázs, Béla. *Theory of the Film.* Trans. Edith Bone, 1952; rpt. New York: Dover, 1970.

Barrios, Richard. *A Song in the Dark: The Birth of the Musical Film.* New York: Oxford University Press, 1995.

Benchley, Robert. *After 1903—What?* New York: Harper & Brothers, 1938.

_____. *From Bed to Worse: Or Comforting Thoughts About the Bison.* New York: Harper & Brothers, 1934.

Berg, A. Scott. *Goldwyn: A Biography.* New York: Riverhead Books, 1989.

Bergman, Andrew. *We're in the Money: Depression America and Its Films.* New York: Harper and Row, 1972.

Blair, Walter. *Horse Sense in American Humor.* Chicago: University of Chicago Press, 1942.

_____. *Native American Humor.* 1937; rpt. Scranton, Pennsylvania: Chandler Publishing, 1960.

Bowman, John, and Zoel Zoss. *Diamonds in the Rough: The Untold History of Baseball.* New York: Macmillan, 1989.

Brown, Joe E. (as told to Ralph Hancock). *Laughter Is a Wonderful Thing.* New York: A. S. Barnes, 1956.

_____. (with Margaret Lee Runbeck). *Your Kids and Mine.* Garden City, New York: Doubleday, Doran, 1944.

Brownlow, Kevin. *The Parades Gone By....* 1968; rpt. New York: Ballantine Books, 1970.

Cantor, Eddie (with Jane Kesner Ardmore). *Take My Life.* Garden City, New York: Doubleday, 1957.

Capra, Frank. *The Name Above the Title.* New York: Macmillan, 1971.

Carr, Jay. *The A List: The National Society of Film Critics' 100 Essential Films.* Cambridge, Massachusetts: Da Capo Press, 2002.

Chaplin, Charlie. *A Comedian Sees the World.* New York: Crowell, 1933.

Chaplin, Charles. *My Autobiography.* 1964; rpt. New York: Pocket Books, 1966.

Chaplin, Charles, Jr. (with N. and M. Rau). *My Father, Charlie Chaplin.* New York: Random House, 1960.

Chaplin, Lita Grey (with Morton Cooper). *My Life with Chaplin.* New York: Bernard Geis Associates, 1966.

Clymer, Floyd. *Those Wonderful Old Automobiles.* New York: Bonanza Books, 1953.

Cobb, Elizabeth. *My Wayward Parent: A Book About Irvin S. Cobb.* Indianapolis: Bobbs-Merrill, 1945.

Cobb, Irvin S. *Exit Laughing.* 1941; rpt. Garden City, New York: Garden City Publishing, 1942.

Curtis, James. *W. C. Fields: A Biography.* New York: Alfred A. Knopf, 2003.

Dale, Alan. *Comedy Is a Man in Trouble: Slapstick in American Movies.* Minneapolis: University of Minnesota Press, 2000.

Dawidoff, Nicholas (ed.) *Baseball: A Literary Anthology.* New York: Library of America, 2002.

Dickson, Paul. *Baseball's Greatest Quotations.* New York: HarperCollins, 1991.

Dmytryk, Edward. *It's a Hell of a Life but Not a Bad Living.* New York: Time Books, 1978.

Dunne, Finley Peter. *The World of Mr. Dooley.* Ed. Louis Filler. New York: Collier Books, 1962.

Eells, George, and Stanley Musgrove. *Mae West: A Biography*. New York: Morrow, 1982.
Eyles, Allen. *The Marx Brothers: Their World of Comedy*. New York: Paperback Library, 1971.
Eyman, Scott. *John Ford: The Searcher, 1894–1973*. Los Angeles: Taschen, 2004.
_____. *Print the Legend: The Life and Times of John Ford*. Baltimore: John Hopkins University Press, 1999.
Faith, William Robert. *Bob Hope: A Life in Comedy*. New York: Putnam's, 1982.
Ferguson, Otis. *The Film Criticism of Otis Ferguson*. Ed. Robert Wilson. Philadelphia: Temple University Press, 1971.
Fields, Ronald J. (ed.). *W. C. Fields by Himself: His Intended Autobiography*. Englewood Cliffs, New Jersey: Prentice-Hall, 1973.
Franklin, Joe. *Joe Franklin's Encyclopedia of Comedians*. Secaucus, New Jersey: Citadel Press, 1979.
Franklin, Sidney. *Bullfighter from Brooklyn*. New York: Prentice-Hall, 1952.
Gehring, Wes D. *American Dark Comedy: Beyond Satire*. Westport, Connecticut: Greenwood Press, 1996.
_____. *Charlie Chaplin: A Bio-Bibliography*. Westport, Connecticut: Greenwood Press, 1983.
_____. *Groucho & W. C. Fields: Huckster Comedians*. Jackson: University Press of Mississippi, 1994.
_____. *Joe E. Brown: Film Comedian and Baseball Buffoon*. Jefferson, North Carolina: McFarland, 2006.
_____. *Laurel & Hardy: A Bio-Bibliography*. Westport, Connecticut: Greenwood Press, 1990.
_____. *Leo McCarey and the Comic Anti-Hero in American Film*. New York: Arno Press, 1980.
_____. *Leo McCarey: From Marx to McCarthy*. Lanham, Maryland: Scarecrow Press, 2005.
_____. *The Marx Brothers: A Bio-Bibliography*. Westport, Connecticut: Greenwood Press, 1987.
_____. *Mr. Deeds Goes to Yankee Stadium: Baseball Films in the Capra Tradition*. Jefferson, North Carolina: McFarland, 2004.
_____. *Parody as Film Genre: "Never Give a Saga an Even Break."* Westport, Connecticut: Greenwood Press, 1999.
_____. *Personality Comedians as Genre: Selected Players*. Westport, Connecticut: Greenwood Press, 1997.
_____. *Populism and the Capra Legacy*. Westport, Connecticut: Greenwood Press, 1995.
_____. *W. C. Fields: A Bio-Bibliography*. Westport, Connecticut: Greenwood Press, 1984.
Gelbert, Larry. *Laughing Matters*. New York: Random House, 1998.
Goff, Robert. *The Essential Salvador Dali*. New York: Wonderland Press, 1998.
Gombrich, E.H. *The Story of Art*. 1950; rpt. and enlarged. New York: Phaidon Press, 1975.
Hale, Georgia (ed. Heather Kiernan). *Charlie Chaplin: Intimate Close-Ups*. 1995; rpt. Lanham, Maryland: Scarecrow Press, 1999.
Hemingway, Ernest. *Death in the Afternoon*. New York: Scribner's, 1932.
Hilfer, Anthony Channell. *The Revolt from the Village: 1915–1930*. Chapel Hill: University of North Carolina, 1969.
Hope, Bob. *They Got Me Covered*. Hollywood, California: no publisher credited, 1941.
Hope, Bob, and Bob Thomas. *The Road to Hollywood: My 40-Year Love Affair with the Movies*. Garden City, New York: Doubleday, 1977.
Huff, Theodore. *Charlie Chaplin*. 1951; rpt. New York: Henry Schuman, 1972.
Jacobs, Lewis. *The Rise of the American Film: A Critical History*. 1939; rpt. New York: Teachers College Press, Columbia University, 1971.
Jenkins, Henry. *What Made Pistachio Nuts? Early Sound Comedy and the Vaudeville Aesthetic*. New York: Columbia University Press, 1992.
Kerr, Walter. *The Silent Clowns*. New York: Alfred A. Knopf, 1975.
Kitses, Jim. *Horizons West*. Bloomington: Indiana University Press, 1969.
Knight, Arthur. *The Liveliest Art: A Panoramic History of the Movies*. New York: Macmillan, 1978.
Knipfel, Jim. *Quitting the Nairobi Trio*. 2000; rpt. New York: Berkley Books, 2001.
_____. *Slackjaw*. 1999; rpt. New York: Berkley Books, 2000.
Kracauer, Siegfried. *Theory of Film: The Redemption of Physical Reality*. New York: Oxford University Press, 1960.
Lait, Jack (ed.). *Will Rogers: Wit and Wisdom*. New York: Frederick A. Stokes, 1936.
Lardner, Ring. *You Know Me Al: A Busher's Letters*. 1914; rpt. New York: Colliers Books, 1991.
Lax, Eric. *Woody Allen: A Biography*. New York: Alfred A. Knopf, 1991.
Leff, Leonard J., and Jerold L. Simmons. *The Dame in the Kimono: Hollywood Censorship, and the Production Code*. Lexington: University Press of Kentucky, 2001).
Lewis, Jerry, and James Kaplan. *Dean & Me: A Love Story*. New York: Doubleday, 2005.
Lewis, Sinclair. *Babbitt*. 1922; rpt. New York: Signet Classics, 1980.
Louvish, Simon. *Man on the Flying Trapeze: The Life and Times of W. C. Fields*. New York: W. W. Norton, 1997.
Maland, Charles. *Chaplin and American Culture: The Evolution of a Star Image*. Princeton, New Jersey: Princeton University Press, 1989.
Maltin, Leonard. *The Great Movie Comedians: From Charlie Chaplin to Woody Allen*. New York: Crown, 1978.

Marx, Arthur. *Life with Father: A Son's-Eye View.* New York: Simon and Schuster, 1954.

_____. *Son of Groucho.* New York: David McKay, 1972.

Marx, Groucho. *Groucho and Me.* 1959; rpt. New York: Manor Books, 1974.

Marx, Groucho, and Richard J. Anobile. *The Marx Brothers Scrapbook.* New York: Grosset & Dunlap, 1974.

Marx, Harpo (with Rowland Barber). *Harpo Speaks!.* 1961; rpt. New York: Freeway Press, 1974.

Marx, Maxine. *Growing Up with Chico.* Englewood Cliffs, New Jersey: Prentice-Hall, 1980.

Mast, Gerald. *The Comic Mind: Comedy and the Movies.* Indianapolis: Bobbs-Merrill, 1973.

_____. *A Short History of the Movies.* 1971; rpt. Indianapolis: Bobbs-Merrill, 1981.

McCabe, John. *Charlie Chaplin.* Garden City, New York: Doubleday, 1978.

_____. *The Comedy World of Stan Laurel.* Garden City, New York: Doubleday, 1974.

_____. *Laurel & Hardy.* Ed. Al Kilgore. 1975; rpt. New York: Ballantine Books, 1976.

McCaffrey, Donald W. *The Golden Age of Sound Comedy: Comic Films and Comedians of the Thirties.* New York: A. S. Barnes, 1973.

McElvaine, Robert S. *The Depression and the New Deal: A History in Documents.* New York: Oxford University Press, 2000.

McKenna, George (ed.). *American Populism.* New York: Putnam's, 1974.

Monti, Carolotta (with Cy Rice). *W. C. Fields & Me.* 1971; rpt. New York: Warner Books, 1973.

Moss, Robert F. *Charlie Chaplin.* 1975; rpt. New York: Harcourt Brace Jovanovich, 1977.

Murray, Edward. *Fellini the Artist.* New York: Frederick Ungar, 1976.

Novick, Peter. *The Noble Dream: The "Objectivity Question" and the American Historical Profession.* Cambridge: Cambridge University Press, 1988.

Orwell, George. *1984.* 1949; rpt. New York: Signet Classic, 1961.

Payne, Robert. *The Great God Pan: A Biography of the Tramp Played by Charles Chaplin.* New York: Hermitage House, 1952.

Quigly, Isabel. *Charlie Chaplin: Early Comedies.* London: Studio Vista, 1968.

Reidenbaugh, Lowell. *Baseball's Hall of Fame: Cooperstown: Where the Legends Live Forever.* 1983; rpt. New York: Crescent Books, 1997.

Robinson, David. *Chaplin: His Life and Art.* New York: McGraw-Hill, 1985.

Rogers, Will. *Letters of a Self-Made Diplomat to His President.* New York: Albert & Charles Boni, 1926.

_____. *There's Not a Bathing Suit in Russia & Other Bare Facts.* New York: Albert & Charles Boni, 1927.

Ross, Lillian. *Moments with Chaplin.* New York: Dodd, Mead, 1980.

Ross, Lillian (with Mike Connolly and Gerold Frank). *I'll Cry Tomorrow.* New York: Frederick Fell, 1954.

Schmitz, Neil. *Of Huck and Alice: Humorous Writing in American Literature.* Minneapolis: University of Minnesota Press, 1983.

Schultz, Max. *Black Humor Fiction of the Sixties.* Athens: Ohio University Press, 1973.

Seidman, Steve. *Comedian Comedy: A Tradition in Hollywood.* Ann Arbor: University of Michigan Research Press, 1981.

Seldes, Gilbert. *The Movies Come from America.* New York: Scribner's, 1937.

Shelden, Michael. *Orwell: The Authorized Biography.* New York: HarperCollins, 1991.

Skretvedt, Randy. *Laurel and Hardy: The Magic Behind the Movies.* Beverly Hills, California: Moonstone Press, 1987.

Smith, Seba. *The Life and Writings of Major Jack Downing.* 1833; rpt. New York: AMS Press, 1973.

Spragg, Mark. *An Unfinished Life.* 2004; rpt. New York: Vintage Contemporaries, 2005.

Steinberg, Cobbett. *Reel Facts: The Movie Book of Records.* New York: Vintage Books, 1978.

Sterling, Bryan B., and Frances N. Sterling. *Will Rogers in Hollywood.* New York: Crown, 1984.

Sterling, Bryan B. (ed.). *The Will Rogers Scrapbook.* New York: Grosset & Dunlap, 1976.

Summers, Harrison B. (ed.). *A Thirty-Year History of Programs Carried on National Radio Networks in the United States, 1926–1956.* New York: Arno Press, 1971.

Thomson, David. *The New Biographical Dictionary of Film.* New York: Alfred A. Knopf, 2003.

Thorn, John, and Pete Palmer (eds.). *Total Baseball.* New York: Warner Books, 1989.

Thurber, James. *The Owl in the Attic.* 1931; rpt. New York: Harper & Row, 1965.

Tuska, Jon. *The Films of Mae West.* Secaucus, New Jersey: Citadel Press, 1973.

Twain, Mark. *Huckleberry Finn.* 1885; rpt. New York: W. W. Norton, 1962.

Vonnegut, Kurt. *Slapstick.* New York: Delacorte Press/Seymour Lawrence, 1976.

Wansell, Geoffrey. *Haunted Idol: The Story of the Real Cary Grant.* New York: William Morrow, 1983.

Watkins, Mel. *Stepin Fetchit: The Life & Times of Lincoln Perry.* New York: Pantheon Books, 2005.

Watts, Jill. *Mae West: An Icon in Black and White.* New York: Oxford University Press, 2001.

Watz, Edward. *Wheeler & Woolsey: The Vaudeville Comic Duo and Their Films, 1929–1937.* 1994; rpt. Jefferson, North Carolina: McFarland, 2001.

Weales, Gerald. *Canned Goods as Caviar: American*

Film Comedy of the 1930s. Chicago: University of Chicago Press, 1985.
West, Mae. *Goodness Had Nothing to Do with It*. 1959; rpt. New York: MacFadden-Bartell, 1970.
Woollcott, Alexander. *While Rome Burns*. New York: Grosset and Dunlap, 1934.
Yagoda, Ben. *Will Rogers: A Biography*. 1993; rpt. New York: HarperCollins, 1994.

Shorter Works

Agee, James. "Comedy's Greatest Era." *Life* (September 3, 1949).
"*Alibi Ike* Comedy Home Run." *The Hollywood Reporter* (June 8, 1935): 3.
Alibi Ike review. *Los Angeles Times* (June 7, 1935).
Als, Hilton. "Mammy For the Masses." *The New Yorker* (September 26, 2005): 148–51.
Alsop, Joseph, Jr. "Surrealism Beaten at Its Own Game." *New York Herald Tribune* (December 15, 1935).
Artaud, Antonin. "Les Frères Marx au Cinéma du Panthéon." *Nouvelle Revue Française* (January 1, 1932).
"At the Paramount." *New York World Telegram* (November 24, 1939): 28.
Bailey, Blake. "Proto Beat." *New York Times* (January 29, 2006): Book Review Section: 12.
Barnes, Howard. "*The Ghost Breakers*— Paramount." *New York Herald Tribune* (July 4, 1940): 6.
"Baseball Post to Joe E. Brown." *New York Times* (April 1, 1953): 38.
Bazin, André. "The Virtues and Limitations of Montage." In *What Is Cinema? Vol. 1*. Ed. and translator Hugh Gray. 1958; rpt. Los Angeles: University of California Press, 1967.
Beebe, Lucius. "*Elmer the Great*— Radio City Music Hall." *New York Herald Tribune* (May 26, 1933): 18.
Benchley, Robert. "Kiddie-Kar Travel." In *Pluck and Luck*. Henry Holt, 1925: 6–15.
Bergson, Henri. "Laughter" (1900). In *Comedy*. Ed. Wylie Sypher. Garden City, New York: Doubleday Anchor Books, 1956.
"Big Deal For London." *The Hollywood Reporter* (December 19, 1930): 1.
Birrell, Francis. "The Marx Brothers." *New Statesman and Nation* (October 1, 1932): 374–75.
Boehnel, William. "Chaplin Still Supreme in His *Modern Times*." *New York World Telegram* (February 6, 1936): 27.
_____. "Horseplay's the Thing in New Fields Picture." *New York World Telegram* (July 14, 1934): 9.
_____. "Irvin Cobb's Old South Seen in Rogers Comedy." *New York World Telegram* (October 12, 1934): 25.
_____. "Laurel and Hardy in Lively Comedy." *New York World Telegram* (May 4, 1937).
_____. "Lively Screen Infants Greet the New Year." *New York World Telegram* (January 5, 1935): 18.
_____. "*A Night at the Opera* Causes Jaws to Ache." *New York World Telegram* (December 7, 1935): 21.
_____. "*She Done Him Wrong* Crisp Picture of the '90s." *New York World Telegram* (February 10, 1933): 18.
Bogdanovich, Peter. "Modern Screen." *New York Observer* (March 6, 2000): 23.
Brown, Joe E. "The Role I Liked Best ..." *Saturday Evening Post* (November 9, 1946): 97.
Brown, John Mason. "Mae West as an Actress On the Stage and Screen — Her Performance in *She Done Him Wrong*." *New York Post* (March 25, 1933): Section 2: 4.
Burdett, Winston. "*Modern Times*, with Charlie Chaplin, Opens at the Rivoli." *Brooklyn Eagle* (February 6, 1936).
Butterfield, Roger. "The Legend of Will Rogers." *Life* (July 1949): 92, 94.
Cameron, Kate. "Babies, Just Babies, on Music Hall Screen." *New York Daily News* (March 4, 1938): 46.
_____. "*Cat and the Canary* a Wow at Paramount." *New York Daily News* (November 23, 1939): 52.
_____. "Marx Brothers Full of Fun in *Duck Soup*." *New York Daily News* (November 23, 1933): 44.
"Cantor For Vaude Tour." *The Hollywood Reporter* (October 6, 1932): 2.
Carle, Teet. "Laughing Stock: Common and Preferred." *Stage* (March 1937): 48–50.
Carroll, Sidney. "Everything Happens to McCarey: During those sparse times when he isn't breaking his valuable neck, Leo McCarey does direct some extraordinary pictures." *Esquire* (May 1943): 57, 140–42.
Cat and the Canary review. *Variety* (November 1, 1939).
"*Cat and Canary* Sparkling Comedy Murder Mystery." *The Hollywood Reporter* (October 25, 1939): 3.
Cavett, Dick. "I Was Bob Hope." *Film Comment* (May/June 1979): 18–19.
"Chaplin: A Bewildered 'Little Feller' Bucking Modern Times." *Newsweek* (February 8, 1936): 19.
"Chaplin and Movie Hailed by Broadway." *New York World* (February 7, 1931): 11.
Chaplin, Charlie. "Pantomime and Comedy." *New York Times* (January 23, 1931): Section 8: 6.
"Chaplin Gets Legion of Honor, First for Foreign Film Actor." *New York Times* (March 28, 1931): 1.
"Chaplin Set on All Silent for Next." *The Hollywood Reporter* (January 26, 1934): 1.

"Chaplin to Direct the 'Perfect' Talkie." *The Hollywood Reporter* (August 25, 1932): 1.

"Chaplin Will Talk in Production No. 5." *The Hollywood Reporter* (October 13, 1934): 1.

"Charlie Chaplin." In *Current Biography 1940*. Ed. Maxine Block. New York: H. H. Wilson, 1940: 157–59.

"Charlie Chaplin Comes to Town." Uncited New York newspaper (February 4, 1931). In the *City Lights* file. Performing Arts Library, New York Public Library at Lincoln Center.

Chavance, Louis. "The Four Marx Brothers as Seen by a Frenchman." *The Canadian Forum* (February 1933): 175.

Cheatham, Maude. "Juggler of Laughs." *Silver Screen* (April 1935): 30–31, 62.

"*City Lights* A Cinch For Big Money Everywhere." *The Hollywood Reporter* (January 30, 1931): 3.

City Lights review. *Variety* (February 11, 1931).

Clark, Gerald. "She Was What She Was: Mae West, 1893–1980." *Time* (December 1, 1980): 80.

"Classic Scene: *A Night at the Opera*." *Premiere* (November 1996): 115.

Cobb, Irvin S. "Irvin Cobb Recalls His Pal Bill." *Los Angeles Examiner* (August 17, 1935).

Cohen, John S. "Chaplin Triumphs Anew in *City Lights*." *New York Sun* (February 7, 1931): 6.

_____. "*The Kid from Spain*, or Bullfights with Eddie Cantor and Sidney Franklin." *New York Sun* (November 18, 1932): 27.

_____. "*Let's Go Native*, Wherein Jack Oakie and Others Spread Mirth on a Tropical Island." *New York Sun* (August 30, 1930): 4.

_____. "*Sons of the Desert*, with Laurel and Hardy, at the Rialto." *New York Sun* (January 1, 1934).

Cohn, Herbert. "Hope in Top Form in *Cat and Canary*." *Brooklyn Eagle* (November 23, 1939).

Coleman, Robert. "*Cat and Canary* Film Outdoes Stage Play." *New York Daily Mirror* (November 23, 1939).

"Comic Relief." *The New Yorker* (February 18, 1933).

Couchman, Jeffrey. "Bob Hope: More Than a Gagster?" *New York Times* (May 6, 1979): Section 2: 1, 15.

Creelman, Eileen. "Five Pictures, Melodrama and Comedy, Open on the Holidays." *New York Sun* (November 24, 1939): 30.

_____. "Joe E. Brown as a Ring Lardner Ball Player in *Alibi Ike*." *New York Sun* (July 17, 1935).

_____. *Judge Priest* review. *New York Sun* (October 12, 1934): 27.

Crewe, Regina. "*Alibi Ike* Amusing Ring Lardner Tale, Stars Joe Brown." *New York American* (July 17, 1935).

_____. "Chaplin Film Test Tonight of Silent Versus the Talkies." *New York American* (February 6, 1931): 18.

_____. "*Kid from Spain*, Shown at Palace, Gay and Tuneful." *New York American* (November 18, 1932): 10.

_____. "Wheeler, Woolsey in *Diplomaniacs* at the RKO — Roxy." *New York American* (May 2, 1933).

_____. "Will Rogers Acts One of Best Roles as *Judge Priest*." *New York American* (October 12, 1934): 30.

Crowther, Bosley. *Earthworm Tractors* review. *New York Times* (July 25, 1936): 16.

Dabb, William. *Elmer the Great* mini-review. *Motion Picture Herald* (May 13, 1933): 53.

Dali, Salvador. "Surrealism in Hollywood." *Harper's Bazaar* (June 1937): 68–69, 132.

Daney, Serge, and Jean-Louis Noames. "Taking Chances: Interview with Leo McCarey." *Cahiers du cinema in English* (January 1967): 42–54.

Delehanty, Thornton. "Charles Chaplin Contributes a Generous Sample of His Genius in *City Lights*." *New York Post* (February 7, 1931): Section 4: 3.

_____. "*The Kid from Spain*, Starring Eddie Cantor, Inaugurates New Policy at the Palace." *New York Post* (November 18, 1932): 22.

_____. "Mae West in *She Done Him Wrong* as Shown on the Paramount Screen." *New York Post* (February 10, 1933).

_____. "The Marx Brothers At the Capitol." *New York Post* (December 7, 1935).

Dickstein, Martin. "Mae West Adorns the Brooklyn Paramount's Screen in *She Done Him Wrong*. *Brooklyn Daily Eagle* (February 24, 1933).

Dixon, Campbell. "New Triumph by Chaplin." *London Daily Telegraph* (February 12, 1936).

Duck Soup review. *Newsweek* (December 2, 1933): 33.

Duck Soup review. *Variety* (November 28, 1933).

"*Duck Soup* Typical Marx Whirligig of Laughter." *The Hollywood Reporter* (November 2, 1933): 3.

"Einstein Waves Aside Luring Movie Offers." *New York Times* (January 11, 1931): Section 2: 2.

"*Elmer the Great* Gives Plenty of Belly-Laughs." *The Hollywood Reporter* (March 23, 1933): 3.

Elmer the Great review. *New York Sun* (May 27, 1933): 27.

Erskine, Carl. "Foreword." In *Mr. Deeds Goes to Yankee Stadium: Baseball Films in the Capra Tradition*. By Wes D. Gehring. Jefferson, North Carolina: McFarland, 2004.

Fadiman, Clifton. "A New High in Low Comedy." *Stage* (January 1936).

Ferguson, Otis. "The Marxian Epileptic." *New Republic* (December 11, 1935): 130.

_____. *Modern Times* review. *New Republic* (February 19, 1936).

_____. "While We Were Laughing" (1940). In *The Film Criticism of Otis Ferguson*. Ed. Robert

Wilson. Philadelphia: Temple University Press, 1971: 18–24.

Fields, W. C. "The Family Ford." In the "W. C. Fields Papers" (copyrighted October 16, 1919 — first of three versions). Library of Congress.

_____. "Life Begins at 20 — Says W. C. Fields." *Motion Picture* (September 1935): 49, 70–71

"Fireman Corking Comedy." *Hollywood Reporter* (January 27, 1932): 3.

Fireman, Save My Child review. *New York Sun* (February 20, 1932): 6.

Fireman, Save My Child review. *Variety* (February 23, 1932).

Forsythe, Robert. *Modern Times* review. *New Masses* (February 18, 1936).

Gehring, Wes D. "Chaplin and the Progressive Era: The Neglected Politics of a Clown." *Indiana Social Studies Quarterly* (Autumn 1981): 10–18.

_____. "The Comic Anti-Hero in American Fiction: Its First Full Articulation." *Thalia: Studies in Literary Humor* (Winter 1979–80): 11–14.

_____. Conversation with John Hampton, silent film collector and original owner-operator of Los Angeles' Silent Movie Theatre. Los Angeles (June 1975): author's files.

_____. Correspondence with William Goldman. (October 5, 1980): author's files.

_____. "Fields and Falstaff" (cover article). *Thalia: Studies in Literary Humor* (Fall & Winter 1985): 36–42.

_____. "Film's First Comic Anti-Heroes: Leo McCarey's Laurel & Hardy." *Ball State University Forum* (Autumn 1979): 46–56.

_____. "The Many Faces of Movie Comedy." *USA Today Magazine* (July 1998): 80–89.

_____. "On the 'Road' with Hope & Crosby." *USA Today Magazine* (November 2000): 68–73.

_____. "Reel World: Baseball's Comic All-Star." *USA Today Magazine* (May 2005): 75.

_____. "Reel World: Chaplin's [*City*] *Lights* Still Shines." *USA Today Magazine* (March 2006): 59.

_____. "Reel World: Everything Is Ducky." *USA Today Magazine* (July 2004): 75.

_____. "Reel World: The Gears of a Clown." *USA Today Magazine* (November 2003): 71.

_____. "Reel World: Groucho and Leo in the Soup." *USA Today Magazine* (July 2005): 73.

_____. "Reel World: A Salute to the Genius of Director Leo McCarey." *USA Today Magazine* (September 2003): 61.

_____. "Reel World: 'You Said a Mouthful!' " *USA Today Magazine* (May 2004): 69.

_____. "Television's Other Groucho." *Humor: International Journal of Humor Research* (5–3, 1992): 267–82.

_____. "W. C. Fields: The Copyrighted Sketches." *Journal of Popular Film & Television* (Summer 1986): 65–75.

"*Ghost Breakers* At the Paramount." *PM* (July 4, 1940).

The Ghost Breakers review. *New York Post* (July 5, 1940): 8.

"*Ghost Breakers* Riotous..." *The Hollywood Reporter* (June 6, 1940): 3.

"Goldwyn to Hit #2 Spots with Cantor." *The Hollywood Reporter* (September 23, 1932): 1.

Gow, James. "Art Without Words." *New York World* (February 7, 1931): 11.

Grady, Sandy. "The Forum." *USA Today* (August 22, 2002): 12-A.

Grant, Jack. "That Nose of W. C. Fields." *Movie Classic* (February 1935): 56, 60.

Greene, Graham. *A Chump at Oxford* review. *Spectator* (February 23, 1940): 248.

Grierson, John. "The Logic of Comedy" (1935). In *Grierson on Documentary*. Ed. Forsyth Hardy. New York: Praeger, 1971: 45–58.

"Hails Chaplin Aid to Blind." *New York Times* (February 23, 1931): 5.

Hale, Wanda. "*Alibi Ike* Cheers Joe E. Brown Fans." *New York Daily News* (July 17, 1935).

_____. "*The Ghost Breakers* A Mirthful Thriller." *New York Daily News* (July 4, 1940): 22.

_____. "Laurel and Hardy Okay in *Sons of the Desert*." *New York Daily News* (January 12, 1934): 54.

Hall, Gladys. "Charlie Chaplin Attacks the Talkies." *Motion Pictures* (May 1929): 28+.

Hall, Mordaunt. "Chaplin Hilarious in His *City Lights*." *New York Times* (February 7, 1931): 11.

_____. "Eddie Cantor in an Uproaring Farce with Interludes of Singing and Dancing." *New York Times* (November 18, 1932): 23.

_____. "Joe E. Brown and Patricia Ellis in a Film of a Baseball Comedy by Ring Lardner." *New York Times* (May 26, 1933): 24.

Hill, Hamlin. "Modern American Humor: The Janus Laugh." *College English* (December 1963): 174.

Hofstadter, Richard. "North America." In *Populism: Its Meanings and National Characteristics*. Eds. Ghita Ionescu and Ernest Gellner. London: Weidenfeld and Nicholson, 1969.

Hudson, Rochelle (as told to Reginald Taviner). "On the Set with Will Rogers." *Photoplay* (August 1935): 108.

It's a Gift capsule review. *Film Comment* (May/June 1983).

"*It's a Gift* Grand Nonsense." *The Hollywood Reporter* (November 8, 1934): 3.

"*It's a Gift* (Paramount)." *Time* (January 14, 1935): 34, 36.

It's a Gift review. *Literary Digest* (January 19, 1935): 30.

It's a Gift review. *London Times* (December 31, 1934).

It's a Gift review. *Variety* (January 8, 1935).
"Japanese Captives Wanted Baseball Talk." *New York Times* (April 25, 1943): Section 1: 13.
Jefferson, Margo. "A Serious Look at a Humorous Man." *New York Times* (September 29, 1993): C-20.
"Joe Brown Wants to Play Rube Waddell." *The Hollywood Reporter* (December 28, 1942): 3.
"Joe E. Brown Returns in a Merry Film Version of Ring Lardner's *Alibi Ike* at the Cameo." *New York Times* (July 17, 1935): 22.
Johaneson, Bland. *Alibi Ike* review. *New York Daily Mirror* (July 17, 1935).
"John Ford Gives Old-Timers Chance For a Film Comeback." *New York World Telegram* (May 6, 1933): 9.
"John Ford Rejoins Fox." *Los Angeles Times* (September 15, 1934): Section 1: 4.
Johnston, Alva. "Close-Up: Bob Hope." *Life* (October 27, 1941): 102+.
_____. "The Scientific Side of Lunacy." *Woman's Home Companion* (September 1936): 12–13, 73–74.
Judge Priest press release. (Fox, 1934). In the Will Rogers file, Margaret Herrick Library, Academy of Motion Picture Arts and Sciences, Beverly Hills, California.
Judge Priest print ad. *Los Angeles Times* (September 27, 1934): Part 1: 13.
Judge Priest review. *Variety* (October 16, 1934).
Judge Priest "subpoena" invitation. In the *Judge Priest* file. Performing Arts Library, New York Public Library at Lincoln Center.
Kendall, Read. "Around and About in Hollywood." *Los Angeles Times* (November 2, 1934): Section 1: 15.
Kent, George. "The Mammy and Daddy of Us All." *Photoplay* (May 1934): 32–33, 100–03.
"*The Kid from Spain* a Hit; Gay Gorgeous Production." *The Hollywood Reporter* (October 20, 1932): 3.
Knight, Arthur. "One Man's Movie." *Saturday Review* (May 6, 1972): 14.
Lahr, John. "Bring Me Sunshine." *The New Yorker* (January 21, 2002): 84–85.
_____. "The C. E. O. of Comedy." *The New Yorker* (December 21, 1998): 62+.
Lane, Anthony. "Looking For Heroes." *The New Yorker* (June 6, 2005): 106–07.
Lardner, Ring. "Alibi Ike." In *Haircut and Other Stories*. 1922; rpt. New York: Scribner's, 1954: 35–56.
"Laurel and Hardy Film Farce Seen at Loew's Metropolitan." *New York American* (January 8, 1934).
"Leo McCarey Oral History." American Film Institute (Los Angeles, 1972). Interviewer Peter Bogdanovich.

"London in Raptures At Chaplin Movie." *New York Times* (February 28, 1931): 22.
Lorentz, Pare. *She Done Him Wrong* review. *Vanity Fair* (March 1933).
Lowell, James Russell. "The Biglow Papers: Second Series." In *The Complete Poetical Works of James Russell Lowell*. Ed. Horace E. Scuddler. 1894; rpt. Cambridge, Massachusetts: Riverside Press, 1924.
"Lusty Shake: Joe Brown's Grip May Have Cost Game." *Toledo Times* (October 9, 1934): 2.
"Marx Break Reported." *New York Times* (March 10, 1933): 18.
"The Marx Brothers in *A Night at the Opera*, a Mad, Merry Comedy, at the Capitol." *New York Sun* (December 7, 1935): 10.
"Marx Brothers Plans Unusual." *Los Angeles Times* (November 15, 1934): Section 1: 13.
Maslin, Janet. "Nothing Stands in the Way of a Laugh." *New York Times* (September 23, 1992).
Masters, Dorothy. "Laurel-Hardy Comedy Jeopardizes Theatre." *New York Daily News* (May 4, 1937).
Masters, Edgar Lee. "Deacon Taylor." In *Spoon River Anthology*. 1915; rpt. New York: Collier Books, 1962: 80.
McCarey, Leo. "The Audience Must Go On." *Hollywood Reporter* (November 2, 1943—Thirteenth Anniversary Issue).
_____. "The Could-Be Quality." *Hollywood Reporter* (October 28, 1939)—9th Anniversary Issue.
_____. "Mae West Can Play Anything." *Photoplay* (June 1935): 30–31, 126–27.
"Me 'n Paul" (cover story). *Time* (April 15, 1935): 52.
Meryman, Richard. "Ageless Master's Anatomy of Comedy: Chaplin, An Interview." *Life* (March 10, 1967): 82+.
"*Modern Times* at the Rivoli." *New York Daily Mirror* (February 7, 1936).
Modern Times review. *Variety* (February 12, 1936).
Mooring, W. H. "With MacLaurel & MacHardy in Bonnie Scotland." *Film Weekly* (June 28, 1935): 8, 9, 28.
Mullett, Mary B. "Bill Fields Disliked His Label, So He Laughed It Off." *American Magazine* (January 1926): 19, 143–47.
My Man Godfrey review. *Variety* (September 23, 1936).
"New Laurel and Hardy Feature Is Good Fun." *The Hollywood Reporter* (November 10, 1933): 3.
"New York Reviews: *Judge Priest*." *The Hollywood Reporter* (October 20, 1934): 2.
A Night at the Opera ad. *New York American* (December 6, 1935): 17.
"*A Night at the Opera* Will Win Converts to Marxism." *Newsweek* (November 23, 1935): 29–30.

"1937 — An Interview with L & H." Prefaced by Eldon K. Everett. *Classic Film Collector* (1976).

Nugent, Frank S. *The Cat and the Canary* review. *New York Times* (November 23, 1939): 38.

_____. "Heralding the Return, After an Undue Absence, of Charlie Chaplin in *Modern Times*." *New York Times* (February 6, 1936): 23.

_____. "The Reign of Good King Charlie." *New York Times* (February 9, 1936): Section 10: 5.

_____. *Way Out West* review. *New York Times* (May 4, 1937): 29.

"Old Chaplin Dead? Say It's Not True, Charlie: Cane, Derby and Mustache Doomed If He Enters Talkies." *New York American* (February 5, 1931): 17.

"Para's *She Done Him Wrong* Bawdy but Plenty Funny." *The Hollywood Reporter* (January 10, 1933): 3.

"Paris Hails Chaplin with Delirious Joy." *New York Times* (March 23, 1931): 24.

Parsons, Louella O. "Chaplin to Take *City Lights* to Europe, Being Only Actor Who Can Show Original Film." *New York American* (February 5, 1931): 19.

Parsons, Louella. "Paulette Goddard and Bob Hope Scheduled For Another Thriller, *The Ghost Breakers*." *Los Angeles Examiner* (November 22, 1939): Section 1: 17.

Paul, William. "Way Out West." *Village Voice* (January 29, 1970): 58.

Pelswick, Rose. "*Cat and the Canary* Opens at Paramount." *New York Journal American* (November 24, 1939): 14.

_____. "Chaplin Returns in Old Role but Brings New Laughs and Sings to Film Fans." *New York Evening Journal* (February 6, 1936): 16.

_____. "Eddie Cantor Film Inaugurates Straight Movie Policy for Palace Theatre." *New York Evening Journal* (November 18, 1932): 24.

_____. "Hilarious Lunacy Makes Marx Film — Diverting Comedy at Roxy." *New York Evening Journal* (December 7, 1935): 8.

_____. "Joe E. Brown Amusingly Plays Goofy Pitcher in Baseball Classic." *New York Evening Journal* (July 17, 1935).

_____. "Mae West Film Rich in Slang and Humor." *New York Evening Journal* (February 10, 1933): 13.

_____. "Rogers Brings Fine Humor to Judge's Role." *New York Evening Journal* (October 12, 1934): 19.

_____. "Rose Pelswick Reviews Chaplin Premiere." *New York Evening Journal* (February 7, 1931): 12.

Poppy review. *London Times* (July 13, 1936).

"Prague Angry At Chaplin." *New York Times* (June 14, 1931): 14.

Purdum, Todd S. "Bob Hope, Before He Became the Comedy Establishment." *New York Times* (April 20, 2003): Section 2: 7.

"Radio Poll." *The Hollywood Reporter* (December 21, 1941): 1.

"Red Skelton Scores in First Starring Role." *New York Morning Telegram* (August 28, 1941).

Redway, Sara. "W. C. Fields Pleads for Rough Humor." *Motion Picture Classic* (September 1925): 32–33, 73.

"Reich Has Yet to Act on New Chaplin Film." *New York Times* (February 18, 1936): 8.

"Ricky Successor Pledges Pennant." *New York Times* (October 26, 1955): 36.

Riley, Brooks. "Words of Hope." *Film Comment* (May/June 1979): 20–25.

"Ring Lardner Story Offers Joe Brown Familiar Material." *New York Post* (July 17, 1935).

"*Road to Singapore* Swell; Crosby and Hope Fine Team." *The Hollywood Reporter* (February 21, 1940): 3.

"Rogers' Kindness Recalled by Cobb." *Philadelphia Bulletin* (August 22, 1935).

Rogers, Will. "All I Know Is What They Say in Their Wires" (June 3, 1934). In *Will Rogers' Weekly Articles: The Roosevelt Years, 1933–1935*. Ed. Steven K. Gragert. Stillwater: Oklahoma State University Press, 1982: 123–25.

_____. "Good Sportsmanship Among the Movie Actors" (July 1, 1934). In *Will Rogers' Weekly Articles: The Roosevelt Years, 1933–1935*. Ed. Steven K. Gragert. Stillwater: Oklahoma State University Press, 1982: 130–32.

_____. "Mr. Rogers Makes His Official Report on World Series Finale and the Riot." (October 10, 1934). In *Will Rogers' Daily Telegrams: The Roosevelt Years, 1933–1935*. Ed. James M. Smallwood. Stillwater: Oklahoma State University Press, 1979: 226–28.

_____. "Rogers Gets a History Lesson" (June 24, 1934). In *Will Rogers' Weekly Articles: The Roosevelt Years, 1933–1935*. Ed. Steven K. Gragert. Stillwater: Oklahoma State University Press, 1982: 128–30.

_____. "Some Vivas For Mexico" (November 15, 1931). In *Will Rogers' Weekly Articles: The Hoover Years: 1931–1933*. Ed. Steven K. Gragert. Stillwater: Oklahoma State University Press, 1982: 87–88, 90.

"Rogue's Progress." *Newsweek* (January 6, 1947): 19.

Rollins, Peter C. "Will Rogers: Symbolic Man and Film Image." *Journal of Popular Film* (Fall 1973): 323–52.

Rushmore, Howard. "Horror Stuff, but Pleasant, at Paramount." *New York Daily Worker* (November 23, 1939).

Sandburg, Carl. "Carl Sandburg Says Chaplin Could Play Drama" (1931). In *Authors on Film*. Ed. Harry M. Geduld. Bloomington: Indiana University Press, 1972.

Schjeldahl, Peter. "Rule Like an Egyptian." *The New Yorker* (April 3, 2006): 86.

Scott, John. "*Judge Priest* Scores in Studio's Preview Showing." *Los Angeles Times* (September 14, 1934).

Sennwald, Andre. *It's a Gift* review. *New York Times* (January 5, 1935): 20.

———. *Judge Priest* review. *New York Times* (October 12, 1934): 33.

———. "Lines For a Mae West Scrap-Book." *New York Times* (September 30, 1934): Section 9: 4.

———. *Sons of the Desert* review. *New York Times* (January 12, 1934): 29.

———. "W. C. Fields Buffoon." *New York Times* (January 13, 1935): Section 9: 5.

"Sennwald's Death Laid to Gas Fumes." *New York Times* (January 13, 1936): 18.

Seton, Marie. "S. Dali + 3 Marxes =." *Theatre Arts* (October 1939): 734–40.

She Done Him Wrong review. *London Times* (April 3, 1933).

Silver, Charles. "Leo McCarey: From Marx to McCarthy." *Film Comment* (September 1973): 8+.

Siskel, Gene. "Woody Allen, A Joker More Mild Than Wild." *Chicago Tribune* (September 24, 1978): Section 6: 3.

"$650,000 Radio Offer Refused by Chaplin." *New York Times* (February 12, 1931): 13.

"So Mae West's Slipping? Not So She Can Notice It!" *Los Angeles Times* (May 20, 1934): Section 2: 3.

Sons of the Desert review. *Liberty Magazine* (February 17, 1934).

Sons of the Desert review. *New York Post* (January 9, 1934).

Sons of the Desert review. *Newsweek* (January 20, 1934): 35.

Sons of the Desert review. *Variety* (January 9, 1934).

"Sporting Life." *Time* (April 27, 1935).

"Star Scores Screen Hit." *Los Angeles Times* (September 28, 1934): Section 1: 13.

Tallmer, Jerry. "Book and Author: Robert Parrish." *New York Post* (May 29, 1976): 33.

"Testing a Film—For Laughs." *Brooklyn Eagle* (December 10, 1935).

Thirer, Irene. "*Kid from Spain* Mirth Film." *New York Daily News* (November 18, 1932): 54.

"Thomas J. McCarey." *New York Times* (February 2, 1936): Section 2: 8.

Thorp, Dunham. "The Up-to-Date Old Times." *Motion Picture Classic* (September 1926): 38–39, 88–89.

Thurber, James. "The Day the Dam Broke." In *My Life and Hard Times*. 1933; rpt. New York: Bantam Books, 1947: 49–65.

———. "James Thurber Presents *Der Tag Aux Courses*." *Stage* (March 1937): 49.

"Top Male Stars." *The Hollywood Reporter* (October 31, 1941).

Van Doren, Carl. "The Revolt from the Village." *Nation* (October 12, 1921).

Van Doren, Mark. "Charlie Chaplin." *Nation* (February 19, 1936): 232.

Veseth, Carl. *Elmer the Great* mini-review. *Motion Picture Herald* (July 22, 1933): 69.

"Vienna Won't Let Chaplin Wave Red Flag in Picture." *New York Times* (April 3, 1936): 27.

"A Voiceless Chaplin." *New York Times* (January 11, 1931): Section 8: 6.

"W.C. Fields Stars in Hilarious Film at the Paramount," *New York American* (July 14, 1934): 9.

Warshow, Robert. "Monsieur Verdoux." In *The Immediate Experience*. 1962; rpt. New York: Antheneum, 1972: 207–21.

Watkins, Mel. "Richard Pryor, Who Turned Ghetto Humor Into Biting Social Satire, Dies at 65." *New York Times* (December 11, 2005): 42.

Watts, Richard, Jr. *Alibi Ike* review. *New York Herald Tribune* (July 17, 1935): 10.

———. "Charlie Chaplin in *City Lights*." *New York Herald Tribune* (February 7, 1931): 8.

———. "*Duck Soup*—Rivoli." *New York Herald Tribune* (November 23, 1933): 15.

———. *Fireman, Save My Child* review. *New York Herald Tribune* (February 19, 1932): 12.

———. "*It's a Gift*—Roxy." *New York Herald Tribune* (January 5, 1935): 10.

———. "*Judge Priest*: Radio City Music Hall." *New York Herald Tribune* (October 12, 1934): 27.

———. "*A Night at the Opera*—Capitol." *New York Herald Tribune* (December 7, 1935): 10.

———. "*She Done Him Wrong*—Paramount." *New York Herald Tribune* (February 10, 1933): 11.

Way Out West review. *London Times* (May 3, 1937).

Way Out West review. *Variety* (May 5, 1937): 16.

"Wife Leaves for East to Greet Joe E. Brown." *Hollywood Citizen-News* (February 11, 1944).

Winsten, Archer. "*The Cat and the Canary* Opens at the Paramount." *New York Post* (November 24, 1939): 13.

———. "Laurel and Hardy Panic Rialto with Their Act." *New York Post* (May 4, 1937).

Wolfe, Sheila. "Joe E. Brown Grins, Waits For Surgery." *Chicago Tribune* (April 16, 1965): Section 1: 3.

Woodbury, Mitchell. "Strolling Around [Series Trophies Given Joe Brown]." *Toledo Times* (October 14, 1934): 5-D.

Wright, Basil. "Blest Pair of Sirens." *World Film News* (June 1937): 3.

Young, Stark. *Diamond Lil* review. *New Republic* (June 27, 1928): 145–46.

Index

Numbers in ***bold italics*** represent pages with photographs.

A Nous la Liberté 144
Abbott and Costello 153
Adamson, Joe 51
The Adventurer 70, 145, 146
Agee, James 11, 18, 49, 108
Alda, Alan 139
Alibi Ike 2, 3, 9, 10, 110–119, ***120***, 121–125, 178
Allen, Steve 28
Allen, Woody 23, 54–55, 105, 144, 148, 164–165, 169, 175
Ambassador Bill 31
American Gothic 76, 99
An American Werewolf in London 40–41
Andalusian Dog 61, 134
Angora Love 56
Animal Crackers 55, 61, 128, 129, 130–131, 136, 137, 138
Annie Hall 9, 54
Arbuckle, Fatty 22
Autry, Gene 157
The Awful Truth 45, 55, 60, 72, 129

Babbitt 99
Babes in Toyland 74
Baker, Eddie 21
Balázs, Béla 146, 148
Ball, Lucille 144
Bananas 144
The Bank 17
Barzun, Jacques 111
The Battle of the Century 71
Bazin, André 18–19, 21
Beatles 102
Beavers, Louise 43–44
Beckett, Samuel 79
Beery, Noah 32, 42, 44, 45, 46
Belle of the Nineties ***8***, 39, 48–49, 77
Benchley, Robert 7, 68, 70, 71, 106, 135
Benny, Jack 165, 167
Bergman, Andrew 61, 62

Bergman, Henry 20
Bergson, Henri 20
Berkeley, Busby 30, 31
Big Business 71, 72
The Big Store 137, 147
Black-Heads 72
Blair, Walter 81
Blotto 70
Boetticher, Budd 94
Bogdanovich, Peter 11
Bonnie and Clyde 41
Boudu Saved from Drowning 24
Brats 69
Breen, Joseph 48
Brice, Fanny 29
Brook, Mel 40
Brown, Joe E. 2, 3, 4, 9, 10, 28, 96, 110–111, ***112***, 113–115, ***116***, 117–119, ***120***, 121–125, 137, 178
Brown, Tom 84, 85, ***90***
Brownlow, Kevin 144
Bull Durham 123
Buñuel, Luis 61, 134
Bunyan, Paul 40
Buscemi, Steve 29
Busch, Mae 73, 74, 77

Cagney, James 49
Calhern, Louis 62, ***63***
Call of the Cuckoos 56
The Cameraman 115
Cantor, Eddie 3, 4, 10, 27, ***28***, 29–32, ***33***, 34, ***35***, 36, 38, 55, 77, 117, 178
Capra, Frank 82, 86, 87, 91, 94–95, 154–155, 161, 176
Carey, Harry 82, 93
Carrey, Jim 174
Carroll, Lewis 134–135
The Cat and the Canary 2, 9, 10, 42, 164–165, ***166***, 167, ***168***, 169, 178
Caught in a Cabaret 148
The Champion 22
Chaplin, Charlie 30, 36, 39, 41,
46, 50, 57, 70, 71, 89, 97, 102, 106, 108, 120, 128, 135, 152, 159, 160, 162, 164; *City Lights* and 10, 11–14, ***15***, 16–18, ***19***, 20–21, ***22***, 23–26, 140, 141, 145, 146, 147, 149, 158, 177, 178, 180; *Modern Times* and 2, 4, 7, 9–10, 17, 24, 140, ***141***, 142, ***143***, 144–149, ***150***, 151, 165, 171, 177, 178, 179
Chaplin, Charles, Jr. 12, 148
Chaplin, Victoria 24
Chase, Charley 55, 57–58, 59, 60, 72, ***75***, 77
Cherrill, Virginia 13, 14, ***15***, 16, 17–18, 19, 25
Chicago Cubs 114, 117, 118, 120, 122, 123, 124
A Chump at Oxford 71, 74
Churchill, Berton 87, 88, 94
The Circus 17, 146
Clair, René 137, 144
Clive, Henry 13, 23
The Clowns 24
Cobb, Irvin S. 82, 84, 85, ***86***, 88, 89–90, 91, 93, 94
Cobb, Ty 111, 114, 121
The Cocoanuts 128, 129, 138, 159
Cohan, George M. 115, 117
Colbert, Claudette 154–155
The Comic Supplement 40, 97
A Connecticut Yankee in King Arthur's Court 92
Coogan, Jackie 147, 179
Coppola, Sofia 19
The Count 24
Cracked Ice 51, 62
Cracked Nuts 31, 62
Crosby, Bing 144, 164, 165, 173, ***174***, 175

Dalí, Salvador 52, 56, 61, 134, 135
"Dance of the Cuckoos" 76
Daughters of Revolution 76, 99

David Copperfield 39
David Harum 87, 88
Davidson, Max 56
A Day at the Races 53, 129, 130, 137
Dean, Dizzy 121, 123, 124, 125
Death in the Afternoon 34
De Havilland, Olivia 119, 122, 123
The Devil's Brother 74, 77
Diamond Lil 39, 40, 43, 46, 47, 48, 49
Dickens, Charles 30, 39, 99, 100, 147
Dietrich, Marlene 45, 48
Diplomaniacs 62
Dmytryk, Edward 56
Dr. Bull 9, 87, 89
Dr. Strangelove, Or: How I Learned to Stop Worrying and Love the Bomb 9, 54, 178
Donnelly, Dorothy 40, 97
Duck Soup 2, 7, 9, 10, 24, 30, 31, 39, 51, *52*, 53–56, *57*, 58–62, *63*, *64*, 65–66, 105, 126, 127, 128, 129, 136, 159, 177, 178, 179
Dumont, Margaret 51, 59, 126, 130, 135, *136*, 179
Dunne, Finley Peter 43
Dunne, Irene 60
Durante, Jimmy 28, 29, 110

Early to Bed 60
Earthworm Tractors 110
Easy Street 21, 145
Einstein, Albert 25
Eisenstein, Sergei 12
Elmer the Great 9, 111, 113, 113, 115, 117–119, 122, 125
Exit Laughing 85
Eyles, Allen 56, 58

Fairbanks, Douglas 26, 36
"Far Side" 79
Fargo 29
Feldman, Marty 41
Fellini, Federico 23–24
Ferguson, Otis 48–49, 131, 138, 143, 149
Fetchit, Stepin 80, 82, 88–89, 179
Field of Dreams 83
Fields, W.C. 1, 9, 10, 21, 28, 29–30, 31, 38, 39, 40, 45, 48, 53, 54, 73, 74, 96–100, *101*, 102, *103*, *104*, 105–109, 110, 111, 127, 131, 135, 137, 146, 153, 167, 171, 176, 177, 179, 180
Fighting Fluid 60
Finlayson, James 72, 153, *154*, 155, *156*, 157, 159
Fireman, Save My Child 9, 111, 113, 115, *116*, 117, 118, 123

The Floorwalker 57
Fonda, Henry 84, 94
Ford, Francis 94
Ford, John 9, 39, 44, 83, 86, 87, 88, 89–90, 92, 93–95, 162, 173, 176
Franklin, Joe 29
Franklin, Sidney 34, 36
Frawley, William *120*, 121, 123
Free and Easy 13
Frost, Robert 125

Gable, Clark 154–155
Gallagher and Shean 53
Gehrig, Lou 118,
Gehring, Emily v, 5, 79
Gehring, Sarah v, 5, 79
The General 24, 41–42, 61
The Ghost Breakers 169, 170, 171, *172*, 173, 174
Goddard, Paulette 31, 141, 146, 147, *150*, 165, *166*, *168*, 169, *172*, 173, 174, 175, 177, 179
Going My Way 30, 55
The Gold Rush 14, 17, 25, 147, 149, 159, 160, 180
Goldman, William 41
Goldwyn, Samuel 30–31, 36–37, 49
Grable, Betty 31
Grand Illusion 24
Grant, Cary 43, 44, *45*, 48, 60, 129
The Great Dictator 71, 142, 144, 149
Greene, Graham 71
Grierson, John 152–153
Griffith, D.W. 30

Hale, Georgia 14, 16, 25
Hall, Ruth 32
Hannah and Her Sisters 55
Hatley, T. Marvin 76
Hearst, William Randolph 26
Hemingway, Ernest 34
Hill, Hamlin 70
Hog Wild 69
Holloway, Sterling 111
Hooper, Johnson J. 96
Hope, Bob 2, 9, 10, 40, 42, 80, 120, 144, 153, 164–165, *166*, 167, *168*, 169–171, *172*, *174*, 178
Horizons West 94
Horse Feathers 61, 62, 129, 160
Horse Sense in American Humor 81
Howard, Kathleen 73, 104, 105, 106, 107, 109, 179
Huckleberry Finn 16, 88, 89, 117, 177, 179
Hudson, Rochelle 89, *90*
Huff, Theodore 17, 143, 147, 150

If I Had a Million 1
I'm No Angel 45
In the Night Kitchen 79
It Happened One Night 137, 154–155, 161
It's a Gift 9, 10, 73, 96–100, *101*, 102, *103*, *104*, 105–109, 131, 176, 177, 179
It's the Old Army Game 96

Jackson, Shoeless Joe 124
Jacobs, Lewis 13, 49
The Jazz Singer 12
Jefferson, Thomas 86, 87
Jenkins, Henry 28, 29
Jones, Allan 129, 132
Judge Priest 3, 9, 39, 44, 77, 80–82, *83*, 84–89, *90*, 91–95, 176, 179

Kalmar, Bert 31, 55
Kaufman, George S. 55, 126, 128, 138
Kaye, Danny 164, 175
Keaton, Buster 13, 24, 38, 41–42, 61, 110, 113, 115, 118, 152, 153
Kennedy, Edgar 56, 60, 70
Kerr, Walter 16, 146
The Kid 147, 179
The Kid from Spain 3, 9, 10, 27, *28*, 29–32, *33*, 34, *35*, 36–37, 55, 178
Kiss Kiss, Bang Bang 175
Knipfel, Jim 63, 138
The Knockout 22
Knotts, Don 170–171
Kovacs, Ernie 28, 138
Kracauer, Siegfried 21, 158, 177

Lamour, Dorothy 173, 174–175
Lane, Anthony 26
Langdon, Harry 13, 38, 146, 161
Lardner, Ring 115, 117, 120, 121, 122, 123, 124, 125
Larson, Gary 79
Laurel, Stan 146, *157*
Laurel and Hardy 56, 60, 81, 97, 98, 128, 179; *Sons of the Desert* and 9, 10, 67–74, *75*, 76–77, *78*, 79, 152, 153, 159, 162; *Way Out West* and 9, 10, 73, 152–153, *154*, 155, *156*, *157*, *158*, 159–163, 176, 177, 178
Lawrence, Rosina 153, 158, 159
LeBaron, William 45
LeRoy, Baby 97, 102, 104, 105, 177
Let's Go Native 55
Letters of a Self-Made Diplomat to His President 80, 91
Lewis, Jerry 16–17, 153
Lewis, Sinclair 99
Linder, Max 57

Lloyd, Harold 13, 38, 110, 115, 120, 146
Long Fliv the King 55
Lorentz, Pave 42
Lost in Translation 19
Love and Death 165
Lynne, Sharon 152, **154**, 155, **156**, **157**, 159

Main Street 99
Maltin, Leonard 152
Manhattan 23
Martin, Steve 153, 176
Marx, Arthur 128
Marx, Chico 31, 51, **52**, 53–54, 56, **57**, 58–61, 62, **63**, **64**, 65, 66, 126, **127**, 129, **131**, 132, 133, 134, 135, 137, 159, 160, 161, 177, 179
Marx, Groucho 28, 29, 31, 38, 48, 51, **52**, 53–54, 55, **57**, 58–59, 60–62, **64**, 110, 126, **127**, 128, 129–130, **131**, 132, 133, 134, 135, **136**, 137, 146, 147, 160, 161, 170, 171, 177, 178, 179, 180
Marx, Gummo 51
Marx, Harpo 13, 28, 31, 51, **52**, 53–54, 56, 58–61, 62, **63**, **64**, 65, 66, 126, **127**, 128, 129, 130, **131**, 132, 133, 134–135, 137, 159, 160, 161, 177, 179
Marx, Minnie 53
Marx, Zeppo 51, **52**, 53, 60, **64**, 65, 126, 132, 179
Marx Brothers 13, 38, 74, 80, 180; *Duck Soup* and 2, 7, 9, 10, 24, 30, 31, 39, 51, **52**, 53–56, **57**, 58–62, **63**, **64**, 65–66, 105, 126, 127, 128, 129, 136, 159, 177, 178, 179; *A Night at the Opera* and 4, 126, **127**, 128–130, **131**, 132–135, **136**, 137–139, 176, 177, 179
Masina, Giulietta 23, 24
Mast, Gerald 16, 20, 26, 67, 70, 177
Masters, Edgar Lee 98
Mathewson, Christy 123–124
McCarey, Leo **8**, 9, 10, 22, 23, 30, 34–37, 39, 44, 45, 54, 55–61, 65–66, 68–73, 77, 79, 129, 155, 156, 159, 160, 161, 178
McDaniel, Hattie 88, 89
McEvoy, J.P. 40, 97, 101
McHugh, Frank 118
McKenna, George 81, 87
Mencken, H.L. 115
Mickey's Polo Team 128
A Midsummer Night's Dream 119–120
The Milky Way 23
Million Dollar Legs 31, 32

Mr. Smith Goes to Washington 82, 86, 91, 161
Monkey Business 61, 129, 132–133
Monsieur Verdoux 25, 151
Mum's the Word 57–58, 59
Murray, Bill 19
The Music Box 21
My Darling Clementine 84, 94
My Favorite Brunette 164, 165, 167
My Little Chickadee 39, 153
My Man Godfrey 137–138,
Myers, Harry 10, 13, **22**, 23

Nathan, George Jean 26, 49
Never Give a Sucker an Even Break 109
New York Yankees 113, 114, 115, 118, 125
Night After Night 40
A Night at the Opera 4, 126, **127**, 128–130, **131**, 132–135, **136**, 137–139, 176, 177, 179
A Night in Casablanca 137
Nights of Cabiria 24

O'Brien, Conan 27
Of Thee I Sing 55, 126
The Old-Fashioned Way 9, 97, 99, 102, 107
Open City 23
Orwell, George 144

Paige, Satchel 123
Parrish, Robert 14
Parsons, Louella O. 12, 173
A Perfect Day 70
Pickford, Mary 12, 36, 49
The Pilgrim 25, 145
Poppy (stage) 30, 40, 97
The Potters 105
Pryor, Richard 79
Purviance, Edna 14, 17, 19, 147
Putting Pants on Philip 155

Redford, Robert 85
Renoir, Jean 24
"the revolt from the village" 98
The Rink 145, 146, 148
Roach, Hal 74, 75
Road to Bali 173
Road to Hong Kong 144, 173
Road to Morocco 173
Road to Rio 173
The Road to Singapore 173, **174**
Road to Utopia 173, 174–175
Road to Zanzibar 173
Roberti, Lydia 32, **33**
Rogers, Will 3, 4, 9, 29, 31, 38, 39, 42–43, 44, 77, 80, **81**, 82, **83**, 84–85, **86**, 87–89, **90**, 91–95, 106, 107, 110, 113, 117, 124, 152, 176, 179

Roosevelt, Franklin D. 61, 92
Rose, Pete 118
Rossellini, Roberto 23
Roth, Lillian 130–131
Ruby, Harry 31, 55
Rules of the Game 24
Ruth, Babe 111, 114, 115, 125
Ryskind, Morrie 55, 65, 126, 138

St. Louis Cardinals 117, 118, 121
Sally of the Sawdust 30
Sandburg, Carl 17
Sandford, Tiny 71
Saps at Sea 74
Scott, Randolph 94
Seinfeld 70
Seldes, Gilbert 135
Sendak, Maurice 79
Sennett, Mack 41, 70–71
Sennwald, Andre 48, 77, 102, 108–109
Seven Years Bad Luck 57
Shaw, George Bernard 24
She Done Him Wrong 2, 9, 10, 38–44, **45**, 46, **47**, 48–50, 165
Should Married Men Go Home? 68
Shrine Quartet 76
Silver, Charles 56
Sinclair, Upton 63
Skelton, Red 118, 145, 164, 169, 175
Skipworth, Alison 1
Sleeper 165
Smith, Seba 86, 91
So This Is London 84
Some Like It Hot 9, 54, 128
Sons of the Desert 9, 10, 67–74, **75**, 76–77, **78**, 79, 152, 153, 159, 162
Soundergaard, Gale 167, **168**
Spoon River Anthology 98, 99
Steamboat Round the Bend 9, 85, **86**, 88, 89–90, 92
Stewart, Donald Ogden 135
Stewart, Jimmy 82
La Strada 23–24
Sunnyside 146, 147

Take the Money and Run 105
Thalberg, Irving 126–127, 128, 129, 132, 136
That's My Wife 70
Their First Mistake 73
Their Purple Moment 70
Them Thar Hills 73, 160
They Had to See Paris 80
Thurber, James 68, 70, 109, 133
Tootsie 9, 54, 175
"The Trail of the Lonesome Pine" 157, 158
The Tramp 17
Twain, Mark 16, 92, 98, 153

Twentieth Century 137, 138
Two Tars 71

An Unfinished Life 85

The Vagabond 19, 147
Vonnegut, Kurt 67, 180
von Stroheim, Erich 24

Waddell, Rube 116–117, 123
Waiting for Godot 79
Walthall, Henry B. 82, *83*, 87
Warshow, Robert 142
Way Out West 9, 10, 73, 152–153, *154*, 155, *156*, *157*, *158*, 159–163, 176, 177, 178
We Faw Down 68, 72–73, 76, 77
Weales, Gerald 48, 59
Welcome Danger 13
West, Mae 2, *8*, 9, 10, 38–44, *45*, 46, *47*, 54, 77, 107, 110, 111, 117, 136, 153, 165, 179
Wheeler, Bert 28
Wheeler and Woolsey 31, 62, 77
Whitman, Walt 111
Williams, Bert 29
Williams, Robin 27, 29

A Woman of Paris 141
Wood, Grant 76, 99
Woolf, Virginia 115
Woollcott, Alexander 149, 180
Wright, Basil 152–153

Yagoda, Ben 91–92, 94
Young, Robert *28*, 32, *33*
Young Frankenstein 41
Young Mr. Lincoln 83, 84

Ziegfeld, Florenz 29, 30
Ziegfeld Follies 29–30, 37, 40, 80, 97, 101, 108

www.ingramcontent.com/pod-product-compliance
Lightning Source LLC
Chambersburg PA
CBHW081556300426
44116CB00015B/2901